SUPER SYNCHRONICITY

Super Synchronicity

Where Science and Spirit Meet

Gary E. Schwartz, PhD
The University of Arizona

Foreword by
William Gladstone
Author of *The Twelve* and *Tapping the Source*

Introduction by
Stephen Brewer, MD
Medical Director, Canyon Ranch in Tucson, Arizona
Co-author of *The Everest Principle*

Commentary by
John H. Spencer, PhD
Author of the multiple award winning
The Eternal Law: Ancient Greek Philosophy, Modern Physics, and Ultimate Reality

PARAM MEDIA INC
Vancouver, BC

ISBN: 978-1945949586

Distributed by Waterside Digital Press

Cover design by Param Media

ParamMedia.com

AUTHOR'S NOTE
SUPER SYNCHRONICITY AND SUPERSYNCHRONICITY

Although the title of this book is called *Super Synchronicity* (two words) the scientific phenomenon is called supersynchronicity (one word). The reason is that scientific words often join the prefix super with the designated term. Examples include supercomputers, superconductors, superclusters (of galaxies), and supernormal (abilities).

Praise for *Super Synchronicity*

"Gary Schwartz is the Master of Serial Coincidences. No one else has experienced and reported so many coincidences made up of similar, repeated observable elements. At the start of this energetic book, he demolishes the statisticians' favorite explanation for coincidences: the Law of Very Large Numbers. He then encourages all of us to become self-scientists to test for ourselves the reality of serial coincidences the most grand of which he calls "supersynchronicities". In a mind-expanding ending, he urges us to see that synchronicities alert us to the mysterious hiding in plain sight—the Greater Mind in its many variations. Dr. Schwartz has made a major contribution to the study of coincidences."

Bernard D Beitman, MD
Author of *Connecting with Coincidence*

"The emerging image of consciousness is that our minds are united—from Bateson's 'pattern that connects,' to Schrödinger's 'one mind,' to Jung's 'collective unconscious.' Now consciousness researcher Gary Schwartz adds another thread to this tapestry, that of synchronicity. *Super Synchronicity* is a valuable contribution that affirms what most of us experience from time to time—that beyond our individual minds lies an infinite reality in which consciousness is fundamental and unitary. On this realization our future as humans may depend.

It is arrogant to think that Nature would reveal itself only in scientific laboratories through the language of physics and mathematics, as eloquent as that language is. As Gary Schwartz shows in *Super Synchronicity,* Nature is multilingual, and one of its dialects is synchronicities. The message? Intelligence, meaning, and connectedness are intrinsic features of life itself. *Super Synchronicity* is an extension of science, not a refutation. It is a refreshing antidote to the suffocating, deadening effects of the ideology of materialism in our time. Beautifully done, Gary, congratulations."

Larry Dossey, MD
Author of *Healing Words,*
The Power of Premonitions, and *One Mind*

"In the exciting emergence of the more mature science that is eliminating the paltry fiction of pure scientific materialism, Dr. Gary Schwartz has provided a pivotal work that strikes right at the heart of the old world view, by illuminating the reality of synchronicities in all of our lives. Written in a wonderfully personal style, Dr. Schwartz's *Super Synchronicity* offers all of the tools one needs to perform their own investigations into how we are all part of the One Mind, offering great meaning and purpose to our existence."

Eben Alexander, MD
Neurosurgeon, author of *Proof of Heaven* and
The Map of Heaven

"According to CG Jung, synchronicity is an "acausal connecting principle" which is the underlying mechanism by which our reality actually works. For over 40 years I have admired the sheer genius of Dr. Gary Schwartz to bring rigorous science to bear on such formidable issues. As both a scientist and visionary, he has achieved major insights into the nature of the mind and reality with his new breakthrough research and writing... Bravo!"

Kenneth R. Pelletier, PhD, MD,
Clinical Professor of Medicine and Professor of Public Health, University of California School of Medicine (UCSF), San Francisco, and University of Arizona School of Medicine, author of *Mind as Healer—Mind as Slayer, Sound Mind—Sound Body,* and *New Medicine*

"What a delightful nest of synchronicities we are served here. Synchronicities, multiple-synchronicities, supersynchronicities, and more! Professor Schwartz does with numbers what physicist and colleague of Carl Jung, Wolfgang Pauli, did with puns. Brings warm memories of John Barth's wonderful stories, Lost in the Funhouse."

Allan Leslie Combs, PhD
Navin and Pratima Doshi Professor, California Institute of Integral Studies, author of *Synchronicity and Consciousness Explained Better*

"What is the meaning of those meaningful coincidences called synchronicities? *Super Synchronicity* explores this question in detail through a series of increasingly striking examples, and then proposes a thought provoking set of explanations. Written in Schwartz's clear and entertaining style, this book will make your head spin, in a good way."

Dean Radin, PhD
Chief Scientist, Institute of Noetic Sciences, author of *The Consciousness Universe, Supernormal* and other books

"As a person whose own life has been profoundly shaped by what Gary Schwartz calls "supersynchronicities" I know how powerful these experiences can be. Gary has written an excellent and very helpful book about understanding these meaningful coincidences, and it contains real insight and wisdom."

Stephan A. Schwartz
Author of *The 8 Laws of Change,*
Opening to the Infinite, Secret Vaults of Time,
and *The Alexandria Project*

"Gary Schwartz has written a book that is both entertaining and highly significant. It addresses the question whether synchronicity is just a chance event—or something real and meaningful. It is the latter. We should be grateful to Gary for bringing together all these shining examples that testify to it—we live in a non-chance, meaningful, and truly interconnected—and therefore truly synchronicity-filled—universe."

Ervin Laszlo, PhD
The Laszlo Institute of New Paradigm Research,
author of *What Is Consciousness?,*
The New Map of Cosmos and Consciousness, and other books

"Dr. Gary Schwartz has done it again: helped us to appreciate the wonder of the Universe while keeping us grounded with scientific methods. *Super Synchronicity* serves as a primer for noticing and appreciating the signs of our innate interconnectedness. This magical book holds the keys to finding that connection within ourselves and ultimately coming to the realization that their is only one Self. Bravo to Dr. Schwartz for this gift of a book."

Suzanne Giesemann
Former Navy Commander, evidential medium,
and author of *Messages of Hope* and *Wolfs Message*

"Dr. Gary Schwartz of the University of Arizona at Tucson is the leading research scientist in the broad field of afterlife investigation. His groundbreaking 2003 book, *The Afterlife Experiments,* demonstrated conclusively that psychic mediumship is a real phenomenon; and his later work in this field, documented in books like

The Truth about Medium and *The Sacred Promise,* has added immeasurably to our understanding of what in fact is going on.

Studying synchronicities is a project of the heart for Dr. Schwartz. His delight in it shows in this extraordinary book. Simply put, synchronicities are two or more events that happen close in time and seem to "rhyme" in some fashion. They come in many flavors, from the day that everyone came to work wearing a blue shirt with a red tie to the amazing day when you saw seventeen separate references to flamingos. Synchronicities happen to all of us, so we seldom ever realize how statistically unlikely they are; but to those who study them, their frequency and the odds against their happening by chance are strong indications that something big is going on.

Part of the delight of Dr. Schwartz's book is his documentation of supersynchronicity chains that include as many as two dozen events and had me laughing aloud; but what I most enjoyed was his penetrating analysis of what synchronicities mean, and why they happen. God is winking at all of us! And thanks to another beautiful and groundbreaking book from Dr. Gary Schwartz, now we can joyfully wink right back."

Roberta Grimes, JD
Author of *The Fun of Dying, The Fun of Staying in Touch, Liberating Jesus,* and *The Fun of Growing Forever,*
and host of Seeking Reality with Roberta Grimes

"Dr. Gary Schwartz kept me thoroughly entertained in his new book, *Super Synchronicity.* His personal stories remind us that being conscious of who we are and of our surroundings can bring us amazing gifts, such as synchronicity."

Judy Stakee
Former Senior VP of Creative, Warner Chappell Music,
author of *The Songwriter's Survival Guide*

"There is a lot that we do not fully understand, including the beautiful concept of Synchronicity. Gary gives us great lessons in between the lines!"

Phil Hellmuth
NY Times Best Selling author of *Play Poker Like the Pros* and 14 time World Champion of Poker

"If we stay alert, we can sometimes catch God at play/work and see more of the delightful "big picture." Dr. Schwartz's fascinating book has added supersynchronicities to my list of evidence-based signs that our earth-experiences are interconnected, meaningful, and magnificent adventures amidst eternity."

Mark Pitstick, MA, DC
Author of *Soul Proof, The Eleven Questions,* and *Radiant Wellness;* Director and Co-Founder of The SoulPhone Foundation

For Rhonda, Susy, Jerry, Larry,
Michael, Paul, Sophia, and Sam

When Kepler found his long-cherished belief
did not agree with the most precise observation,
he accepted the uncomfortable fact.
He preferred the hard truth
to his dearest illusions;
that is the heart of science.
Carl Sagan, PhD

Coincidence is God's way of remaining anonymous.
Albert Einstein

It's too coincidental to be a coincidence.
Yogi Berra

Table of Contents

SECTION THREE

Theory—Emerging Scientific Understanding

Foreword

William Gladstone
Author of *The Twelve* and *Tapping the Source*

The music is all around us; we just have to listen.
August Rush

I am honored to be writing the foreword to this amazing book about *Super Synchronicity*. My novel *The Twelve* explores the theme of synchronicity and how important it can be to lead a life of joy and purpose. The universe is always trying to tell us what to do, where to go, and how to behave. We just have to listen.

Dr. Gary Schwartz, however, does more than listen: he instructs. First he starts by taking notes, and then as the scientist he was born to be, he begins analyzing the possible meanings of synchronicities in his own life.

I have known Gary for more than fifteen years, and so I know that he is not an impulsive man. He waited decades between experiencing the first synchronicities in his life and accepting such synchronicities as scientific data. When the speed of his personal synchronicities began to accelerate, he started writing about them in his book, *The G.O.D. Experiments.* However, his previous editor and I, as his agent, discouraged him from going public with his key messages. He was, after all, a serious scientist, and some of these synchronicities may have seemed a little too weird and a little too personal for most people.

But the universe did not ignore Gary's newfound interest in noting and analyzing the synchronicities taking place in his own life. These synchronicities just kept coming. Then, to top it off, I sent Gary a copy of my novel *The Twelve*—an act that was, in itself, synchronistic.

Gary could no longer contain himself, and although busy with research and his next book, he went back to the chapters and notes on synchronicities I had previously discouraged him from publishing. What he saw was an even more unified storyline ready to be shared with those who want to know if Jung was right about synchronicities, and whether they could actually be documented and analyzed within a systematic framework.

As a result of his research, Gary has proven that real-life synchronicities can indeed be documented, and not just by him. This book will be heralded for the pioneering work that it is. It is also a rather amusing and entertaining piece of writing, a rarity in scientific analysis.

I am not a scientist, and no doubt some traditional hardline scientists will find much to criticize within these pages. However, the central point of this book is to disprove what traditional scientists claim to be the boundaries of science.

Gary points to the future of science, a future that other great thinkers such as Dr. Ervin Laszlo in *Science and the Akashic Field* confirm must include data that have hitherto been ignored for being inconvenient or nonreplicable. The emerging science allows for both replicable experiments, as well as the kind of more personal "self-science" which Gary expounds and demonstrates in this book.

I hope that this book generates great controversy and great public interest in exploring the true nature of reality.

In my own novel I discuss the concept "A is and is not equal to A". This concept is central to understanding the character of the protagonist, Max Doff, and also the deeper spiritual message of the novel. Some of the early critics of the book confessed to not understanding the meaning and implication of this concept. Gary, however, immediately grasped its significance, because it is not altogether dissimilar to his own work as documented in *The Living Energy Universe*. In Chapter 17 of this book, Gary explains how the statement that "A is and is not equal to A" provides an important insight for helping us to understand the reality of synchronicity.

Neither Gary nor I want to limit our readership to scientists and mathematicians. We have written books that are accessible to readers of varied educational backgrounds. You may rest assured, however, that we have both done the math and that the conclusions we have drawn are not only plausible, but are mathematically and scientifically significant as well.

Gary will always be an obsessive scientist. This is his nature, his passion, his gift. He is also an obsessive teacher, and like any good teacher, he understands that knowledge is more quickly and easily learned if the student is also entertained.

May this book both entertain and enlighten you.

In joy,
William Gladstone

Introduction
The Reality of Synchronicity: My Surprising Awakening

Stephen Brewer, MD
Medical Director, Canyon Ranch, Tucson
Co-author of *The Everest Principle*

This widened consciousness...
is a function of our relationship to the world...
bringing us into an absolute binding
and indissoluble communion with the Universe. ...
There is no individuation on Everest.
Carl Jung

Although I had heard mention of the term synchronicity prior to meeting Dr. Gary Schwartz, it wasn't until our friendship began to flourish that I came to understand what this word really meant, and what impact it would have on my life and the lives of my colleagues, patients, and friends.

After experiencing a highly improbable string of five startling events involving multiple sclerosis, I came to appreciate the reality of synchronicity and the truth behind what Gary was researching.

A Bit of History

I first met Gary in 1999 when I attended an Integrative Medicine conference at the "Research Triangle," a research Mecca that is

North Carolina's equivalent to California's Silicon Valley, where multiple research companies are doing Western-based research in pharmaceuticals and other medical disciplines. It was both interesting and ironic that one of the first major conferences on non-traditional medical care was being held in the middle of this conservative hub of learning and research.

The conference was sponsored by the University of Arizona's Program of Integrative Medicine (today the Arizona Center for Integrative Medicine) and Duke University's Integrative Medicine Center. The big draw was Dr. Andrew Weil, director of the University of Arizona's Center. He had recently received national recognition as the result of his magazine and television features, in addition to the popularity of the books he had written.

Andy may have helped set up the show, but it was Gary who stole it. At the end of Gary's lecture, all five hundred participants gave him a rousing standing ovation. This was my first interchange with Gary.

I got to know Gary some time later when we started having bagels together to discuss his working part-time as the Corporate Director of Development of Energy Healing at the Canyon Ranch Health Resorts, an acclaimed life-enhancement corporation located in Tucson, Arizona. Since those "bagel days," our relationship has grown on both a professional and personal level.

Although I have been involved in integrative medicine and practice medical acupuncture, I remain at heart a conservative in the liberal-minded field of complementary and alternative medicine. With my somewhat reserved thinking, I barely comprehend quantum physics, let alone anything to do with understanding "synchronicities." Before the term "synchronicity" entered my conversations with Gary, I thought it was simply a word made up by Shirley MacLaine. (I later learned that it was, in fact, coined by Dr. Carl Jung.)

After Gary started working at Canyon Ranch, he began attending our weekly "peak performance" team meetings. He always stretched our minds and souls with his thought-provoking questions and keen observations, and continued to do so with his comments on some of the "synchronicities" he had experienced.

At first, his examples seemed to be just coincidences that were fun to discuss. But my belief that these so-called "synchronicities" were merely mind-teasers based on chance came to an abrupt end when I experienced my own insight into synchronicity.

Five Surprising Events

My own transformative chain of synchronicities began in the middle of the night, when I was startled out of a deep sleep by a coherent thought: the chosen topic for our next peak performance meeting should be about individuals suffering from multiple sclerosis, and we should discuss ways in which we, as a group, could improve their lives.

The peak performance team is a remarkable group that personifies the essence of integrative medicine. The team consists of doctors, nurses, behaviorists, nutritionists, exercise physiologists, and other alternative medicine practitioners. Our goal is to establish protocols for improving the emotional and physical well-being of guests at Canyon Ranch, thus allowing them to realize their full potential.

Now, for me to suddenly wake up in the middle of the night with any sort of coherent thought is highly unusual, especially if this thought involves a subject that apparently has no impact on me personally.

That was Event #1, although at the time I was not aware it was the beginning of a synchronicity at all; I merely thought it was strange.

The next day was Friday, a day on which four of us get together from the departments of medicine, life management, nutrition, and exercise physiology to lecture to our patients about what they have learned during their stay at Canyon Ranch.

While waiting for my turn to speak, I was discussing my strange nocturnal awakening with an exercise physiologist friend who is a member of our peak performance team. She, in turn, told me about a woman who had come to her the day before to ask if Canyon

Ranch would be a good place to bring her husband. He was suffering from multiple sclerosis and was frustrated with the therapies he had been receiving at home. Could Canyon Ranch offer a fresh approach in treating his disease?

This became Event #2.

At the time, I chalked this up to mere coincidence. When the exercise physiologist was called in to speak, the previous speaker came back to the waiting area and sat down beside me. I then felt the need to tell this person of the pair of events involved in this particular "synchronicity." As I spoke softly to him, his jaw dropped. He then informed me about his *own* recent diagnosis of multiple sclerosis!

He proceeded to tell me how frustrated he was with multiple sclerosis "support" magazines. He said they depressed him because they only addressed those patients who had the more aggressive forms of the disease, leaving no room for information aimed at improving the lives of functioning MS patients.

This was Event #3.

I returned to my office still convinced that these "events," while surprising, were nothing more than pure coincidence. Just as I was sitting down at my desk, a nutritionist (who is also on our peak performance team) dropped by to ask me a question. Because she had listened to Gary's many examples of synchronistic events, I told her of my three potential synchronicities. As I did so, she sat down and began to shake.

I looked at her and thought, *Not you, too!*

Once she had collected herself, she said, "You are not going to believe this, but I stayed up late last night listening to an educational tape about a woman describing a specific diet that had 'cured' her of multiple sclerosis."

This became Event #4.

Needless to say, the topic of how we can improve the lives of multiple sclerosis patients was presented at our next meeting. At the beginning of the meeting, I told the group about the synchronous events that had led me to discuss this topic.

When I finished my story, I looked across the table at Gary and waited for him to say, 'I told you so.' He was grinning, but these were not the words he said.

Instead, Gary recounted how the woman who had made the audio tape on multiple sclerosis (the one that my nutritionist had randomly decided to listen to) had interviewed him on her radio show just a few days prior to this meeting.

Welcome to Event #5!

At this point, I was hooked. This chain of events was clearly "too coincidental to be accidental", as Gary's dear friend, Susy Smith, used to say. As Gary explains in Chapter 1 (pages 3–44), a conservative estimate of the probability of these five events occurring by chance alone is less than one in a trillion!

From now on, Gary, I promise to keep my heart and mind wide open to life's potential synchronicities. I hope you, the reader, do, too.

Author's note: Dr. Brewer's chain of synchronicities turns out to be extraordinarily improbable. By the most conservative estimate, it would take more than 28 million years for Dr. Brewer's Type II Synchronicity to possibly occur by chance. But a consideration of the more likely estimate leads to the conclusion that it would take more than 200 times longer than the estimated age of our universe to potentially achieve the same result by chance! You will learn how to calculate such super improbabilities in Chapter 1.

Section One
Foundations of Supersynchronicity

May everyone experience at least one supersynchronicity in their personal and professional lives.

Chapter 1
Is Synchronicity Real? Essential Reading for All of Us, Including Skeptics

Whenever you have eliminated the impossible,
whatever remains, however improbable, must be the truth.
Sir Arthur Conan Doyle

This is an ambitious book. It offers a novel synthesis of personal observations, astronomical improbabilities, visionary science, and compelling incentives for us to act in the service of individual and global awakening. As you are about to discover, the wealth of synchronicities—many which are being revealed here for the first time—is sure to be extraordinarily thought-provoking. Chapter 1 is essential reading for all of us, including skeptics. I hope you choose to read it carefully.

A synchronicity, in the most basic sense, refers to the occurrence of two or more events in close proximity that do not seem to have any causal connection, but are still related meaningfully for certain people. As I will explain shortly, I have classified synchronicities as Type I (two events), Type II (three to five events), and Type III (six or more serial events), the latter also being called "supersynchronicity," which are rarer and more powerful.

Over the years, I have come to realize that "it takes a super mind to create and comprehend supersynchronicity." What I mean by this is that the more complex and sophisticated the documented sequences of synchronicities are, the more demanding they are of our minds to understand, and ultimately even to imagine that the patterns of events actually happened in the first place.

My own ability to observe, track, integrate, and interpret supersynchronicities has evolved substantially over the years. In light of the brilliant research on multiple intelligences conducted by Dr. Howard Gardner, a professor of education at Harvard University, it makes sense to envision the concept of "synchronicity intelligence" as a potential new type of multiple intelligence in the twenty-first century mind. Coincidentally (or maybe beyond coincidence?), Howard and I were fellow graduate students in the Department of Social Relations at Harvard in the late 1960s.

I propose that we need to develop our personal "super minds" to understand complex "supersynchronicities." Moreover, it may take a "cosmic Super Mind"—what Dr. Larry Dossey, MD, refers to as "the One Mind" in his seminal book titled *One Mind: How Our Individual Mind is Part of a Greater Consciousness and Why It Matters*—to create and comprehend "cosmic Supersynchronicities" that potentially interconnect and semi-orchestrate billions of beings, including people, animals, and even "spirits."

Some of the factual accounts found in this book, such as the sixteen documented supersynchronicities involving diverse individuals from all walks of life—from professors and physicians to a fictional FBI agent in a novel and a professional poker player—may at first seem difficult, if not impossible, to accept. At times, some readers may find themselves doubting, dismissing, or outright denigrating some of the information presented as evidence in this book. I understand those feelings. I have felt them myself, and often.

I sometimes feel like the skeptic who said to the distinguished anthropologist, Dr. Margaret Mead, "These are the kind of data I would not believe, even if they were true". For the record, in this book, all of the data (to the best of my reporting) are true.

A Banquet of Supersynchronicity Evidence

Part of the challenge for the reader is to successfully digest the full range of supersynchronicity evidence that is provided in this book. Trust me: you are about to be presented with a veritable banquet of supersynchronicities.

Imagine a buffet table the length of a football field offering a smorgasbord of Italian, French, Chinese, Indian, Hungarian, and Russian dishes, spanning appetizers, salads, breads, soups, main courses, side dishes, and desserts. How many dishes could you realistically savor in one sitting?

Similarly, the buffet of compelling supersynchronicity evidence that is presented in this book may seem overwhelming at times, especially if consumed too quickly.

Each individual chapter can be likened to a separate type of cuisine, a distinct seven-course meal to be savored and appreciated on its own. To avoid experiencing supersynchronicity indigestion, I encourage you to savor each of the varieties of synchronistic delicacies at your own pace.

I have crafted this book to be personal, playful, entertaining, and scientific. Indeed, as you will see, I am not averse to poking fun at the evidence. Nor am I averse to poking fun at myself!

Unfortunately, some scientists have a very narrow view of science, and might therefore dismiss any possibility of studying synchronicities scientifically. The irony is that this kind of narrow-mindedness is itself thoroughly anti-scientific. Science should be as open and unbiased as possible, and scientists should remain ready to study these phenomena that so many people experience daily in such a meaningful way.

Being appropriately skeptical is a vital part of the scientific process, but that does not grant us license to refuse to believe overwhelming evidence simply because it makes us feel psychologically or emotionally uncomfortable. The irony is that accusing someone of being unscientific while simultaneously refusing to examine (or even acknowledge) evidence is *itself* unscientific and anti-intellectual. If the sciences were to remain chained only to what is already known, they would never have been able to advance in the first place.

I will also introduce in these pages the concept of "self-science," which is especially important for the study of synchronicities, and which essentially refers to creatively applying the methods of science to the real-life laboratories of our personal lives. By providing you with self-science methods and tools that are easy to apply, you will have the opportunity to discover and evaluate for yourself synchronicities in your own life and in the lives of others.

Essential Reading for All of Us, Including Skeptics

To facilitate your reading the core parts of this book, I have prepared the following "required reading" sections to assist you in understanding the essential information. I have used a different font to highlight theses essential pages.

First, to understand how statistics, properly implemented, reveal the "astronomical improbabilities" of supersynchronicities, read this chapter **(pages 3–44).** As Dr. Bernard Beitman, MD, author of *Connecting with Coincidence: The New Science for Using Synchronicity and Serendipity in Your Life,* describes my analyses:

"At the start of this energetic book, he demolishes the statistician's favorite explanation for coincidences: the Law of Very Large Numbers."

Second, the eight conventional (and inadequate) explanations for supersynchronicity are summarized in Chapter 15 **(pages 228–233).** They are:

Anecdotal
Mistakes of perception and memory
Cherry picking
Pseudo-science
Easily explained by chance
Seeing patterns where none occur
Theoretically impossible
Unethical observer

As you will read, none of these hypotheses can responsibly and justifiably explain the totality of the synchronicity evidence reported in detail in this book.

Third, the eleven primary lessons discovered about supersynchronicities are summarized in Chapter 13 **(pages 209–211).** These lessons are fascinating, challenging, and meaningful, and as such they deserve your serious consideration.

Fourth, the "staircase of twelve possible explanations" for supersynchronicities is summarized in Chapter 16 **(pages 237–254).** They are:

Step 12 The One Mind—Collective
Step 11 The One Mind—Personal
Step 10 Higher Spiritual Beings
Step 9 Human Spirits
Step 8 Human Intention and Energy
Step 7 Biophysical and Social Self-Organization
Step 6 Geophysical and Astrophysical Forces
Step 5 Psychological and Social Causes
Step 4 Beyond Probable Chance
Step 3 Chance Coincidences
Step 2 Selective Attention
Step 1 Deception—Self or Other

As you will learn, genuine supersynchronicities require that we seriously consider physical (Steps 6–7), psychological (Step 8), and/or spiritual (Steps 9–12) explanations. Moreover, various *combinations* of Steps 8–12 may be involved in complex supersynchronicities.

Finally, my responses to twelve frequently asked questions about synchronicities can be found on **pages 281–293.**

As an educator as well as a researcher, my goal is to help readers discern what is primary. My responsibility is to provide you with sufficient reasoning and data to help you reach an evidence-based conclusion. My hope is that this book will help you reach your own conclusions, whatever they may be.

The Opportunity of Supersynchronicity

Supersynchronicity reveals what I call "the energy of opportunity," an explosive release or unfolding of latent energetic potential that is made possible by our gradual awakening to the existence, power, and inspiring nature of synchronicities in our increasingly interconnected lives. This extends what Canyon Ranch calls "the power of possibility".

My deeper purpose in writing this book is to give you the opportunity to learn something extraordinary about the underlying nature of life and the universe. As Sir Francis Bacon once said, "A wise man will make more opportunities than he finds." For many of you this will be a new experience, or at least a way to provide a deeper understanding of what you may have already experienced. You will have the opportunity to reexamine and enhance your personal and professional life, and to see life more broadly and grandly in a comprehensible yet increasingly mysterious way.

My ultimate goal was inspired by Bill Gates and Paul Allen's vision of a computer "on every desk and in every home", first mentioned in print in 1977. My hope and vision is that someday, *"every person will experience at least one supersynchronicity in their workplace and home."* I say "workplace" and "home," because it is the experiences of supersynchronicities in these two major contexts of our lives (professional and personal) that will enable us to fully accept and celebrate the core nature of synchronicity in the Greater Reality.

Why are Superynchronicities Important?

Besides being an interesting curiosity, why are supersynchronicities important? As I shall show, the likelihood of these events occurring by pure chance are so low that they only happen at time intervals that extend well beyond the current age of the universe.

And yet, they occur with incredible frequency. Clearly something else is involved besides random chance occurrences. Given this and other emerging evidence, it is becoming obvious that our current mainstream view of reality is flawed and incomplete. And if this is so, what else might be incorrect about our assumptions and understanding about reality?

Humans have lived on the planet for less than 100,000 years in our biological modern form, hardly a drop in the bucket of geological time. Our bodies are products of the earth's natural environment and evolutionary processes. For all of that time but the last few hundred years, most of our ancestors lived out their lives in harmony with nature. All living creatures, including humanity, used only what was needed to survive. Most everything that was taken was reused and recycled back into the environment. There was a sacred and deep connection between the living and the spirit world.

Essentially in the blink of an eye in geologic time we have developed technologies that now give us substantial dominion over the earth. Unfortunately many of us have forgotten our connection to the Earth and with Spirit. Between (1) our large and increasing population, (2) our greedy and self-serving ways, (3) our powerful technologies, and (4) our propensity for resolving conflicts by violent means, the current path that humanity is on is no longer sustainable. This path not only threatens our own survival but now also that of most life on the planet.

How would humanity react if it found clear scientific evidence that consciousness was a fundamental aspect of the universe?

That the consciousness of all living creatures was interconnected in fundamental and deep ways?

That consciousness is eternal and the memories and full emotional impact of all actions and corresponding consequences for every living human being on the planet were carried forever in human spirits, in higher spiritual beings or in the One Mind of all creation?

How would we treat the earth, our fellow humans and all the other creatures we share the planet with? Would we finally come to realize that Love is the organizing principle of Nature?

How would we live with such a realization and how would we treat our fellow travelers here on Earth?

A small mountain of evidence is accumulating that the current modern view of science regarding the nature of reality is not the correct view. Instead of the materialist position that everything is composed of matter and energy, we are now being forced to embrace the post-materialist view where we have to add consciousness and information into the mix as well. Synchronicities, psychic abilities, Near Death Experiences (NDEs), Out of Body Experiences (OBEs), extraordinary abilities (e.g. idiot savants), remote viewing, spontaneous healings, transcendent experiences (epiphanies) and many other phenomena are now providing clues to such a larger reality. And this larger reality also includes the survival of consciousness beyond bodily death.

Supersynchronicities provide one way for everyone to experience a small piece of this larger reality. With enough empirical evidence, from studying supersynchronicities and other related phenomena we can begin to develop models of how this larger reality may function. Theoretical models do not necessarily describe the exact mechanisms that nature and the Cosmos actually use, but models allow us to create testable predictions. From these predictions we can then create experiments and eventually theories. From these theories we will ultimately create or discover processes and technologies that will further enhance our understanding of nature and perhaps utilize nature's mechanisms in ways that were once thought of as fairy tales or pure fiction.

In a future book I will be discussing these theories and technologies that are currently being tested in laboratories around the world. Perhaps one day these technologies will allow us to communicate with what I now consider to be hypothesized collaborative discarnate (HCDs) entities (i.e. spirits). If we are successful in this effort, what then will be the fate and future destiny for humanity and all of the earth's living creatures?

What Do You Believe?

What do you believe about the reality of synchronicity?

If you already believe that synchronicity is real and/or you prefer to experience the delights of some delicious supersynchronicity meals before understanding their recipes and preparations, you may wish to save the rest of this overview chapter for later. This chapter gets a bit technical in places, especially our discussion of some basic statistics. I invite you to read just the next two paragraphs, and then skip to Chapter 2 *(so long as you do not forget to read the rest of this chapter later* ☺).

However, if you question whether synchronicity is real and/or you prefer to understand the discovery and science of supersynchronicity before enjoying the meals, I strongly encourage you to savor the rest of this chapter now.

However, whether you currently do or do not believe in synchronicities, it is still the case that a methodological study can increase our understanding, and thereby enhance our synchronistic abilities. Fortunately, we can accurately confirm the reality of synchronicity through the creative application of the methods of science to the natural and real-life laboratories of our personal lives by engaging in what I refer to as "self-science."

Science, Scientism, and Self-Science

The essence of the scientific method involves the careful observation and recording of information followed by the unbiased and honest evaluation of potential alternative explanations of the data. But as Dr. Charles T. Tart elegantly explains in his book *The End of Materialism,* there is a fundamental distinction between science and "scientism."

Science, in its ideal form, is an unbiased and open process of discovery and learning. It does not dictate which questions or theories are acceptable and which are considered taboo. Scientism, on the other hand, is a set of dogmas about which observations and hypotheses are allowed within the umbrella of science, and which are excluded.

A common characteristic of scientism is the core belief, held by a majority of senior scientists living today, that only those explanations that are "material" in nature can be included in science.

If the scientific method reveals that certain phenomena cannot be adequately explained simply in materialist terms—for example, that A causes B exclusively via physical or chemical means—then by definition these phenomena are not part of science and should be ignored. Those who do wish to scientifically study such phenomena are often labeled as "pseudoscientists" by the adherents of scientism.

However, true science is about "following the data wherever they lead," and seeking truthful explanations about currently unknown areas of possible exploration. Scientism, on the other hand, is about "following the data only if they can be explained in terms of our current assumptions," and rejects any phenomena or explanations that fall beyond this narrow comfort zone. The current reigning paradigm in scientism is known as "materialism," the belief that only physical things are real, despite the fact that such an assumption is not itself scientifically provable.

It should be self-evident that I prefer the process of science to the practice of scientism.

Moreover, I have learned through laboratory experiments, as well as direct personal experience, that certain questions can only be addressed when individuals conduct the research themselves and are allowed to reach their own conclusions.

Synchronicity is a case in point. Although others can be of assistance to the process, you must ultimately discover synchronicities for yourself, and the practice of self-science is a vital part of this discovery process.

Self-science is participatory science, in that we each serve as both experimenters and subjects in the investigation. This fact places extra responsibility on us to function as accurate and cautious scientists in the natural laboratory of our personal lives. It requires that we be creative and open-minded synchronicity detectives.

I first thought about the idea of self-science—though I did not call it by that name at the time—when I was doing systematic research on biofeedback and self-regulation of physiological processes at Harvard and Yale in the late 1960s, 70s, and early 80s. Self-science can be great fun. It can be an adventure for one's entire life, from childhood to advanced adulthood. Self-science fosters self-discovery, self-realization, self-insight, and self-understanding.

My purpose in writing *Super Synchronicity* was not merely to enable you to reach the conclusion that synchronicities are real, but to inspire you to become a synchronicity self-scientist yourself, to have your own adventures in synchronicity, and then to help to awaken others.

As you read this book, I welcome you to enter my mind and heart as I come to discover, slowly but surely, the existence of ever more complex, challenging, and weird patterns of events occurring in my personal life—events which were highly interconnected with similar events involving the lives of numerous colleagues, students, family, and friends. It has been an incredible journey, and it is an honor to share a piece of it with you.

Before discussing the Type III string of synchronicities involving the prefix "super," let's first consider the following set of events that transpired just a few days prior to my editing of this Overview.

A Propitious and Exemplary Set of Spontaneous Synchronicities

Event #1: I had received an email from Dr. Lisa Miller, a professor of psychology and education at Columbia University. In her email she invited me to participate in a small think tank at Columbia to discuss the relationship between contemporary physics and spirituality.

For this event, she had selected those professionals who had contributed chapters to her *Oxford Handbook of Psychology and Spirituality,* which was soon to be released by Oxford University Press (an important point to note as you read further).

Although I was unaware of it at the time, her email contained two striking synchronicities, which I discuss below.

Event #2: Later that day, while I was driving in my car, I was inspired to call my wife Rhonda to tell her about Dr. Miller's surprise invitation, and to ask for her advice on whether I should make the trip to the east coast. As it so happened, I had previously been invited to speak at a meeting called the "Synchro Summit" at Yale University, scheduled to be held a few weeks earlier than the Columbia meeting. Both events intrigued me, but I was reluctant to make two crosscountry trips in such a short span of time.

As I was telling Rhonda about Dr. Miller's invitation, I happened to notice a political campaign sign on the side of the road touting someone named Brian Miller. The timing seemed highly improbable, even more so because during the years Rhonda and I had been married (up to that point in time), we had never discussed anyone by the name of Miller. Now, here we were talking about (Lisa) Miller, while at the same time a roadside poster flashed by trumpeting the political virtues of a fellow named (Brian) Miller. I mentioned this improbable observation to Rhonda literally as it was occurring. Was the Miller/Miller co-occurrence merely a coincidence? Perhaps.

[Note: my writing of this section was just interrupted by an unexpected phone call. The significance of this will become clear in a moment.]

Event #3: I wanted to turn around and take a picture of the Miller sign with my then-new smart phone, which I had purchased specifically for taking photographs of meaningful synchronous events. But at that very moment, I noticed another sign on the side of the road that took my breath away. The sign heralded a business called Oxford Realty!

Think about this: a Miller/Miller combination was immediately followed by an Oxford/Oxford combo. Were these two combinations of events merely an extraordinarily improbable pair of coincidences, or was something more profound at work?

Event #4: As just mentioned above, in the process of my inserting the preceding paragraphs into the introduction of this chapter, I happened to receive a Skype call from Dr. Sonia Doi, a professor in the Department of Medicine at the Uniformed Services University of the Health Sciences. I had to stop writing my account of the Miller/Miller and Oxford/Oxford pair of synchronicities to take her call.

Was this just a coincidence, too? It turned out that the primary purpose of Dr. Doi's call was to invite me to speak at an upcoming conference on spirituality and medicine to be held in São Paulo, Brazil. What was unusual and potentially significant about the timing of Dr. Doi's call was that:

(1) it happened to involve the same practical issue as the Miller/Oxford connection—the need to weigh the pros and cons of making multiple long distance professional trips, and

(2) it happened to coincide with my spontaneous decision to insert the Miller/Miller and Oxford/Oxford examples here in the first place.

As an interesting experiment, let's estimate the probability—or perhaps I should say *improbability*—of my receiving Dr. Doi's phone call just as I was specifically writing about synchronicity and the question of long-distance traveling.

At that point in my career, I typically received three to five invitations a year to speak at a venue outside of the United States, and another three to five invitations to speak somewhere along the east coast. Historically the overwhelming majority (e.g. over 90%) of those invitations were made via email or snail mail. If we limit the phone call "window of opportunity" to the possibility of having four calls per hour (i.e. a 15 minute conversation) during a 40-hour work week, then during a given year there would be 8320 opportunities (4 calls times 40 hours times 52 weeks) to receive a phone call invitation involving long distance travel.

Of course, I could potentially receive a professional call any time outside the regular 40-hour work week (e.g. evenings and weekends, which I regularly do), so this is a conservative assumption.

Dividing 8320 by 1 (the average number of invitations I typically receive by phone per year involving long distance travel) gives us a result of 8320. In other words, the probability of Dr. Doi *interrupting me with a query about traveling while I was typing something about traveling* was conservatively estimated to be a 1 in 8320 probability (or 1 divided by 8320 equals $p < .00012$, where "p" stands for "probability").

In science, a 1 in 20 probability is termed statistically significant—in other words, beyond chance. (1 divided by 20 equals $p < .05$) 1 in 100 ($p < .01$), and especially 1 in a 1000 ($p < .001$) are often termed highly significant.

Therefore, by adopting this definition, 1 in 8320 ($p < .00012$) is clearly highly statistically significant, and the significance would have been even higher ($p < .000001$) for this pair of events had we not used such conservative starting assumptions.

I invite you to take a moment to try to put yourself in my shoes. How would you interpret the observation of improbable co-occurrences, especially those that turn out to be "astronomically improbable" (see below)?

Coincidence, or Something More: What Do You Believe?

Yes, coincidences can (and do) happen, which is only to say that two events can happen without any apparent causal or meaningful relationship. In principle this can happen for any p value, and certainly can happen for values of $p <.05$, $p<.01$, and $p<.001$

And yes, people can (and do) sometimes falsely attribute causality or meaning to patterns of events when there may not be any such inherent causality or meaning at all. This is especially true (1) if the people in question happen to lack the relevant understanding of mathematics and science, (2) if they are biased or irrational, and / or (3) if they are potentially suffering from delusion or some other psychiatric illness.

However, individuals such as Dr. Stephen Brewer, whom you met in the Introduction to this book, are well aware of the existence of coincidence (chance) and the need for caution in interpreting a possible linkage between events.

Furthermore, Dr. Brewer is not a naïve or easily swayed person. He is (1) highly educated in the sciences, (2) relatively conservative in his thinking (yet open to new information that may supersede prior assumptions, as any genuine scientist must be), (3) a successful physician and medical department head, and (4) a first-rate athlete.

The question then arises: why are people of such sound mind and body increasingly drawing the conclusion that synchronicities in everyday life are real?

What about you? Are you intrigued by the possible reality of synchronicity?

Not surprisingly, people's belief systems on the subject run the full gamut from a strong positive belief, such as espoused by the philosophy of New Age spirituality, to a strong negative disbelief, such as expressed by inveterate skeptics.

Most adherents of contemporary spirituality are not only convinced that the phenomenon of synchronicity is real, they believe that synchronicity is the rule rather than the exception in nature and the universe. In their view, chance does not exist. Everything in life happens for a reason, whether or not we are cognizant of the reason.

A well-known fiction writer who advocates the reality of synchronicity is James Redfield. His 1993 novel *The Celestine Prophecy* inspired millions of people worldwide to search for the presence of non-random, meaningful connections in their lives. As of May 2005, *The Celestine Prophecy* had reportedly sold more than 20 million copies worldwide and had been translated into more than thirty languages.

In the late 1990s I was encouraged to read *The Celestine Prophecy* by a student at the University of Arizona. Although this book is a work of fiction, it was apparently Redfield's intention to write it as a parable. Redfield saw his novel as a means of illustrating key points and teaching core lessons.

I enjoy reading novels, particularly those that nurture the imagination and teach valuable lessons about our history and/or our possible future. Despite being a scientist, when I elect to read a novel I typically do not focus on verifying which aspects of the novel are fact and which are fiction. I tend to treat novels primarily as entertainment, not as tools for scientific education.

However, I was motivated to investigate the real-life theme of synchronicity as fictionalized in Redfield's novel, because I had been experiencing repeated synchronicities in my own life. Moreover, I had been keeping records of these occurrences and pondering their potential significance with the same kind of inquisitiveness and cautiousness that I apply to my controlled laboratory research.

During the more than three decades I had been exploring the significance of synchronicity in my private life (and the lives of many others), I came to the realization—time and again—that the real-life events I was chronicling were often more bizarre and unbelievable than what I was reading in works of fiction. In fact, I sometimes felt that what I was recording sounded like a rendition of Harry Potter meets the Wizard of Oz!

In 2008, I decided that I had collected sufficient evidence from my personal life, as well as the lives of numerous colleagues, students, and friends. I now needed to write a book describing in significant detail real life evidence for synchronicity. Two-thirds of what was to become this book and its sequel were completed in the summer of 2008. Though the accounts were all real, the truth is that they too often seemed preposterous, and I kept returning to the conclusion that the events, somehow, had to be merely coincidences—in other words, chance occurrences.

Distinguishing Coincidence from Synchronicity, Chance from Purpose, and Fiction from Fact

As mentioned above, it is essential to understand that coincidences do happen. Sometimes two or more events occur in close proximity, and their co-occurrence is random. What this means in statistics is that a given event is independent of prior events. Another way of stating this is that a given event is not causing or influencing another event.

For example, if you flip a two-sided coin many times, you will observe on average an equal number of heads and tails. However, if you flip the coin enough times—and the key word here is "enough"—eventually you will get a string of ten heads in a row simply by chance alone.

This is not a speculation—it is a mathematical certainty. But being an experimental scientist, I prefer to document the evidence for myself.

Prior to writing this chapter, I designed a software program that makes it relatively easy to track complex patterns/sequences/strings of "heads and tails" (1's and 0's) over hundreds of thousands or even millions of coin flips (bits). It could literally take you or me, while working 40 hours a week, 52 weeks a year, a couple of months to perform 100,000 coin flips and then calculate by hand all of the runs of heads in data. A computer, however, can do this in an instant.

As a test, I programmed the computer to "flip the bits" 100,000 times using a random number generator (RNG) algorithm. Each time I did this, I received a similar result: there were approximately one hundred strings of ten or more heads or tails (ten or more 1's or 0's) in a row.

No matter how many times I might run the experiment, I would get virtually the same result. Count on it—it's bankable.

On the other hand, using the computer RNG algorithm to flip the bits 100,000 times, I have never observed a single string of thirty or more 1's or 0's in a row. I have performed this experiment several thousands of times, and thus far have never witnessed thirty or more 1's or 0's occurring in a row in the span of 100,000 flips.

The main point here is that some patterns are sufficiently improbable to *virtually* never occur *within a finite amount of time,* which essentially means that they are, practically speaking, *finitely* beyond statistical chance. In fact, sometimes the probability of their occurring *in real time* may literally be beyond the age of the universe. I use the term "astronomically improbable" to describe such an improbability, and I will offer an example of how to make such calculations shortly.

As you have no doubt concluded by this point, I enjoy working with numbers. Moreover, I stand in awe of the ability of the human mind to develop innovative mathematical tools essential for creating the extraordinary technologies that most of us take for granted.

Because I am adept at statistics, I am able to responsibly estimate the statistical probability of obtaining by chance the wealth of co-occurrence evidence I was accumulating in my daily life. And what I have discovered has shaken me to my core.

In truth, the totality of the observations of real-life patterns has been so extraordinarily improbable as to be far beyond statistical chance. *The accumulated evidence is not only beyond a reasonable doubt; it is beyond virtually any doubt from a strictly mathematical viewpoint.*

However, despite such mathematical certainty I was still left with *emotional doubt,* which in this case was essentially equivalent to *unreasonable doubt from a mathematical perspective.* What the statistics were demonstrating was that life is far more complicated, connected, patterned, and ordered than anything I could comfortably, or conceivably, imagine.

I do not, and would not, expect you to take my word for this.

In this book, you will read more than a dozen chapters that present enough evidence for you to draw your own conclusions. I invite you to relive the journey with me as I slowly but inexorably awakened to the conclusion that all of this, and so much more, is real.

Just as science fiction can sometimes become science fact, I was led to the conclusion that what I presumed must be *synchronicity fiction* was actually *synchronicity fact.*

I was inspired to complete the first draft of *Super Synchronicity* in the summer of 2009, partly because of the emergence of new scientific discoveries that readily could explain how synchronicity works, and partly because of a novel which was then to be published, curiously titled *The Twelve.* The novel was written by William Gladstone, a brilliant and inspired science-minded, spiritually-hearted literary agent, businessman, and author.

The Twelve was taken from Gladstone's life experiences, and like *The Celestine Prophecy,* it was intended to be a parable. Like *The Celestine Prophecy,* some of *The Twelve* was intentionally and explicitly fictional.

However, in addition to certain factual parallels between the main character Max and the author—for example, both Max and Bill had fathers who were publishers, both completed their undergraduate education at Yale University, both did graduate studies at Harvard University, and left prior to finishing their PhD's—the foundation of the novel was based upon the presumed reality of synchronicity.

As you can appreciate from having read the Foreword, I happen to know Bill well. Bill edited my first book, *The Living Energy Universe,* and like Max in his novel, whose single equation "A is and is not equal to A" was featured in *The Twelve, The Living Energy Universe* also included a single equation which was what convinced Bill that my scientific theory about feedback memory was real.

As I read the pre-publication galley of Bill's book, I realized that supersynchronicity provided the scientific evidence and foundation for the parable of *The Twelve.* Since Bill happens to be my literary agent, it seemed propitious to follow the publication of his fictional story about synchronicity with a non-fiction book about the reality of synchronicity.

What is curious is that if I did not know the absolute factual basis of supersynchronicity, I would be hard pressed to decide which of the two books was driven more by the imagination of its respective author.

Though the first draft of this book was completed at that time, we decided it was prudent to delay its publication until I had completed other books and projects. The version you are now reading benefits greatly from our having made this decision.

Three Categories of Synchronicities

In my work and research, I have discovered that it is possible to divide synchronicities into three basic categories, based upon the number of events that occur within a given period of time.

Type I Synchronicity: Single Pair of Events

A Type I Synchronicity is when a single pair of improbable events happens to occur. To no one's surprise, this is the most common type of synchronicity. For example, you might be spontaneously thinking about a friend you have not spoken with in years, and then, seemingly out of the blue, they call you.

I recently learned of a striking Type I Synchronicity from a husband and wife who were admirers of Dr. Paul Pearsall, one of the individuals to whom I have dedicated this book. I happened to have had dinner with this couple a few months before I started writing my book. They told me that they had participated in a workshop given by Dr. Pearsall in California, and they wanted to invite him to speak at one of their educational functions.

Dr. Pearsall lived in Hawaii, thousands of miles from where the couple lived in the Midwest. While they were vacationing in Manhattan and exploring Central Park, they spontaneously happened to be discussing how they might contact Dr. Pearsall.

Guess who they happened to bump into in Central Park at just that moment? You got it: Dr. Pearsall and his wife, Celeste. The couple experienced this coincidence as a strikingly improbable and meaningful synchronicity.

The problem with such Type I Synchronicities is that regardless of how improbable a given pair of events might be, the fact is that improbable events *do* happen, especially given enough time. (Think back to the example of flipping the coins.) You can read about this in Dr. David Hand's statistics book *The Improbability Principle.*

In another example profiled earlier in this chapter, had Dr. Brewer simply experienced his strange dream about multiple sclerosis, and then met the exercise physiologist who had had the memorable conversation with a Canyon Ranch guest about multiple sclerosis—and nothing else had transpired—this would be classified as a Type I Synchronicity, and might well have been a chance and non-meaningful coincidence.

Type II Synchronicity: Three to Five Events

A Type II Synchronicity occurs when three to five improbable events of a similar nature happen within a relatively short span of time. In statistics, the more events that happen in a given period of time, the more improbable is the pattern or sequence of events. These are called "conditional probabilities." For those who may not be familiar with statistics, I offer a few examples to help make the concept easier to understand.

There is very little math in this book, but it is important in this short section to draw from basic statistics in order to emphasize the extraordinary improbability of a Type II Synchronicity, such as Dr. Brewer's, occurring merely by chance.

If you prefer to skim this section, you need only know that by the most conservative estimate, it would take more than 28 million years for Dr. Brewer's Type II Synchronicity to possibly occur by chance. But a consideration of the more likely estimate leads to the conclusion that it would take more than 200 times longer than the estimated age of our universe to potentially achieve the same result by chance! And as incredible as this might sound, for the Dr. Peasall Type I Synchronicity, it would take approximately 1,388 times the age of the universe to achieve the same result by chance!

Conditional probabilities are calculated by multiplying the individual probabilities per event. In the case of coin flips—the simplest case—the probability of getting a head on a given flip is 50/50, or 1 out of 2. The probability of getting two heads in a row is ½ multiplied by ½, or ¼. In other words, the probability of getting two heads in a row is 1 in 4, or 25 percent (indicated as $p = .25$).

The probability of getting 3 heads in a row is ½ x ½ x ½ = 1/8. The probability of getting three heads in a row is therefore 1 in 8, or 12.5 percent. Four heads in a row becomes 1/16 or 6.25 percent; five heads in a row becomes 1/32 or 3.125 percent, and so forth.

In psychological science, if the probability of something happening by chance is less than 5 percent (indicated as $p < .05$, as mentioned previously), it is said to be "statistically significant" and interpreted as possibly "non-random."

Notice that if instead of flipping coins we were flipping a six-sided die, the probability of getting a 1, for example, would be 1/6. Getting two 1's in a row would be 1/6 x 1/6, which is 1/36, or 2.778 percent. So this event is already "statistically significant."

The probability of getting five l's in a row is 1/6 x 1/6 x 1/6 x 1/6 x 1/6, which is 1/7776 or 0.012 percent ($p < .00012$). This would be termed "highly statistically significant."

Type II Synchronicities are by definition less common, especially those involving five events. In the case of Dr. Brewer, he experienced four of the events involving multiple sclerosis in the span of a few hours, and the fifth a few days later.

Since the five events happened within a short span of time, it is possible to make conservative probability calculations of his Type II Synchronicity.

Here is a review of the five events experienced by Dr. Brewer, with our conservative probability estimates:

(1) Dr. Brewer having such an unusual and vivid dream (1 in 1000), and
(2) his spontaneously speaking with a person about multiple sclerosis (1 in 100), and
(3) his spontaneously sharing events concerning multiple sclerosis with another person, and discovering that they had just been diagnosed with multiple sclerosis (1 in 10,000), and
(4) his hearing a story about a person listening to an educational tape about a diet that had allegedly cured a woman of her multiple sclerosis (1 in 10,000), and
(5) me being on a radio program whose star happened to be discussing her multiple sclerosis in the educational tape mentioned above (1 in 10,000).

We then calculated the total conditional probability of this Type II Synchronicity (1000 x 100 x 10,000 x 10,000 x 10,000) occurring by chance to be less than 1 in 100,000,000,000,000,000, or, *1 in 100,000 trillion.*

If you prefer to reduce each of our subjective estimates by a factor of 10 (100 x 10 x 1,000 x 1,000 x 1,000), this still comes out to be 1 in 1,000,000,000,000, or, *1 in a trillion,* a very highly improbable number.

How can we understand such gigantic numbers? It helps if we convert the probability number into how much time it would take, under ideal circumstances, to observe a Type II pattern of events to occur by chance. We will use Dr. Brewer's pattern of events as our example, and first consider the smaller number, 1 in 1,000,000,000,000.

What one in a trillion means in terms of total time is that it would take us 1,000,000,000,000 times or trials of attempting to observe the pattern by chance to see it happen just once.

The question arises: how long would it take us to observe the Dr. Brewer Type II Synchronicity pattern if we could collect data 24 hours a day, 365 days a year (recognizing that this is not biologically possible to do)?

How long would it take: A month? A year? Ten years? A hundred years? The answer is rather extraordinary: it would take approximately 28.5 million years!

How do we calculate such a number?

First, we determine how many minutes there are in a year. 60 minutes per hour times 24 hours a day times 365 days a year equals 525,600 minutes a year.

Second, we estimate how many minutes it would take for all five of Dr. Brewer's types of events to occur.

- Event #1: How long, on the average, does it take to have a dream? Let's say 5 minutes.
- Event #2: How long, on the average, does it take to spontaneously speak with someone? Let's say 2 minutes.
- Event #3: How long, on the average, does it take to share an event with someone and have them respond in kind? Let's say 3 minutes.
- Event #4: How long, on the average, does it take to hear someone share an experience? Let's say 2 minutes.
- Event #5: It is similar to Event #3. Let's say 3 minutes.

The shortest amount of time for all five events to occur on the average—if they could somehow occur one after the other—would be 5 + 2 + 3 + 2 + 3 = 15 minutes.

The exact lengths of time are not important here. Debating whether the estimated total amount of time should be shorter or longer misses the important take-home message. *The reason is that even if the total time for all five events was estimated to be only 1 minute, we would still be left with a number in excess of a million years, far beyond the lifespan of a person—or the entire human species, for that matter!*

Third, we divide the total number of minutes per year by the total number of minutes it would take for the five events to occur. 525,600 minutes per year times 15 minutes per pattern of events is 35,040 possible patterns of events per year in terms of time taken for them to occur.

Finally, we divide 1,000,000,000,000 (1 in a trillion chance) by the 35,040 possible patterns of events per year. This gives us 28,538,812 years.

It follows that if we use the larger number (1 in 100,000 trillion), the total time would increase to approximately 2,853,881,200,000 years, or 2,853 billion years. Since the universe is generally believed to be "only" 13.7 billion years old, this would mean that it would take 208 times longer than the age of the universe for Dr. Brewer's Type II Synchronicity to occur by chance!

And as astounding as these Type II Synchronicity numbers are, the values for Type III Synchronicities are typically even more incredible. It is appropriate to describe such values as *"astronomically improbable."*

The simplest instance of calculating a conditional probability is for a single pair of events—a Type I Synchronicity. It turns out that every now and again, even a single pair of events can generate a conditional probability that is astronomically improbable.

Let's consider how we would calculate the conditional probability of Couple A, who lives in the Midwest, spontaneously bumping into Couple B, who lives in Hawaii, in New York City, just around the time that Couple A were talking about Couple B. Then, let's convert this value into the time it would take for this precise pairing of events to happen by chance.

Let's be conservative and say there are a hundred million couples living on the planet today.

Of course, if the specific couples happened to live nearby to each other, there would be a reasonably high probability that they would cross paths in a relatively short period of time.

However, if they lived thousands of miles apart, the probability of their spontaneously bumping into each other at any given moment would become extraordinarily low.

Moreover, in order for the two couples to actually cross paths, they have to not only have the ability to travel, but the circumstances must be such that they end up traveling to the same general location at the same time, and then find themselves in precisely the same place at exactly the same time.

While being mindful of these straightforward qualifications, we can still consider what the implications would be of our using the value of one hundred million couples, and calculate the conditional probability of one hundred million times one hundred million, which equals 10,000,000,000,000,000. That is 10,000 trillion, or 10,000,000 billion.

Now, how does this value translate into time?

How long would it take for a specific Couple A, who are talking about a specific Couple B, to be walking along and notice Couple B and then say something like, "Wow—could that be Couple B? Amazing.... That's them!" For ease of calculation, let's estimate that this takes maybe one minute in earth time to occur.

Being conservative again, let's give Couple A every opportunity to bump into Couple B. Let's imagine that our two couples can be walking around, possibly bumping into each other, 24 hours a day, 356 days a year (even though this is not biologically possible—people have to sleep, eat, etc.).

Using the values we have already calculated, we know there are 525,600 minutes a year. When we divide 10,000 trillion by 525,600, we get 19,025,875,190,258. When we divide this number by 13.7 billion, the age of the universe, the result is approximately 1,388 times the age of the universe! This is a truly astronomical amount of time.

Yes, these are over-simplified estimates, and we can certainly be more conservative. Let's say we wanted to be ultra conservative, and we decided to make the unrealistic assumption that Couple A could register and respond to Couple B in one second rather than in one minute.

The calculation is straightforward: we would divide 1388 by 60. This number tells us that it would now take approximately 23.1 times the age of the universe for Couple A to bump into Couple B by chance. The number is still astronomical.

If we wanted to be even more conservative, we could reduce the number of couples living on the planet today to 10 million rather than 100 million (obviously a gross underestimation of the number of couples living on the planet today). Doing so would reduce the estimated time for Couple A to bump into Couple B to only 190 million years.

However, it is essential that we remember that most people living today do not live more than 100 years. Moreover, the actual ability of one couple on the planet to bump into another couple living thousands of miles away only became practical in the twentieth century with the invention of air travel. Furthermore, it is believed that our species has only been on the planet for 200,000 years.

The bottom line is that in terms of actual real life, if chance were the correct explanation for these kinds of improbable events, then none of us would live long enough to ever experience them.

Type III Synchronicity: Six or More Events

A Type III Synchronicity is when six or more events of a given kind happen within a relatively short period of time. As you can imagine, Type III Synchronicities are so rare that many people never experience one.

As you will discover, however, Type III Synchronicities can and do happen. In fact, they can even happen frequently to certain individuals—and sometimes so frequently it can be downright uncanny. I sometimes jokingly describe Type III Synchronicities as being "synchronicities of the third kind."

Indeed, they often seem to have an "otherworldly" quality. They are typically very complex, if not super-complex. In this book I will share with you many Type III Synchronicities, and how I came to discover them.

What you are about to read might be described as being "when the real becomes surreal." And if we could calculate the conditional probability for this set of events, it would be super-astronomically improbable.

My Awakening to Supersynchronicity, and Ultimately to the Three Categories of Synchronicities

On August 9, 2008, I was scheduled to give an invited address at a one-day meeting held at the Four Seasons Hotel in Santa Barbara, California. The subject of my talk was my then-recently published book, *The Energy Healing Experiments*.

The event was sponsored by Mr. Robert Heiman, founder of SAIOE: The Gift of Knowing. SAIEO stands for Sense of Appreciation, Inspiration, Openness, and Essence.

At 8:00 in the morning, an hour and a half before the SAIOE meeting was to begin, I called Rhonda in Tucson and discussed with her an intriguing emerging realization about my unfolding synchronicity journey.

I was just beginning to realize that most of the diverse synchronicities I was recounting in this book shared a core statistical characteristic. As you are learning, the chapters in this book describe the unfolding of complex combinations and sequential patterns of multiple improbable events that, when taken together, go so far beyond plausible levels of chance as to seem almost impossible.

I was in the process of discovering that the common evidential theme connecting all of these accounts was that each involved the occurrence of complex patterns of multiple synchronicities, what we might think of as "synchronicities of synchronicities."

I was coming to realize that these surprisingly sophisticated sequences of synchronicities were expressing a newly observed replicated phenomenon that deserved a precise term to describe them. I imagined various possible new terms to describe such extensive sequences or strings of synchronicities, including mega-synchronicities, macro-synchronicities, and supersynchronicities.

I asked Rhonda what she thought of the term mega-synchronicity. Other words in science that use the prefix "mega" include megabits, megabacterium, and megafauna, so my suggestion had scientific precedent. In response, Rhonda reminded me that words beginning with "mega" were not always positive in connotation (for example, megalomania). She wondered what I thought of using the prefix "super" (which I had also considered, but had not yet mentioned to her).

Rhonda and I discussed a number of well-known examples of respected words in science that used the prefix "super," including supercollider, supercomputer, and superclusters of galaxies.

Notice that we were not using the prefix "super" here like the word "supernatural," meaning "beyond" natural, but rather like the terms "superstar" or "super bowl" meaning "really big" or "biggest."

I smiled as I listened to Rhonda say the word "supersynchronicity" because prior to that phone call I had never heard it spoken aloud, and I must say, it sounded pretty super to me.

I thanked Rhonda for her insightful suggestion and I told her I would ponder it.

At the time Rhonda and I were engaged in this creative conversation, I did not imagine the possibility that the word "super" might soon show up repeatedly, in ever more improbable ways, and eventually become a supersynchronicity itself.

In fact, it was the immediate emergence of a complex and extensive sequence of synchronicities involving the word "super" that led me to conclude that supersynchronicity was an accurate and meaningful scientific term to describe what I was experiencing.

I typed "supersynchronicity" into my smart phone, and went to the meeting.

This would turn out to be Event #1.

The first speaker, at 9:30, was Robert Heiman. He gave an inspired speech about the origin and implications of SAIOE.

Midway through his presentation, he spoke about quantum physics and emphasized the concept of "superposition."

Passionately engrossed in his subject, Robert explained the paradox of an electron being similar to a cloud of possibilities: its potential existence is present in multiple regions of space simultaneously until it is observed. It then collapses (as physicists describe it) into a finite localized particle. While it is not vitally important for our purpose here to understand this important concept in quantum physics, what is significant is that Robert was emphasizing the concept of *superposition,* which happens to be a "super" word. For the record, this was not a meeting on quantum physics or engineering; it was a conference for psychotherapists and healers and anyone else interested in the topics we were discussing.

I typed the word "superposition" into my smart phone. At this point I did not consider it to be, by itself, a synchronicity.

However, it turned out to be Event #2.

The next speaker, Greg Moers, the creator of LifeCamp Coaching and the moderator of the meeting, gave a brief but passionate presentation about SAIOE in relation to life coaching, and he happened to speak about his work with "super-achievers"! First the audience was lectured about superposition, and now about super-achievers? I began to wonder if more super-words would pop up during the meeting.

This was Event #3.

Then, just before Greg was about to introduce me, he spontaneously recounted a recent experience that had taught him a great lesson. Neither the experience nor the lesson is important here; what is important is that Greg's experience occurred, of all places, in a supermarket, and he repeated the word "supermarket" several times!

I could not remember the last time I had been to a clinical or scientific meeting in which the presenter told a story involving a supermarket. I typed "supermarket" into my smart phone.

This was Event #4.

My lecture was next, and I had also included a term using the prefix "super" in my talk. I presented data using a device called the SQUID, an acronym that stands for "Superconducting Quantum Interference Device." The SQUID is an instrument that measures tiny magnetic fields (called microteslas). Since I typically mention the SQUID when I lecture about energy healing, I did not include it in the emerging sequence of synchronicities involving the prefix "super."

However, the next speaker, Dr. Asher Milgrom, founder of American Medical Aesthetics Corporation (now called AMA Skincare), discussed the concept of "superimposition" as it applies to the use of cold lasers in aesthetic medical treatments. While the technical meaning of superimposition is not important to us here, the fact that the word "super" was mentioned again is very significant.

This became Event #5.

As I typed "superimposition" into my smart phone, I tried to recall the last time I had attended a conference in which the first four speakers (including myself) had all employed one or more concepts containing the prefix "super." I could not recall a single one. Since I am neither a physicist nor an engineer, I do not attend meetings that regularly employ terms with this prefix.

In light of hearing about superpositions, super-achievers, supermarkets, and superimpositions—all within a single conference—I started thinking more seriously about the emerging concept of supersynchronicities.

The following morning, as I was reading the novel *The Narrows* by Michael Connelly, I came across the following phrase on page 145: "You left your superhero in here, Buddy".

I realized that in the types of mystery and science fiction novels I tend to read, the term "superhero" is *not* a common word—hence it became Event #6.

As I pondered the word "superhero" and its curious appearance at that moment, I was reminded that on my way to Santa Barbara, I had spent the afternoon in Palo Alto, California with a superstar named Phil Hellmuth, who is known somewhat infamously as the "Poker Brat". Phil was the winner of the most World Series of Poker bracelets (at that time, 11), and he had a special interest in probabilities and synchronicities, hence my reason for seeing him.

I could not recall ever having made a special trip to speak about synchronicity with a celebrity poker superstar.

This became Event #7.

Think about it—here we have a combination of:

- (1) my first ever intentional meeting with a superstar to discuss probabilities and synchronicities on August 8, 2008 with
- (2) the birthing of the concept of supersynchronicity as spoken aloud by my wife Rhonda on the morning of August 9, followed on that same day by
- (3–6) multiple lectures emphasizing superposition, superachiever, supermarket, and superimposition, and then, on the next day,
- (7) my coming across the word "superhero" in the first few pages of a novel I was reading.

Quite a string, isn't it? Is it any wonder that on August 10, I was entertaining the possibility that I was experiencing a supersynchronicity regarding the prefix "super"? Wouldn't *you* be entertaining that possibility?

However, it was the next super improbable and meaningful event that occurred on August 10 that convinced me that this book should include the term supersynchronicity.

Rhonda and I had planned to see the blockbuster movie *Dark Knight,* which happened to be about a superhero (Batman) and featured numerous Hollywood superstars. Since many movies involve superheroes and feature superstars, I did not consider the movie to be part of a potential supersynchronicity. Because Rhonda and I had a few minutes to spare before the previews were to begin, we decided to visit the local bookstore.

Rhonda happened to notice a book titled *The Case for a Creator: A Journalist Investigates Scientific Evidence That Points Toward God.* The book was written by Lee Strobel and published by Zondervan.

Without giving it a thought, Rhonda spontaneously opened the book to pages 144–145. There, in capitalized and bolded letters, she read a chapter subheading titled **"THE SUPERMIND"**.

No way could she miss *that* title!

As you can imagine, she was startled by this novel super-word presented in such a bold fashion. The quality of her voice when she called out to me suggested that she had come across something of note, and so I hurried to her side.

When she told me what she had found, I had a hard time believing what I was hearing and seeing. I felt as though I was having an "Alice in Wonderland" moment—real life had become surreal.

When I asked Rhonda if she had ever heard of the term "supermind," she said she hadn't. Neither had I.

This was Event #8.

I flipped to the index at the back of the book and searched for the word "supermind." To my surprise, the word was not listed.

I flipped back to pages 144 and 145. As I started reading the paragraphs under the subheading, I learned that the word "supermind" was created not by the author, but was used by a man named Collins who had stated the following:

"So postulating the existence of a supermind—or God—as the explanation for the fine-tuning of the Universe makes all the sense in the world. It would simply be a natural extrapolation of what we already know that minds can do."

By this point, I had already concluded that the explanation for the existence of supersynchronicities required the existence of some kind of universal and infinite intelligence.

However, I had never heard of, or thought about, using the term "supermind" to refer to this or any other hypothesis. I doubt many people have.

Clearly, I had to have that book. The previews were about to start, so Rhonda raced to the movie theatre while I purchased the book.

When I arrived at the theatre, Rhonda greeted me with a smile. One of the advertisements shown on the screen, she said, had been for "supersavers."

For the record, since that day Rhonda and I have seen many hundreds of ads on movie screens in theatres. During all that time and in all of those ads, the word "supersaver" has cropped up only a handful of times.

Was Rhonda's witnessing an ad for supersavers part of the emerging supersynchronicity about supersynchronicity?

I include it as Event #9.

My decision to introduce you to the existence of Type III Synchronicities with the account of how the term "supersynchronicity" came to be was reached after I looked up the word "supermind" on the Internet.

When I did, I discovered that one of India's greatest spiritual leaders and mystics of the twentieth century, Sri Aurobindo, frequently used the word "supermind" and the evolution of what he calls "Supramental consciousness." A full understanding of Sri Aurobindo's notion of supermind (sometimes noted as "Supermind" and often spelled as "Super Mind") would require going a bit too far afield for our purposes here, but the basic idea refers to a higher level of mind beyond our normal (discursive) consciousness that is fully attuned to the supreme unity, the absolute divine One.

Although at first this may sound rather mystifying, in plain English it is essentially what Einstein meant when he said that his ultimate goal was "to know the Mind of God".

You will recall that I mentioned that Type III Synchronicities often have a surreal, "otherworldly" quality. I think we can agree that my discovery of the word "supermind," preceded by superstar, the birthing of supersynchronicity, superposition, super achievers, supermarkets, superimposition, and superheroes—and then punctuated by the appearance of the word "supersaver"—is more than just an extraordinarily improbable sequence of super-words!

Is it possible that their propitious appearance has a deeper meaning that links the timing of the discovery of the idea of supersynchronicity with the idea of the supermind?

The answer is yes, presuming you are open to the possibility of this potentially meaningful connection.

As scientists, or as anyone who wants to discover truth, we need to be skeptical, in the sense of employing a reasonable sense of doubt to help keep us on the right track. However, being skeptical is very different from being a "skeptic," which is essentially someone who stubbornly refuses to believe anything beyond so-called "normal" science, no matter how much evidence is presented.

Unfortunately, this sort of skeptic would ultimately destroy science, because only by searching beyond the known can we ever discover what is currently unknown. If we didn't proceed that way, science would never make any progress. If the skeptics had their way, quantum physics would never have been discovered in the first place.

So, skeptics may summarily dismiss the sequence of superword related events that occurred on August 9 as reflecting chance coincidences combined with selective attention on my part. But in doing so, it is very unlikely that they will make the effort to attempt to calculate a conditional probability to determine how astoundingly improbable this set of events really is (it is more improbable than the Dr. Brewer example).

However, the subsequent occurrence of the word "supermind" on August 10 was an added improbability. In addition, and despite the already extraordinary improbability surrounding the word "super" in relation to pondering the title of this book, the relevant synchronistic events have continued.

For example, about two years later, on August 6, 2010, after I had just finished editing the above section—which I had not read in a year—I decided to check my email and do some other work. What I saw gave me quite a start: ten of the top sixteen email subject lines in my inbox had the term "Super PSI" in the subject heading, while two other subjects contained the word "terminology" which happened to be referring to Super PSI.

Apparently, a group of my colleagues had started a dialogue about Super PSI, which refers to a class of extraordinary paranormal phenomena that cannot be explained by conventional/simple psychic mechanisms such as telepathy, remote viewing, and precognition.

On no more than five occasions in the preceding two years had I written on the origin of the term supersynchronicity. And yet, I received a flurry of emails regarding Super PSI beginning at around 10:16 am, shortly after I finished what I had assumed would be the final edit of the above section. I have never, to the best of my memory, ever received a string of emails with the word "super" in the subject line (nor have I since then). And I have a file of over 50,000 emails….

As you can see, highly improbable and meaningful synchronicities are continuing, even as I am editing this manuscript, which should serve to remind us to keep an open mind when pondering how such "super-improbable" events can and do occur. I hope that you find yourself inspired to travel with me as I aim to investigate, discover, and understand the possible nature and purpose of all types of synchronicities.

The title *Super Synchronicity* and the scientific term supersynchronicity honors this super hypothesis!

Just the Beginning!

Although this may be hard for you believe, the present book presents *only a small subset of all the supersynchronicities I have experienced.* If I tried to include all of them, this book would be thousands of pages in length. Table I (at the end of this section) provides a fairly complete listing of the Type III Synchronicities I have witnessed over a twenty-year period. Note that there was a dramatic increase in their occurrence, and re-occurrence, in the last few years represented in the table.

I should explain that in September of 2009, I stopped counting every Type III Synchronicity I was experiencing because it was taking too much of my time and energy. Today I carefully document only those sets of supersynchronicities that are the most improbable, meaningful, and insightful about the nature and evolution of synchronicities in twenty-first century life.

For the record, I have *not* selected for inclusion in this book many of the most startling, improbable, or evidential examples of supersynchronicity I have experienced. The supersynchronicities presented in this book are sufficient in their individual and collective astronomical improbability. In fact, I am saving a set of truly exceptional examples for a second book that will document how supersynchronicities can grow, multiply, and evolve in receptive minds and hearts.

The truth is, the more skilled I have become in documenting and processing the unfolding supersynchronicities in my life, the more numerous, complex, and meaningful they have become. In fact, one of the recent supersynchronicities I have documented with Rhonda (plus two research assistants in my laboratory at the University of Arizona) involves more than 120 events occurring during a two-week period that involved wolves, a deceased super-celebrity (Michael Jackson), and the need for the protection of humanity and the planet in the twenty-first century. The immensity and profundity of this supersynchronicity can only be appreciated and understood after carefully savoring and digesting the representative supersynchronicity delicacies revealed in this volume. This book is just the beginning!

TABLE I

List of Key Type III Synchronicities up to September 2009

1. 11s (1982)
2. Benjamin Franklin (2001)
3. Diamonds (2001)
4. Dragonflies (2002)
5. Plans and Story Creation (2003)
6. Deception and Illusions (2003)
7. Evil and Demons (2003)
8. Ravens(2004)
9. Roses (2004)
10. Symbols and Signs (2004)
11. Combinations/Integrations over days (2005)
12. Sequences over days (e.g. Cussler Novels) (2005)
13. Guardians (2005)
14. Blues and Grays (2006)
15. Cats (2006)
16. Spirals and Spiral Stars (2006)
17. Suicide (2006)
18. Ducks (2007)
19. Bows and Arrows (2007)
20. Swarms (2007)
21. Bridges (2007)
22. Angels (2007)
23. Bears (2007)
24. Hawks (2007)
25. Gaps (2007)
26. Perfection (2007)
27. Gratitude (2007)
28. Wolves (2007)
29. Arks/Arcs (2007)
30. Circles (2007)
31. Crosses (2007)
32. Infinite (2007)

33. Skulls (2007)
34. Gold (2007)
35. Ladders (2007)
36. Cookies (2008)
37. Goats (2008)
38. Houdini and Doyle (2008)
39. Green Emeralds / Green (2008)
40. Light (2008)
41. More Ravens (2008)
42. Humming (2008)
43. Fullness and Fulfillment (2008)
44. Freedom (2008)
45. French (2008)
46. Candles (2008)
47. Stones (2008)
48. Elephants (2008)
49. Zebras (2008)
50. Circus (2008)
51. Supersynchronicity Days and Dreams (2008)
52. Butterflies (2008)
53. Wind (2008)
54. Eagles (2008)
55. More Ducks (2008)
56. Horses (2008)
57. Connections (2008)
58. Clowns/Circus (2008)
59. Hearts (2008)
60. John Lennon (2008)
61. Confirmations in Two or More Books at the Same Time(2008)
62. Supersynchronicity Moments (in less than 15 minutes) (2008)
63. Fear and Terror (2008)
64. Heaven (2008)
65. Monsters (2008)
66. Dark (2008)
67. Synchronicities (2008)

68. Secrets/Silence (2008)
69. Anonymous (2008)
70. Fun (2008)
71. Sun (2008)
72. Sunflowers (2008)
73. Fire and Fire Trucks (2008)
74. Doves (2008)
75. Multi-Person Synchronicities in the Same Time Period (2008)
76. Tigers (2008)
77. Farmers (2008)
78. Bees (2008)
79. Opportunity (2008)
80. Buzzing (2008)
81. Rainbows (2008)
82. Cobras (2008)
83. Multiple Deceased Persons (2008)
84. Frogs (2008)
85. Superman (2008)
86. Last Names (2008)
87. Stories (2008)
88. Buffalos (2008)
89. Buddha (2008)
90. Illusions (2008)
91. Moon (2008)
92. Here Comes the Sun (2008)
93. Funeral (2008)
94. On Broadway (2009)
95. August Rush (2009)
96. Star Guitar (2009)
97. Sparks (2009)
98. Clouds (2009)
99. Bobo(2009)
100. Silver (2009)
101. Bond (2009)

102. Plans (2009)
103. More Ravens (2009)
104. Telepathy (2009)
105. Numerology (2009)
106. Interference (2009)
107. More Ducks (2009)
108. Kachinas (2009)
109. Multiple supersynchronicities in books (2009)
110. Dancing (2009)
111. Gratitude (2009)
112. More Roses Parker (2009)
113. Names (2009)
114. Birds over Cars (2009)
115. More Bridges (2009)
116. Single Evening Four-Person Super-Synch (2009)
117. Labs (2009)
118. More Ben Franklin (2009)
119. Mickey Mouse (2009)
120. Breaking (2009)
121. Being Bugged (2009)
122. More Tigers (2009)
123. Parker (2009)
124. Thomas Jefferson (2009)
125. Trumpets (2009)
126. More Ravens (2009)
127. Bunnies (2009)
128. French and France (2009)
129. Montreal and Canada (2009)
130. More Ducks (2009)
131. More Bees (2009)
132. More Ravens (2009)
133. Baseball (2009)
134. Max (2009)
135. Change (2009)
136. Twelves (2009)

Section Two
Evidence—Thirteen Synchronicity Lessons

"Data! Data! Data!" he cried impatiently.
"I can't make bricks without clay."
Sherlock Holmes

Chapter 2
Supersynchronicity in New York City

Lesson: Follow the Evidence that is Way Beyond Chance

The intellect has little to do on the road to discovery. There comes a leap in consciousness, call it intuition or what you will, the solution comes to you and you don't know how or why.
Albert Einstein

Is it possible that a specific number can appear, in various guises (if not disguises), at key stages in our lives?

Is it possible that by discovering a ubiquitous number in our life we can be led to a cascade of extraordinarily improbable events linking ancient wisdom with the everyday lives of a diverse set of seemingly disconnected people?

Can this unfolding trail of interconnected events foretell not only an implicit purpose and direction in our lives, but ultimately reveal the essence of how the universe evolves?

I had originally planned to highlight this real-life set of events as a critical chapter in my book, *The G.O.D. Experiments.* However, both my writing partner on this book, William Simon, and my editor, Brenda Copeland, then at Simon & Schuster, concluded that the set of events and their implications may have seemed too far-fetched for many readers to accept.

Though I appreciated their realistic concerns, for the sake of integrity I could not allow this true-life happening to be banished from the book. Though the totality of the events that occurred were exceptionally hard to believe, the fact is they played a foundational role in leading me to develop self-science as a personal research strategy for applied self-discovery.

I proposed to William and Brenda that we quietly include this evidence in Appendix C of the *The G.O.D. Experiments.* They agreed, and the account was for all practical purposes buried there.

However, it is now time for this extraordinary set of events to take center stage, for it represents my initial awakening to the reality of synchronicity and its possible sacredness. While the phenomena and events that I recount may sometimes seem unbelievable—from 11s and dragonflies, through ravens and roses, to ducks, bears, and beyond—it is important to remember that I am reporting accurately and not exaggerating. Each section of the book becomes ever more challenging to what many of us believe is possible in everyday life. In this book, Alice in Wonderland moments are the rule, and not the exception.

Setting the Stage, Understanding the Events in Context: A Bit of Personal History

It was the early 1980s. At that time I was a mainstream health psychologist and psychophysiologist (someone who studies the relationship between mind and body) at Yale University. In addition to being a tenured professor of Psychology and Psychiatry, and the director of the Yale Psychophysiology Center, I co-directed the Yale Behavioral Medicine Clinic (which included me seeing patients for stress management and biofeedback one day a week).

My research at the time was funded by the National Sciences Foundation, the National Institute of Mental Health, the National

Heart, Lung, and Blood Institute, as well as private foundations, and I was serving as the President of the Health Psychology Division of the American Psychological Association. Partly because of my early background in electronics and electrical engineering, my academic interests also extended beyond psychology and psychiatry to special relativity, quantum physics, and general systems science (described in *The G.O.D. Experiments, The Energy Healing Experiments,* and *The Living Energy Universe*).

However, my world unexpectedly turned upside down—as well as inside out—when I noticed a particular anomaly associated with the number 11 occurring in my environment. Because I was committed to data and evidence, I followed where the apparent numerical anomaly was taking me.

It is also important to clarify that when I describe below the appearance of a replicated pattern of the number 11 that occurred, I do so as a scientist and mathematician, not as a numerologist.

Interestingly, while it can be tempting to dismiss numerology as being unscientific, we cannot dismiss the fact that an unavoidable reliance on numbers forms a foundational part of science. Indeed, one of the most important factors in the development of modern science, as beautifully expressed in Dr. John H Spencer's book *The Eternal Law,* has been an unwavering belief that our ability to discover truths about physical reality is directly dependent on a proper understanding of the relations between numbers (as in the laws of physics written in mathematics).

However, during this unique window of time at Yale University, numbers seemed no longer to be my friends.

Discovering the Number 11 at Yale

In some sense, it feels like it was only yesterday as I recall the initial insight—the first "11" observation—which began with my pondering the number of my office, 1A in the basement of Yale's Sterling-Strathcona-Sheffield Hall. For some reason it occurred to me that the letter A was the first letter in the alphabet—which created the number 11. This would become Event #1.

The Psychology Building was on "Hillhouse Av" (which is how the sign was printed). It had 11 letters. Event #2.

The exit I took off the Connecticut Turnpike was exit 56. 5 plus 6 equals 11. This was Event #3.

I then realized that I took Route 1A to get to my house. Another 11. Event #4.

I lived at 326 Colonial Road. 326 added up to 11. Event #6.

Even the state name, Connecticut, had 11 letters! Event #7.

My birthday is June 14. June was the 6th month of year. Adding together 6 plus the digits in 14 (1 plus 4) equals 11. Event #8.

Though I do not recall now my precise phone numbers, license plates, and such from that time period, I do remember that the numbers—or combinations of numbers and letters—more often than not added up to 11. Lacking these details, I am not listing them here.

Of course, I considered various explanations to account for the apparent anomaly of being surrounded by all these 11s, including what is sometimes called the "VW Bug Phenomenon," Simply stated, when you start looking for VW Bugs, you find them because they are there. Their existence and patterns are not anomalous, and they are not related to you.

I realized that if the 11s seemingly surrounding me were merely analogous to VW Bugs in the above example, then anyone who looked for 11s would find them surrounding them, on the average, just as frequently as I did. In other words, like VW bugs, if you began looking for 11s all around you, not only would you find them, but they would appear, on the average, just as frequently for you as they did for me (or for anyone else, for that matter).

However, I did not have to actively search for 11s in my vicinity; they were literally all around me. All I had to do was analyze the numbers and letters in my everyday life. Moreover, if you examined the pattern of office numbers, street names, house numbers, phone numbers, and so forth, for randomly selected people (which I did), you would be able to verify that the frequency of the pattern of 11s that I was experiencing at the time was way beyond chance.

Of further importance is that when I left Connecticut and moved to Arizona, my 11 synchronicity greatly diminished (although it was replaced by the number 9), indicating that there was some sort of statistical anomaly happening at that time.

However, though the collection of 11s was clearly highly improbable, I thought that it could possibly have happened by chance. At the time I had no idea whether this numeric anomaly (in terms of its statistical significance) had any meaning (in terms of personal significance).

In fact, if the rest of events I am about to describe had not unfolded, I would have likely dismissed the "11 anomaly" as being just a highly improbable and amusing fluke.

"Sometimes You Say Things that are Prophetic"

One day a young medical student came to see me to ask if I would be his advisor for his dissertation (to preserve his anonymity, I will call him Jason). Unlike most American universities that require dissertations of PhD students only, Yale honored the older European tradition of requiring that MD students do a dissertation (albeit somewhat less extensive in nature) as well.

Jason wanted to do a dissertation that integrated quantum physics, acupuncture, and ancient African philosophy. I told him that I knew a fair amount about quantum physics, very little about acupuncture, and absolutely nothing at all about ancient African philosophy. However, I suggested that if he were willing to meet weekly with me to discuss the writing of his dissertation, I would be happy to provide what advice I could.

Approximately six weeks into our meetings, Jason said (and I paraphrase), "Dr. Schwartz, are you aware that every now and again—especially when you talk about systems theory, order, and patterns of numbers—that what you say is prophetic?"

"Prophetic?" I said. "What do you mean?"

He replied, "You say things that are right out of the Kabbalah."

"The Ka Ba Wah?" I had no idea what he was talking about.

"No, the Kabbalah."

"The Kabbalah, what's that?"

"Ancient secret Jewish mysticism."

"Ancient secret Jewish mysticism?" I had never been taught that there was anything remotely mystical about Judaism.

"Yes. Sometimes what you say reflects these secret teachings."

The thought popped into my head, *I wonder if this relates to my strange observations concerning the number 11.* Of course, I did not mention this to Jason.

I asked, "How can I learn about these secret teachings?"

Jason replied, "You are fortunate. Books are beginning to appear in English that describe these traditions. I suspect if you go to New York City, you can find a book on it there."

Needless to say, that weekend I went to New York City (a city whose name, curiously, contains 11 letters).

I went to Scribner's bookstore on 5th Avenue, and looked for books on the Kabbalah. Remember, this was the early 1980s, and there were very few books published in English on the Kabbalah at that time.

I can vividly recall climbing the stairs to the second floor and finding, on the second shelf along the wall on the right hand side, a few books on the Kabbalah.

One was called *Kabbalah for the Layman* by Rabbi Berg. *I'm a layman!* I thought to myself and decided to purchase the book.

What I read took me completely by surprise. Just as Jason had said, the underlying philosophical tenets of the Kabbalah were virtually the same as those of contemporary systems science.

More amazingly, I learned that there was an ancient practice known as numerology where the letters from the Hebrew alphabet were converted into numbers and summed. The resulting summary number was allowed to be only one digit (or, in special cases, two digits).

For example, consider the word GARY. G is the seventh letter of the alphabet, A is the first, R is the eighteenth, and Y is the twenty-fifth. We add the numbers: 7+1+18+25 to get 51. We then add together the digits of resulting number 51: 5+1 = 6.

Now, consider the word NUMBERS. N is the fourteenth letter of the alphabet, U is the twenty-first, M is the thirteenth, B is the second, E is the fifth, R is the eighteenth, and S is the nineteenth. We add the numbers together: 14+21+13+2+5+18+19 equals 92. We then add together the digits of the resulting number 92: 9+2 =11.

However, in this instance, 11 would not be reduced further (i.e., it would not be summed to 2).

It turned out that the number 11 was said to be a "master number." In fact, according to some texts, the number 11 was the number for God. I wondered, *had I unknowingly "rediscovered" ancient Hebrew numerology and applied it to the English alphabet?* I further wondered, *was I somehow meant to learn the Kabbalah?*

I told my then wife, Jeannie, about this remarkable coincidence—the number 11, the medical student, the Kabbalah, and then numerology. I told her that I had decided that I wanted to take Kabbalah classes in New York City with Rabbi Berg.

Jeannie said, "Absolutely not." She reminded me that I was an Ivy League professor and a highly visible scientist, not a Jewish academic mystic. She was also frankly worried about how I would cope with what I might learn.

I could not argue with her. Jeannie was a smart, loving, and strong person, and her reasoning was justified. However, I felt compelled to stay connected, somehow, to this seemingly synchronous and meaningful set of events that were unfolding in my life.

A few weeks later, the seemingly impossible happened. Emotionally, it felt miracle-like at the time. Today I would add the word "sacred." Here's what happened.

Rescuing a Cardigan Welsh Corgi in New York City

A practical yet seemingly ridiculous idea popped into my head while Jeannie and I were dining in one of our favorite restaurants.

We were in New York City—11 letters again. Event #1.

We were staying at The Yale Club. Although I can't remember the precise room number, I do remember that it added up to 11 (Event #2).

It was a Saturday. We were to spend the afternoon at the Metropolitan Opera. We were having lunch at 65th street in New York City (6+5=11). Event #3.

We were in a restaurant called Shun Lee West (which has a total of 11 letters). Event #4.

I was silently thinking about the eerie frequency of number 11s in New York City, wondering once again if my experience was due to the "VW Bug effect"—or was it something more?

And then I thought to myself, *How am I going to stay connected to the potential synchronicity of the master number 11, the Kabbalah, numerology, and apparent prophesy in my life?*

I didn't consciously or purposely ask the universe the question. I simply asked the question silently in my head.

Immediately, a wild idea popped into my mind, seemingly out of nowhere. What I heard was, *Get a Cardigan Welsh Corgi.*

Get a Cardigan Welsh Corgi?

However, as soon as I pictured the idea, I couldn't help feeling elated.

First, I realized that the name Cardigan Welsh Corgi had connections to the number 11, since the initials CWC work out to 3 + 23 + 3 = 29, and 2+9 = 11. Event #5.

The letter C is especially important, because Kabbalah is sometimes spelled "Caballa." K is the 11th letter of the alphabet, and C is the third. But in the binary numeral system, 3 is expressed as 11. So, whether you spell it with a C or a K, you still get 11. Event #6.

There were other connections to the number 11, but they are not important here. What is important is that I realized that the name of this rare breed of dog could serve as a secret reminder to me of the Kabbalah, as well as the number 11.

Second, I quickly realized that getting a Cardigan Welsh Corgi would be acceptable to Jeannie. At that time we had a Pembroke Welsh Corgi named Thurber (after the late James Thurber). Jeannie was about to begin working in the Yale Behavioral Medicine Clinic, which meant that Thurber would have to be alone during the day. We did not have children, but Thurber was like a child to Jeannie and me.

If we got Thurber a younger brother or sister, then he would have someone to keep him company while we were at work. However, Pembroke Welsh Corgis are fairly rare, and at the time we had our Pembroke, the Queen of England had 11 Pembrokes.

Pembrokes have no tails, although Cardigans do. I had once met a Cardigan Welsh Corgi on Bailey Island in Maine. Though the dog's name was "Killer," he was more like a gentle kitten. Cardigans often have gentle dispositions—perfect for Thurber. It is extraordinarily rare to see someone out walking a Cardigan Welsh Corgi on the street. But guess what happened next?

Without telling Jeannie what was going through my mind, I brought up the subject of Thurber being alone, and gently suggested that maybe we should get him a friend, a Cardigan Welsh Corgi.

To my relief, Jeannie told me that she thought it was a great idea. She suggested that we attempt to rescue an adult Cardigan that needed a home. She suggested that since Cardigans are very rare, we should see if there was a Cardigan Welsh Corgi Club somewhere in the United States where we could let it be known that we were looking to rescue an adult Cardigan in need of a home. I could hardly contain my excitement.

Jeannie didn't know, of course, that if we could somehow, someday, find an adult Cardigan Corgi to rescue, that he or she would become my "secret Kabbalah Corgi."

What happened next was quite extraordinary. Even as I write these words, I still find it virtually impossible to believe that this actually occurred.

We left the restaurant and walked uptown. We purchased two vanilla yogurt cones, and then began crossing 7th Avenue. Around 74th street (yes, another 11, although I did not count it as a synchronous event as we were not actually on that street), Jeannie asked me, "Gary, is that a Cardigan Welsh Corgi?" Event #7.

I couldn't believe what I was seeing. In the middle island separating the uptown and downtown streets was the funniest looking dog I had ever seen.

He was a blue merle and a "fluffy"—which is considered to be a "flaw" for the breed. One of his eyes was brown, and the other was blue. The brown eye had only half a pupil. He had huge ears pointed skyward. He had the typical short legs and long body of a Corgi, with a large fluffy tail. The dog looked positively goofy.

How could this be happening? Out of the blue, an idea pops into my head that I should get a Cardigan Welsh Corgi as a "secret Kabbalah Corgi," and then a few minutes later I bump into a Cardigan Corgi on the streets of New York City? I thought, *That's crazy.*

I bent down on my knees and offered the dog my yogurt (which he enthusiastically accepted). The woman walking the dog looked a bit alarmed. However, I was wearing a jacket and tie for the opera, so I looked reasonably presentable.

I blurted out, "Please excuse me. My name is Dr. Schwartz, and you'll never guess what just happened. We live in Connecticut and have a Pembroke Welsh Corgi named Thurber. Just a few minutes ago we decided that we wanted to get a Cardigan Welsh Corgi as a friend for our dog. We decided we would like to adopt an adult dog who needed a home, and we were just talking about how we might go about finding a Cardigan Welsh Corgi Club. Do you happen to know if there is such a club?"

To my amazement, I saw tears well up in her eyes. And her reply brought tears to my eyes, too. She said, "Dear God, I think my prayers have finally been answered. I am getting a divorce and losing my country home in Connecticut. I have an apartment not far from here. It has become necessary for me to find a home for my dog, Willie. Would you like to talk with me about possibly adopting him?"

There are no words to describe what I felt at that moment, on my knees with Willie finishing my yogurt. The mixture of emotions included awe, wonder, sadness (for her), joy, pain, confusion, and shock. I was stunned.

I asked myself, *What is the statistical probability that this could have happened by chance?* How many dogs are there on the planet? How many are Cardigan Welsh Corgis in need of a home, who are walking near me at precisely the place and time that I am thinking about adopting one?

The timing of all this is critical. We are talking about a truly infinitesimally small number of this set of events happening in such a short period of time. Finding a Cardigan Welsh Corgi only minutes after leaving the restaurant where I had suddenly had the idea of getting a dog of that exact breed is far beyond a mere coincidence, and I had already mentally labelled it as Event #7. But finding Willie, a Cardigan Welsh Corgi who also desperately needed a new home, was an extraordinary additional element, making it Event #8.

Jeannie and I made an appointment to meet with the woman and Willie the following morning. I hardly registered the music of the opera that afternoon, and I don't know how I managed to fall asleep that night.

Note: While working on this section of the book, Rhonda and I spontaneously stopped at the Ventana Canyon Resort to celebrate her completing the first draft of her book *Love Eternal.* We had planned to celebrate at home, but we decided to take a ride, and the idea just popped into my mind as we were driving near the resort. As we walked toward the entrance, I looked down and almost tripped over a Cardigan Welsh Corgi whose name turned out to be Lily (which happens to be the name we plan to give a dog someday).

The next morning we drove uptown to see the woman (we can call her Jennifer) and Willie. I don't remember what street her apartment was on, but I vividly recall the number of her apartment—5F. F is the 6th letter in the alphabet. 5 + 6 = 11. Event #9.

It turned out that Jennifer was an assistant opera coach at the Metropolitan Opera, which, while perhaps not a synchronicity, was still interesting to note given that we were going to the opera the day we met her in the street. Jennifer interviewed us for about an hour. She really loved Willie, and I sensed that the "coincidence" of us being there was almost as meaningful for her as it was for me.

As we became more comfortable with each other, I suddenly felt the need to ask her if she knew anything about the Kabbalah.

Jeannie looked at me cross-eyed. "Where did this come from?" was written on her face.

Meanwhile, Jennifer looked squarely in my eyes, searchingly and knowingly, and said. "Ah. Now I understand. I think you should come with me into the next room."

I followed her. What I saw then was almost as impossible for me to believe as suddenly finding Willie in the street the previous day just after thinking about getting a Cardigan Welsh Corgi.

We were in Jennifer's bedroom. The long wall had floor to ceiling bookshelves. The collection of books was primarily on astrology. Besides being an opera coach, Jennifer was also in training to become a professional astrologer.

If you find it hard to believe what you are now reading, you can imagine how I felt. Jennifer walked over to the right side of the room and from a waist-level shelf pulled out a book about astrology and the Kabbalah (I don't recall the exact title). I asked Jennifer if I could borrow the book, while Jeannie looked at me in complete confusion.

Jennifer insisted on driving out to our home in Guilford, Connecticut. As she was getting Willie ready for the trip, I asked her if she also knew what the number 11 meant.

Jennifer looked up and said, "You know, the number 11 is a very important number."

I said, "Do you know what your apartment number is?"

She said, "Of course. 5F."

I said, "5F equals 11."

Our eyes locked. From that day forward, Willie became my secret Kabbalah Corgi.

The Number 11—Welsh Corgi Connection Continues, Even After Willie's Death

Willie was not known for his intelligence. One of my former Yale PhD students, Geoffrey Ahern, now an MD, PhD, and Professor of Neurology, Psychiatry, Psychology, and the Evelyn F. McKnight Brain Institute at the University of Arizona, and who is a fellow dog lover, used to say that Willie operated on "two neurons."

I, of course, didn't mind his reference to "two." Geof didn't know about the 11 connection then, and therefore did not know that his reference to 2 neurons (i.e., 2 = 1+1) reminded me of the master number 11.

Of the various dogs I have had the privilege to share my life with, Willie was unequivocally my "soul-mate doggie."

However, probably the most extraordinary connection between the Kabbalah, numbers, and Willie emerged seemingly impossibly, of all places, at his funeral.

It was the mid 1990s. Jeannie and I were divorced. Willie was with me in Tucson, Arizona. He had become frail; he was almost 14 years old. I had just rushed home from a visit to Boca Raton, Florida. Debbie, a woman who stayed with Willie when I traveled, had called me explaining that Willie was behaving as if he was in severe pain. He could hardly walk.

I took Willie to an emergency animal hospital. He was diagnosed to be in end stage kidney failure and could not be treated. The veterinarian recommended that he should be let go. I held Willie in my arms as he died.

My grief was severe. It went way beyond just Willie, the dog. As Willie was dying in my arms, I realized that my living secret symbol of the Kabbalah was dying, too.

The veterinarian offered to have someone from his staff take Willie's body to the local animal cemetery, where one of my other Corgis—a Cardigan named Arizona—was buried. I explained that I knew the owner of the cemetery, and would prefer to take Willie myself.

When I arrived at the cemetery, I learned that it had been recently sold to a young married couple. I was introduced to the wife (whom I will call Rebecca), and I explained that I had another dog already buried in her cemetery. As we were preparing the paperwork, she asked if I wanted a footstone.

I explained that I had previously prepared my epitaph for Willie's plaque and that it was on file. She asked me to tell her the epitaph.

I said, "In loving memory of Willie. My Kabbalah Corgi, My Soul-Mate Doggie."

She replied, surprised, "Did you say Kabbalah?"

"Yes", I replied.

She said, "That's remarkable. You must meet my husband."

I could not believe what I was hearing. It was amazing enough that Willie had come to me via the Kabbalah. Could it be possible that he would be leaving me via the Kabbalah as well?

She went to get her husband, whom I will call John. It turned out that this young man, raised a Catholic and in his early 20s, not only had an absolute passion for the Kabbalah, but was also an expert in numerology.

Moreover, with two of his high school friends who also shared a passion for the Kabbalah, John had discovered the secret for calculating the solution to what is known mathematically as the "magic cube."

The details of the magic cube are not important here. What is important is that this extremely difficult numeric calculation was revealed to this young man and his friends though their study of numerology in the Kabbalah.

I spent almost three hours with John, and he came to sympathize with my tears as I confessed to him why Willie was my secret Kabbalah Corgi.

The next day Willie was buried. As his casket was being lowered into the ground, I asked myself, *How many pet cemeteries in the United States are headed by a Kabbalist who has mastered the sacred art of numerology?* and, *What is the probability that a Kabbalah Cardigan from New York City would be buried by a Kabbalah Catholic in the city of Tucson?* This was all clearly far beyond chance.

Taking Stock: Seeing the Complex Pattern and Pondering How It Might Have Occurred

If this had been merely an isolated collection of weird events, a one-time improbable set of circumstances consisting of a web of statistical anomalies, unexpected connections, and clues to an unimaginable collection of relationships, this story would have remained buried in the Appendix of *The G.O.D. Experiments*. Instead, it has become the opening act of a continually expanding physical and spiritual Play of ever-increasing complexity and incredulity—recall Table I in the Overview.

Though I am writing the words you are reading, in a much deeper sense I am neither composing "the Story" nor writing the "larger Play." If anything, what I am trying to do is be a reliable scribe and record the events as they actually happened. As a laboratory scientist, I am attempting to catalogue and analyze the events, and then search for potential patterns and meanings in the findings.

After Willie's death, I learned that numerous people have had collections of synchronicities involving the number 11 that are at least as extraordinary as mine. In a follow-up book, I am planning to provide a detailed account of several of these personal synchronicity discoveries, and when their true yet incredible stories are combined with mine, the larger plot becomes ever more rich, complex, and compelling.

A key aspect of self-science is to focus on rigorously analyzing one's own relevant experiences in various contexts, such as I have been doing in this chapter. However, we are really searching for a clearer understanding of the larger story—the universal and sacred reality of synchronicities unfolding in all our lives. Through offering my own self-science experience in synchronicities as an example, I am hoping to help inspire you to seek your own inner power to discover and benefit from your own synchronicities via self-science.

As in any complex story or mystery, some elements are critical and define the plot, while others are minor and have much less apparent consequence or meaning.

Just because a city has 11 letters, for example, or a student says you sometimes sound like a prophet, does not necessarily mean that these observations have meaning. Observations can be over-interpreted and/or misinterpreted, and no one wishes to fall for fool's gold.

But it is not reasonable to deny the extraordinary sequence of tightly interconnected events I have here provided. Not only did such events often occur far beyond chance, but each such occurrence was also permeated with profound meaning, guiding me in significant life decisions.

After such an incredible synchronistic journey, how could I ever have anticipated, even in my wildest dreams, that this was just the beginning?

Chapter 3
How to Discover Synchronicities: Four Core Principles
Lesson: The Evidence is Always Friendly

Eliminate all other factors, and the one
which remains must be the truth.
Sherlock Holmes

Before continuing with me on my personal journey of discovering synchronicities and their meanings, it is helpful for us to consider some basic principles in conducting exploratory science in general, and self-science in particular. Once you grasp these four principles, you will find it easier not only to make sense of my discovery process, but you will have the opportunity to expand your own.

There are different stages in the practice of science, and I have written a very brief, user-friendly introduction to the art and science of scientific discovery, so we can all be, so to speak, on the same experimental page.

Fundamental to the early stages in scientific methodology is the task of collecting all of the relevant data as carefully and accurately as possible. A prerequisite for good science is good data. If the data are invalid, then the resulting scientific conclusion based on those data must also be invalid.

Another vital component of the beginning of the scientific process involves the creative exploration of possible alternative hypotheses or explanations of the patterns that are observed in the data.

Being able to see patterns in data is critical to the discovery process. Sherlock Holmes was portrayed as a master of seeing patterns, as well as making connections between the individual pieces of information and their potential significance. There is an art to seeing patterns and making valid connections. You will witness the evolution of my own ability to detect and make sense of patterns of increasingly challenging—and at times seemingly bizarre—observations, as my pattern-recognition skills developed and the evidence accumulated.

There is a later stage in science where specific hypotheses are put to the experimental test. It is the "hypothesis testing" stage of science where controls are carefully and systematically introduced, including the well-known "double-blind" experimental design used in conventional medical science (whereby both the investigator and the participants do not know the nature of the treatment the participant is receiving). Indeed, in this book I have already indicated my efforts to insert critical controls into the synchronicity journey by requesting a clear and replicable demonstration of the source of the unfolding evidence.

There are also four simple principles of discovery that are essential to take on this journey. The first two I learned from Matthew Friedman, MD, the third from Jeannie Crawford-Schwartz, MPH, and the fourth is my own extension of the first. Each principle has a brief accompanying story that brings the lessons to life, and I wish to honor Matt and Jeannie (and their wisdom) by sharing their contributions with you.

I also wish to acknowledge Dr. Robert Stek, who inspired me to reread Sir Arthur Conan Doyle and his ingenious creation, Sherlock Holmes. As Dr. Stek taught me, Mr. Holmes modelled these principles in his own way.

Discovery Principle 1: The Data are Always Friendly

It was the early 1970s. At that time I was an assistant professor in the Department of Psychology at Harvard as well as director of the Clinical Psychophysiology Unit at the Erich Lindemann Mental Health Center of the Massachusetts General Hospital. One of my research assistants in the Clinical Psychophysiology Unit was Dr. Paul Fair, who was then working toward his PhD in psychology at Boston University.

Paul's doctoral dissertation involved recording patterns of facial muscle tension (the technical term is facial electromyography) during different emotional states. Paul made a series of predictions about which muscles would be active in particular emotions. As Paul and I examined the findings, some of the patterns did not fit his predictions.

Paul was distraught. He deeply wanted his predictions to be true. I tried to explain that it was not important whether his specific predictions were valid or not, but rather whether we were making discoveries that would lead to valid understandings.

Unfortunately, Paul initially experienced the novel findings as an enemy to his hoped-for results. I sought the assistance of a young psychiatry resident who worked part-time in my Unit, Dr. Matthew Friedman. Matt offered to help Paul through his personal scientific crisis. He made an insightful suggestion that not only caught my attention, but also served as the key for Paul to release his attachment to his predictions.

What Matt said was, "Paul, why don't you try thinking of the data as friendly?"

I shortened Matt's suggestion to the simple sound bite: "The data are always friendly."

(Note that the word "data" is plural, the singular form of data being "datum." Scientists use phrases like "the data are" or the "data reveal" to express the plural quality of data.)

The "friendly data" principle is exceptionally important, because it reminds us that data are here to inform us. The reason we seek evidence in the first place is to understand. The metaphor

"The data are always friendly" reminds us that the process of science, in its purest form, is not only benign; it is benevolent.

Of course, people can abuse information, and use it for deception if not destruction. But this is not the fault of science; it is in its application.

Take-home message: Science is inherently friendly. And thanks to surprises, especially unbelievable surprises (discussed in Principle 4), science can even be fun.

Discovery Principle 2: There are Never Enough Data to Make a Decision

It was the early 1980s. I had moved to Yale University and was a young tenured Professor of Psychology and Psychiatry. Matt had moved to Dartmouth and was an Associate Professor of Psychiatry.

A small group of us convened at a home on the coast of Maine to explore areas of consciousness and health. I had not seen Matt in a number of years. After we hugged, I shared with Matt that some of my experiences with him lived on in my teachings and research, and that I regularly cited his suggestion with the phrase, "The data are always friendly." He was surprised and pleased.

I then asked him if he had unearthed any other general principles about science and data.

He furrowed his brow for a moment and then said, "Actually, Gary, I recently learned another lesson in science. What I now realize is that there are never enough data to make a decision."

As I heard those words, I took a deep breath followed by a long sigh.

What an insight, expressed so simply. "There are never enough data to make a decision." I was in awe.

What Matt meant by this seemingly simple phrase is that scientists typically can collect only limited amounts of information. Sometimes the sample sizes are small, as in the case of human studies, where there may be no more than ten or twenty subjects or patients in specific experiments. Other times the sample sizes are large: in multicenter clinical trials or epidemiological studies, possibly hundreds or thousands of individuals. However, scientists typically want to generalize their findings to millions or billions of people, if not whole species of animals, plants, molecules, or whatever they are studying. In other words, their goal is to be able to generalize their findings from the particular to the universal.

The question is, how much data do we need to collect and analyze in order to make a decision or reach a reasoned conclusion? How much data are enough?

Matt's phrase, "There are never enough data to make a decision" reminds us that we are always making inferences about the future based upon what we have collected in the past, and that what we have collected is inherently limited.

As the famous baseball player Yogi Berra playfully reminds us, "It is difficult to make predictions, especially about the future".

As you take the synchronicity journey, we will keep asking the question, how much evidence is enough to make a decision about personal synchronicity? At what point can we say, "All right, I get it, there is a real phenomenon here"? At what point do we stop asking the question, "Is this real?" and instead begin asking more advanced questions like, "How does it work?", "What does it mean?", and "How can we use it?" When is enough evidence "enough"?

The famous astronomer Dr. Carl Sagan was fond of saying that "Extraordinary claims require extraordinary evidence".

The phrase "extraordinary evidence" not only means an extraordinary *amount* of evidence, but also that the evidence must be *valid.* It must be real. It must be uncontaminated. And it must be replicated.

I ended up writing this book because I reached the point where I had compiled an immense amount of evidence that was extraordinary and real—i.e., observed across many responsible individuals from all walks of life.

Discovery Principle 3: Not Everything is Data

The third principle was shared with me sometime in the early 1990s. I had moved to the University of Arizona, where I was a professor of Psychology and Psychiatry (later adding Neurology, Medicine, and Surgery). The principle was proposed by Jeannie Crawford-Schwartz, at some point after I had given an invited address at a psychotherapy research conference using the title "The Data Are Always Friendly." (I subsequently published a scientific paper in a peer-reviewed journal based on this presentation.)

I remember asking Jeannie if she had any insights about the nature of data. Jeannie said something to the effect of, "Gary, it is worth remembering that not everything is data."

I remember initially appreciating her comment partly because scientists are not allowed to "throw out" data or selectively ignore evidence *unless there is very good reason.* For example, sometimes a piece of data is contaminated or incomplete. And sometimes conclusions actually apply only to a subset of the findings.

However, what Jeannie meant by this phrase was that sometimes data simply have little meaning or importance. In other words, it is worth remembering the classic phrase, sometimes "a cigar is just a cigar". Often times the presence of a cigar does not have any deep psychoanalytic significance—it is just something to smoke.

Principle 3 is of paramount importance as we explore the world of potential synchronicities and what they might mean. Sometimes a given event is just a coincidence, meaning that (1) it has no personally relevant cause (or causes), (2) it is not part of a particularly meaningfully pattern, and (3) it has no explicit or implicit meaning. It is simply an unimportant event, case closed.

The key here is for us to be discerning. We must learn to distinguish the wheat from the chaff, or what Dr. David Shapiro, my wise and playful doctoral advisor at Harvard, described as discerning the "gold in the garbage". He once said that I had a gift, so to speak, for finding the gold in the garbage, a phrase that I have never forgotten.

The challenge, of course, is for us to discern true gold from fool's gold.

Most scientists seek true gold, not fool's gold, and we certainly don't want to be fooled by nature. Nor do we want to fool ourselves.

One of the greatest challenges I have faced in addressing the mystery of synchronicity was in determining who was being fooled—the people who entertained the synchronicity hypothesis and even lived their lives by it, or the people who summarily dismissed it.

Who are the fools here, the "believers" or the "skeptics"?

Discovery Principle 4: Some Data are Extraordinarily Surprising and Seem Unbelievable, if Not Impossible

Principle 4 is my extension of Principle 1, "The data are always friendly." In a previous book, *The Living Energy Universe,* I quoted a former president of the Association for the Advancement of Science, the distinguished economist and systems scientist Dr. Kenneth Boulding.

Dr. Boulding said, "The future is bound to surprise us, but we need not be dumbfounded".

Most of us—scientists included—would prefer not to be dumbfounded as well as not being fooled.

The history of science is overflowing with surprises. Sometimes they are quite extraordinary and seem to be unbelievable, if not impossible. The history of science reminds us that evidence sometimes appears that no one has predicted, and in special cases, which no one has even imagined. Though mathematical theory can be a powerful predictive tool, there is no substitute for collecting the data and "letting the data speak." The fact is, as observed repeatedly in science, nature and the universe are indeed stranger than any one of us has ever imagined.

I live my life as a professional scientist, not only being open to the possibility of surprises, but actively seeking them. I am a fan of mysteries and detective stories. I relish the moments when the experiments do not conform to my predictions (which happens more than 50% of the time), and instead reveal patterns and phenomena that are typically more interesting than anything I (or anyone else) had envisioned.

The truth is, some data are extraordinarily surprising and seem unbelievable, if not impossible. When it comes to researching the mystery of synchronicity, Principle 4 can be viewed as being an understatement.

Armed with these four principles, you can more effectively embark on the journey of synchronicity. And frankly, we will need all the help we can receive.

Becoming a Synchronicity Seeker: The Truth-Seeking Intention is Key

As a general rule, if we do not seek the information, we will not find it. Many synchronicities are small if not subtle, and require that we be continuously vigilant and sensitive.

Searching for synchronicities is akin to searching for distant galaxies deep in space, or searching for biophoton emission in the leaves of plants (described in my previous book *The Energy Healing Experiments).* Both sources of light—from distant galaxies or plant leaves—are extraordinarily weak. Detecting them requires that we use very sensitive, ultra-cooled cameras that are pointed in the right places and focused at the right distances.

However, having the proper equipment—in this instance, "ultra-cooled low-light CCD cameras"—is not enough. You must use the equipment intentionally, with clear focus of purpose. Moreover, knowing how to use the cameras is not enough, either. You must use the equipment wisely, knowing where to point it, and when.

Finally, even knowing how to collect and analyze the data is not enough. You must not only record the information so that it can be located and retrieved at a later date, but you must then put the time and energy into calculating and interpreting or explaining the patterns discovered.

Simply put, if we do not seek synchronicities, most of the time they will pass us by, unnoticed or simply dismissed. There is no substitute for our making the commitment to regularly and reliably seek, collect, and interpret the data as they unfold. Otherwise, we will remain blind to the patterns around us. As Sherlock Holmes said to Dr. Watson, " 'You see, but you do not observe. The distinction is clear".

Simply stated, we must be open to, and believe in, the possibility of synchronicities if we hope to be able to discover them. Or, as Yogi Berra reportedly phrased it, “If I hadn’t believed it, I wouldn’t have seen it”.

Every now and again, the synchronicities are too large to miss. Sometimes they literally hit us between the eyes. However, my accumulated experience is that even the very large and obvious ones only make sense if we actively seek to uncover the smaller ones that surround them. Sherlock Holmes appreciated this even further when he said, “It has long been an axiom of mine that the little things are infinitely the most important”.

My experience is that the big ones do not occur by themselves, as if they are in a vacuum. They virtually always appear as part of a larger pattern, waiting to be discovered. Otherwise, we may be tempted to forget or dismiss even the large ones.

We are ready to continue the synchronicity-seeking process by exploring the story of my second close encounter with a powerful synchronicity. As you participate in my early confusion, concern, and wonder, I encourage you to remember the spirit of the maxim issued by the distinguished neuroscientist Dr. Warren McCulloch, a philosophy I follow devoutly.

He said, “Do not bite my finger; look where I am pointing”.

Chapter 4
From the Late Susy Smith to the Movie *Dragonfly*
Lesson: Spirit Can Play a Role in Synchronicity

It is belief that gets us there. Dragonfly,
the movie

In Chapter 2, we reviewed how I first discovered that patterns of numbers and letters in my life were often adding up to the number 11. A seemingly unconnected meeting with a medical student led me to learn about the existence of Kabbalah and the historic practice of numerology. In the face of continued number 11 synchronicities in New York City, the idea occurred to me that we should try to rescue a very rare breed of dog—a Cardigan Welsh Corgi. Within less than an hour of envisioning this possibility, I came upon a Cardigan Welsh Corgi—Willie—who needed to be rescued. It turned out that 11s and numerology connected directly to Willie and his owner. Willie became my "secret Kabbalah Corgi." Then years later when Willie died and I feared that my connection to Kabbalah synchronicities and related numbers would end, the person who presided over his burial turned out to be a master of Kabbalah numerology.

Taken together, this interconnected combination of real-life events seems almost impossible to imagine occurring by chance.

If a novelist wrote such a story, we would conclude it was too far-fetched to be taken seriously.

Would you believe that my second close encounter with seemingly impossible synchronicities, almost seven years after Willie had died, included an improbable replication—another rescued dog? I ask you this question having only realized this potential connection just as I was beginning to write this chapter!

It appears as if each leg of my unfolding synchronicity journey was part of a carefully crafted, extraordinarily complex mystery of Hollywood proportions. Like any superbly designed mystery novel or movie script, it seems as if every scene—in fact, every line within every scene—has some obvious or subtle meaning or purpose to the unfolding plot (even if the plot seems, at times, like science fiction).

You may have noticed that the more you re-read a treasured book or re-watch a favorite movie, the more you discover details of plot and connection that previously escaped your awareness.

As always, our challenge is to discern the difference between reading connections into a plot that aren't there versus discovering connections that are actually there, but which we had previously missed.

The question before us here is whether the apparent repetition of a rescued dog (what a scientist might describe as a replication) is merely a coincidence, or if it is important to the totality of the unfolding narrative.

Is this a genuine synchronicity, readying itself to be revealed as we explore the story?

How much does the role of love for people, animals, and even insects play in the existence and meaning of synchronicities?

We begin with the movie *Dragonfly* and the importance of its take-home message for this unfolding true-life story.

Setting the Stage: The Movie *Dragonfly* and Its Message about Belief

When I first saw the movie *Dragonfly,* directed by Tom Shadyac, I had no idea that there would be a series of synchronicities attached to it. Though the movie was profoundly moving and meaningful to me, I had no inkling that its unforgettable message would soon bloom into a garden of increasing and unimaginable Type III Synchronicities.

Briefly, the plot of the movie involves two physicians who were very much in love: the husband, Dr. Joe Darrow, who specialized in emergency medicine, and his wife, Dr. Emily Darrow, who worked in pediatric oncology.

Emily was pregnant, and they were eagerly awaiting the birth of a baby girl. Emily went off on a Red Cross mission in South America to help young children. An unanticipated horrific accident occurred and everyone, including the children, the bus driver, and Emily, were presumed to have been killed.

After the accident, Joe—played by Kevin Costner—began experiencing strange happenings in his home involving one of his wife's favorite creatures, the dragonfly. Portrayed as a skeptic, Joe found these dragonfly-related events impossible to believe.

In the process of fulfilling his promise to Emily that if anything were to happen to her, he would take care of her surviving pediatric patients, Joe began to discover that various children whose hearts had stopped beating and had to be resuscitated ("Code Blues") were experiencing unusual near-death experiences (NDEs) that seemingly involved his deceased wife. These children were claiming that Emily was calling out to Joe from the other side with a message. However, the children did not know what the precise message was.

I remember listening attentively to the hauntingly beautiful music accompanying these scenes and wondering who the composer was. Though the story was at various times sensationalized, the movie nonetheless accurately portrayed the controversial claim that people who experience NDEs can sometimes receive important messages, purportedly from deceased people—whether the deceased are their loved ones or are total strangers to them.

As Joe's world is being turned upside down and spinning out of control, he learns that a nun, Sister Madeline, has been collecting data on the children's NDEs. Joe decides that he must speak with the nun to determine if he is simply going crazy, or if what he is experiencing is real.

Joe eventually meets Sister Madeline—movingly portrayed by Linda Hunt—in a chapel lit with hundreds of candles. Sister Madeline explains, scientifically and poetically, how she has reached her conclusion that afterlife experiences associated with NDEs are often real.

Toward the end of this spellbinding and profoundly important scene, she makes a simple statement—a take-home message—that touches Joe deeply. In fact, at the end of the movie, Joe restates Sister Madeline's message.

If you have not seen the movie, I strongly recommend watching it. I will not give away any more details of the plot here or its spectacular ending, but I can reveal the take-home message without detracting from the impact of the story.

Amidst some of the most hauntingly beautiful music I had ever heard in a movie, first Sister Madeline, and later Joe, says, "It is belief that gets us there".

The line "It is belief that gets us there" served as both a reminder and a revelation to me. What the movie expressed was the general principle that although knowledge and skills are essential for doing things successfully, it is personal belief that motivates and inspires us to actually accomplish them.

Dragonfly quickly became one of my top five favorite spiritually-oriented science fiction movies (another one is Carl Sagan's *Contact,* which I also discuss in my books *The Living Energy Universe* and *The Afterlife Experiments).*

However, at the time I first saw *Dragonfly,* I had no idea that my feelings for this movie would herald a completely unanticipated set of future events, the capstone being triggered by my seemingly chance meeting with a giant rescued dog, his rescuer/owner, and his owner's mother.

Enter the Late Susy Smith and Her Messages from the "Other Side"

The story is about to get a bit more complicated and potentially push your boggle button. But remember that this is a completely factual account (save for the changing of certain names and incidentals to preserve anonymity as necessary).

It was early in the morning, around 5:00 am, and I was preparing to leave for a one-week lecture tour in California. My scheduled talks included an invited presentation to the San Francisco chapter of the Institute of Noetic Sciences, where I was speaking on *The Afterlife Experiments,* and a special address at a Deepak Chopra sponsored weekend event at the La Costa Resort. Because I was to be out of town for the week, I had various personal and professional details to attend to. This included paying house bills and packing before leaving for the University and then the airport.

Checking for any emergency emails, I discovered an unexpected message from a medium in the Midwest with whom I had conducted a novel and controversial afterlife experiment during the previous six months. I will call her Jane.

Jane had contacted me by email claiming that she was receiving communication from the late Susy Smith, author of thirty books in the field of parapsychology and survival of consciousness after death. I had written about some of the experiments I had conducted with Susy in *The Afterlife Experiments* (when Susy was still alive) and other experiments conducted with her in *The Truth About Medium* and *The Sacred Promise* (performed with various mediums, including Jane, after Susy's death).

In one of the private experiments conducted after Susy had died, Jane would contact Susy and ask her two questions: (1) what had Susy seen happening in my personal life in the immediately preceding twenty-four hours, and (2) what did Susy foresee happening in my life in the upcoming twenty-four hours. Jane collected and emailed me this information daily, five days a week, and I would score the information for degree of accuracy and specificity.

We need not be sidetracked here with reviewing the details of this personal experiment, or with the two controlled laboratory double-blind experiment that replicated it; suffice it to say that the findings were exceptionally positive. (If you wish, you can read *The Sacred Promise* for various examples of such experiments.) What is important here is to recognize that on the morning I was preparing to travel to California, Jane had sent me a spontaneous email, which she did from time to time, providing supposedly special messages from Susy.

In this particular email, Jane mentioned that Susy was bringing up the movie *Dragonfly,* and that this was important. Also, Susy was claiming that I would shortly be meeting a well-known person who was important to the study of the afterlife.

This was a novel email to say the least. Why, seemingly out of the blue, was Susy (according to Jane) bringing my attention to the movie *Dragonfly?* And why, at this moment, was Susy (via Jane) preparing me to meet a potentially famous person who would be important to research on life after death?

As I pondered this information, I remembered that I was scheduled to meet with a person who said he wrote music for the movies. His name was not familiar to me, and I did not look him up online at the time.

This person had read *The Afterlife Experiments,* and was sufficiently intrigued that both he and his wife had requested private readings with one of the mediums I had tested and reported on in the book (I have been requested not to disclose the name of this particular medium—what is important is that the medium was not Jane, and Jane had not yet met this medium).

This composer had contacted me, saying that he was deeply interested in afterlife research and whether science could address the question of life after death. He and his family lived in California, and we decided to meet during my lecture tour.

As I pondered Jane's email, the thought popped into my head, *Could this person somehow be related to the movie Dragonfly?* I typed his name—John Debney—into Google, and quickly found his website. To my astonishment, I discovered that the person I was about to meet was the composer of the hauntingly beautiful music for *Dragonfly!*

I cannot adequately express in words the excitement I experienced in that moment. I had just discovered that I was shortly to meet the composer of the music for not just any movie I liked—or even any favorite spiritual movie—but *Dragonfly,* a movie whose music really stood out and seemingly spoke to me.

But more importantly, I had been led to this discovery via a spontaneous email from a medium in the Midwest who claimed to have received this information from the late Susy Smith, a woman I deeply admired and grew to love as an adopted grandmother.

In a moment of enthusiastic gratitude, I emailed both Jane and John and told them how I was led to discover the John Debney/*Dragonfly* connection. I confessed how much I loved the music from the film, and therefore was especially interested in meeting John.

Jane wrote back and reminded me that she, too, had a connection with the movie *Dragonfly*.

At a certain point in her life, Jane discovered that she spoke a language she did not understand and which she had never been taught. It took her years to determine whether she was speaking gibberish or a real language. A scholar at the Smithsonian, an expert in indigenous languages in South America, discerned that the language Jane uttered was a relatively unknown dialect called Yanomami.

It turns out that the language spoken by the tribe that played a critical and dramatic role in *Dragonfly* was—you guessed it—Yanomami!

I had now experienced three *Dragonfly* synchronicities: the purported communication from Susy was Event #1; my upcoming meeting with the composer of the score for *Dragonfly* was Event #2; and Jane's extraordinary linguistic connection to *Dragonfly* was Event #3. (I later heard tapes of Jane speaking this language, and I have even personally witnessed her produce the language on various occasions.)

That fateful morning, my mind was soaring with possibilities. Could it be that Susy, from the other side, was preparing me to meet the composer of the music for *Dragonfly?* After all, the theme of *Dragonfly*—getting a message from beyond the world of the living—was clearly related to our research on life after death.

But I did not have time to ponder these sorts of questions. I had to pay my bills, pack, and so forth. Around 6 am, I went outside to check the mailbox. I typically collected my mail every few days, so the box was usually full, and that morning was no exception.

Amongst the letters and catalogues was a gold-colored plastic bubble wrapped envelope. I had never seen such an envelope before (or since). To my amazement, I saw that the package was from John Debney! Had John sent me some CD's of the soundtracks he had composed for several movies? Could one of the CD's be the score from *Dragonfly?*

My hands trembled as I opened the golden-bubbled envelope. Sure enough, inside was a collection of CD's representing a small subset of his movies. I could not believe my eyes: one of them was the soundtrack for *Dragonfly*. Event #4.

Holding back tears, I opened the package and played the CD on my home stereo system. Out poured the glorious music John had composed for *Dragonfly*.

I raced back to my computer and sent a follow-up email to John and Jane. I shared the synchronicity of Jane's email, Susy's comments about *Dragonfly* and the person I was about to meet, my going to Google and ultimately discovering that John had composed the music for *Dragonfly*, and then going out to get the mail and discovering that John had sent me a copy of the soundtrack for *Dragonfly*.

At this point, I knew that something special was happening. It felt "Willie-like." I wondered, *what could possibly happen next?*

A week later, the seemingly impossible happened, and it happened in spades.

Returning to Tucson: The Rescued Great Dane, and a Story More Extraordinary than Any I Had Ever Witnessed

Though my trip to California was memorable, it merely set the stage for what was to transpire upon my return to Tucson.

For example, after my lecture at the Deepak Chopra event, I met a participant who was a Senior Vice President for a major financial services company. Her history with 11s and 11-11s was even more extraordinary than mine. She had experienced dragonfly synchronicities, too. This was Event #5.

I was beginning to discover that synchronicities were happening to all kinds of people—not just to "new age" people, but also executives, lawyers, and even scientists.

It turned out that I did not actually meet the Debneys on this trip. They had to unexpectedly cancel, and we rescheduled for the following month. This turned out to be propitious; by the time we finally met, I had seemingly been inadvertently led to firm evidence indicating that the foundation of the movie *Dragonfly*—the premise that messages can be spontaneously conveyed during NDEs—was, in fact, real.

Here's what happened. I returned to Tucson on a Monday afternoon, where I had a dinner meeting scheduled that night at 6 pm with one of my research colleagues, Dr. Kathy Creath, at a Chinese restaurant not far from my home.

It is worth noting that Kathy and I have had at least fifty dinners out together, but only once—that fateful night—did we eat at that Chinese restaurant, or any Chinese restaurant for that manner.

Because I happened to arrive at the restaurant fifteen minutes early, I had the unanticipated opportunity to meet the biggest dog I had ever seen. And curiously, connected with this dog was a genuine, real-life NDE story even more unbelievable than the fictional stories in *Dragonfly*.

Around the corner from the Chinese restaurant was a Starbucks with an outdoor patio. Sitting around one of the patio tables were three women and the biggest dog I had ever seen, a gigantic Great Dane. Great Danes are typically large; this one was exceptionally so.

Being a dog lover, I felt the need to meet this dog. As I gently approached the dog, it became excited and showed an obvious desire to make contact with me (which included licking my face – quite an experience, given the size of its tongue).

The woman holding the dog's leash was surprised and pleased. I introduced myself and asked her about her dog. She explained that she had recently adopted the dog from a Great Dane rescue center in Phoenix, that it apparently had been abused, and was shy of most men. For some reason the dog sensed I was safe, and responded with great affection.

I explained that I taught at the University of Arizona, to which the young woman replied, "Really? I'm a junior at the University of Arizona."

Then one of the other women asked, "Are you the Gary Schwartz who wrote a book called *The Afterlife Experiments?*" For the record, most people I spontaneously meet do not recognize my name, nor do they know that I am the author of *The Afterlife Experiments.*

I said, "Yes, why do you ask?"

She replied, "Because I was recently given your book, and I am reading it right now."

"Really? Who gave it to you?" I asked.

She said, "Jerry Cohen, the CEO of Canyon Ranch. Do you know him?"

"Yes", I said, "In fact, one of the experiments in the book is called The Canyon Ranch Experiment because it took place at the Ranch. Also, I give talks there on various topics, including this work. How do you know Jerry?"

"I have worked at Canyon Ranch for years," she said. "You may not know this," she continued, "but a friend of mine who also works at the Ranch has had an experience that is more extraordinary than any account you provide in your book."

Was I hearing her correctly? Was her friend's experience truly more extraordinary than any account in my book? Needless to say, I was intrigued.

"How interesting," I replied. "Would your friend be willing to speak with me?"

"Actually," she replied, "my friend wrote up an account of her experience over six months ago and has wanted to contact you ever since, but she has been afraid to."

"Really?" I said. "Let me give you my cell phone number. Please tell your friend I would be happy to meet with her and discuss her experience."

The next day, I received a phone call from her friend. Her story turned out to be so unbelievable and evidential that I requested that she and her husband meet with me to record the events for posterity. Part of what made her story so unbelievable was that it related directly to the movie *Dragonfly*.

A few days after the phone call, we held our meeting, which I videotaped. What I can share here is a synopsis of the key points of her story, changing names and a few other details to preserve the anonymity of those involved. We shall refer to her as Claire. Though I never spoke with the surgeon in the story, I did ask Claire to call him and ask if he would be willing to be contacted by me to confirm certain key components of her account. Claire informed me that he was willing to be interviewed if I so requested.

Claire had been suffering from a repetitive-motion injury and was about to have it surgically repaired. During the anesthesia process, she suffered what was apparently a severe allergic reaction and had to be resuscitated. Once she had stabilized, the surgical team decided it was safe to proceed with the operation.

In the recovery room, the lead surgeon informed Claire and her husband that although there had been a problem during the anesthesia, it had thankfully been caught in time. Also, although something unusual (and upsetting) had happened immediately following the surgery concerning one of the surgical team members, the operation itself had been successful and uneventful, and the doctor expected Claire to have a smooth and full recovery. The surgeon did not offer any details about what exactly had transpired immediately following the surgery, and Claire and her husband did not request additional information at that time.

Meanwhile, vague memories of her surgery began to come to Claire: she had a surprising and disconcerting "out-of-body" experience, where she felt as if she were floating above the operating table. She had relatively little memory of what else had transpired during the surgery. Claire was embarrassed to confess this strange experience, and though she did tell her husband about it later, she did not share it with her surgeon at that time.

Here's where the story gets eerie. A few weeks later, Claire and her husband happened to see the movie *Dragonfly*. As she watched the various scenes of children having near-death experiences and supposedly receiving communication from the other side, she began to wonder if her own out-of-body experience was somehow accompanied by afterlife events that might have upset one of the members of the surgical team.

After mustering her courage, Claire called the lead surgeon and asked him if he would tell her what had happened to the team member following the surgery. What he told Claire and her husband would have been completely unbelievable to her had she not been prepared by seeing the movie *Dragonfly,* which is Event #6.

According to the surgeon, as Claire was lying on the operating table and still under anesthesia, she suddenly sat bolt upright and looked around the room, scanning the five people in surgical masks. She then selected one person in particular and said:

"There is a woman here. Her name is Sarah. She has a message for you. She wants you to know that it is not your fault that she died."

Apparently Claire then collapsed back onto the table, unconscious again.

Meanwhile, the person to whom she had directed this startling message fled the room in tears.

The surgeon carefully explained to Claire that the person who had left the room had indeed been married to a woman named Sarah (this is not her real name; I have changed it in the story to preserve her anonymity).

According to the surgeon, Sarah had been suffering from an incurable and deadly disease, and she had become severely depressed. It was claimed that she had decided to end her life and had attempted suicide by slitting her own throat.

Sarah's husband happened to come home as she was bleeding to death. He attempted CPR, but was unsuccessful.

As a result, Sarah's husband lived with extreme guilt, believing that had he only come home sooner, he might have been able to save her life.

To better appreciate what has happened in this story, I encourage you to try to imagine placing yourself in the shoes of three different people, and consider how you would feel.

First, try to imagine how you might feel if you worked as the member of a surgical team:

- that your spouse had committed suicide and you felt personally responsible for your beloved's death, and then
- an anesthetized patient—a complete stranger to you—somehow sits up in the presence of your colleagues and provides you with a message from your deceased spouse, saying that her death was not your fault.

Second, imagine how you might feel if you were the patient:

- that you underwent surgery during which you had a strange out-of-body experience,
- that you later saw a movie suggesting that out-of-body experiences could be accompanied by messages provided by people who had died, and then
- you called your surgeon and discovered that you had conveyed a profoundly healing message to a member of the surgical team, apparently from his deceased wife.

And third, imagine how you might feel if you were me, a conventionally trained scientist:

- that one of your all-time favorite (fictional) movies claimed that children suffering from cancer who had NDEs could sometimes receive important messages from people who have died,
- that through an unsolicited email from a medium in the Midwest, a deceased person you deeply admired and loved was telling you about this movie and that you would soon meet a well-known person who would be important to the work,

- that because of this email you discovered that you were about to meet the very person who wrote the music for this movie, music that you deeply admired,
- that while giving lectures about research addressing life after death, you met credible people with incredible stories related to synchronicities you had personally experienced (replicating connections to the number 11, and even dragonflies),
- that via a seemingly chance meeting with a gigantic rescued dog, you would end up connecting with a woman whose real-life experience replicated the essence of the movie whose story and music you so admired (and whose composer you were about to meet), and
- that her true-life account would be more extraordinary than anything you had written about in your then-latest book.

It would appear that combinations of sets of synchronicities—in this case, from 11s and rescued dogs to dragonflies and life after death—were unfolding in a very powerful way, suggesting that a degree of interconnection was somehow extending across a diverse range of people living in different locations, over extended periods of time, and even involving deceased individuals.

If This Happened (And It Really Did), Then How Did it Happen, and What Did it Mean?

When we examine this complex set of events, and presuming we accept that the events actually happened—that is, that they were not made up, misperceived, or falsely remembered and presented—we are then left with a challenging mystery. How could these events possibly occur, and what might they conceivably mean or imply?

The truth is, at the time I was so taken aback by the events themselves that I could not wrap my mind around such mechanical (the "how") and philosophical (the "why") questions.

I was in the "this can't possibly be happening" state of mind, and I could not get past that conclusion. Though I knew in my heart that this set of events was somehow very important, my head could not handle the totality of the information, and I tried to ignore the emerging evidence and its implications. For example, the spirit of a deceased woman (Susy Smith) via an evidential medium (Jane) could forewarn me about a future synchronistic evident of profound importance.

However, driven partly by curiosity and partly by a sense of responsibility, I knew I had to keep searching to see if the phenomenon (whatever it was) would happen again. So I kept my mind open to the possibility of collecting additional information about 11s and dragonflies, and whatever else might show up next.

Much to my dismay, synchronicities involving ravens began to appear, and I went from a state of disbelief and confusion to outright stress, and finally anger toward the cosmos. Fortunately, as my understanding deepened, this anger dissipated and what remained was an overwhelming feeling of awe. But the path was not an easy one.

CHAPTER 5
RAVENS IN THE ARIZONA INN, ISTANBUL, AND SAINT PETERSBURG
LESSON: SYMBOLS CAN PLAY A ROLE IN SYNCHRONICITY

In order to disprove the law that all crows are black, it is enough to find one white crow
William James, MD

It has been my experience never to know precisely when a new set of synchronicities will begin in my life. However, over time I have come to learn that if I experience something that is highly unusual or "out of the blue," I will begin wondering almost immediately *why* it is happening and *what* it might mean.

Also, I have come to learn that if a particular class of synchronicities appears in earnest, it usually extends further back in time than I was previously aware.

I learned these two lessons in the process of dealing with a completely preposterous sequence of events involving, of all things, ravens. The 11 and dragonfly synchronicities were somewhat like training wheels for what I would discover next.

Setting the Stage: A Historical Unconscious Connection with Ravens Revealed at the Westward Look Resort

Since 1965, when I was 21 years old, I have had a passion for Native American art. My introduction to this type of art occurred, of all places, in Greenwich Village, New York City. I was taken to a shop called Amron, which is the owner's name, Norma, spelled backwards. Amron specialized in Southwest, Pacific Northwest, and Alaskan art, and I immediately fell in love with the genre.

I began collecting Native American art in graduate school, and my collecting continues to the present day. Part of the reason I was a visiting professor at the University of British Columbia in Vancouver, Canada from 1975–1976 was to immerse myself in Pacific Northwest Coast Native American art. Likewise, part of my motivation for moving to the University of Arizona in 1978 was for the experience of Southwest Native American art.

Historically, my focus had been on the aesthetic appeal of the art rather than its deeper meaning and significance. In fact, until my fateful encounter with raven synchronicities beginning in 2005, I paid virtually no attention to what kinds of animals I had been collecting or what they might symbolize.

In the winter of 2005, a team of women came to visit with me at the University of Arizona about the possibility of my doing research related to the late Dr. John Mack, professor of Psychiatry at Harvard Medical School. One of the women was Dr. Diane Hennacy Powell, also a psychiatrist, and I was struck by her intelligence, creativity, and wit.

Dr. Powell had completed her medical training at Johns Hopkins School of Medicine, she had been an Assistant Professor of Psychiatry at Harvard (where she had first met Dr. Mack), and had been on the faculty at the University of California Medical School in San Diego before moving to Ashland, Oregon. Her interests span from neuropharmacology to parapsychology, and her book *The ESP Enigma* is essential reading concerning the bridge between scientific research on mind, brain, and paranormal phenomena.

I invited Dr. Powell to lunch at the Westward Look Resort on Sunday so that we could have some time for private conversation. At first I was a bit surprised, as she spent most of our meeting sharing her remarkable history with ravens. Her synchronicities with ravens are jaw-dropping, and they include the apparent role of ravens in her psychotherapy with patients—but this is her story to tell, not mine. What is important here is that in the back of my mind I was wondering, *Why is this brilliant psychiatrist feeling the need to share this seemingly bizarre information with me? What's with the psychiatrist and the ravens?* Though I was not immediately aware of it, this turned out to be Event #1.

As I listened to Dr. Powell, I wondered if I had any connections with ravens. The truth was that save for Edgar Allan Poe's poem *The Raven,* I knew virtually nothing about ravens at the time. However, I did have a lot of carvings and paintings of birds in my home, and I wondered whether any of them could be ravens. I knew I had some eagles, and an owl or two, but I did not recall having any ravens among my collection.

I asked Dr. Powell if she would like to see my collection of Native American art. She was curious and agreed. It is hard to describe the glee she expressed, as well as my shock, upon discovering that I had been collecting ravens for years and did not know it!

I had a Pacific Northwest Coast Kachina-like dancing figure with a large mask of a bird on a man's heads. The mask turned out to be a raven.

I had a foot-long Pacific Northwest Coast wooden carving of what I presumed to be a duck. It turned out to be a raven mask.

I had two Pacific Northwest ceremonial aprons. One was clearly of an eagle. The other was of a strange bird; Dr. Powell showed me that it was, in fact, a raven.

I had a Pacific Northwest Coast rattle of a bird that turned out to be a raven.

I had a Pacific Northwest Coast print with multiple birds on it. These birds turned out to be ravens.

At least one of the birds on one of my three-foot tall Pacific Northwest Coast totem poles was a raven.

I had been living with ravens for years and had not known it.

Rather than counting all of these ravens as individual synchronicities, I simply thought of them collectively as Event #2. I was well aware that this might all have been just a coincidence, until something truly extraordinary happened the following night. Because of Dr. Powell's connection with ravens, and the fact that it was her intuition to share her raven story with me, I ended up sharing my extraordinary raven journey with her as it unfolded.

An Extraordinary Raven Account at the Arizona Inn

Dr. Powell returned to Ashland, and I resumed my activities in Tucson. I had been scheduled to have dinner that Monday night with a husband and wife who had been trying to meet with me for months. They wintered in the Phoenix area, and desperately wanted to share with me their experiences involving purported after death communications from their deceased son.

My administrative assistant had arranged the appointment, and I knew virtually nothing about their story.

When we met at the Arizona Inn, they brought a photo album that provided visual evidence for some of the experiences they had been having. The key ones involved ravens. Event #3.

Briefly, they claimed that their son, who had died when he was in his early 40s, loved animals. They claimed that after he died, a raven persisted in spending time on their porch at their home in the Midwest, and they were convinced that it was somehow connected to their son. They claimed that this raven followed them all the way from the Midwest to the Phoenix area, and spent time in a tree near their winter home. They showed me pictures of the raven on their porch, from their car, and in the tree. Some of the photos contained imperfections, which they interpreted as possible photographic evidence of the spirit of their son.

Had I not met Dr. Powell and heard her incredible story involving purported communications with ravens, consequently discovered my own longtime connection with ravens, and then learned that to aboriginal peoples of the Pacific Northwest, the raven is often described as a messenger from spirit, I probably would have kindly and gently dismissed this family's experiences as likely reflecting misperceptions and misinterpretations associated with their grief. However, after my 11 and dragonfly experiences, coupled with the curious timing of Dr. Powell's story and the discovery of my apparent raven connection, I could not be so cavalier as to dismiss their claims.

This open-mindedness turned out to be propitious, because the raven synchronicities not only continued, but actually escalated.

Jim Eppler's Raven Statue and White Ravens in Santa Fe

I was scheduled to give a major address about *The Afterlife Experiments* at the Science and Consciousness meetings in Santa Fe, and I invited Dr. Powell to meet me there. I had shared the Arizona Inn conversation with her, and she sensed that this was just the beginning.

Given my passion for Native American art, it is not surprising that Santa Fe is one of my favorite places to visit. I arrived at the conference early, and spent the afternoon exploring the numerous Native American art galleries nearby.

As I passed a town square, I noticed a large black bird sitting on a bench near the Manitou Gallery. I looked more closely, and to my amazement discovered that it was a raven.

I had never before come upon a raven sitting on a bench, and I stopped in my tracks. I did not want to frighten it, as I quickly recognized this as Event #4.

As I looked at the raven, I noticed it was standing quite still—too still, in fact. I slowly walked up to it and discovered that it was actually a life-sized (and remarkably lifelike) statue of a raven.

How often have you chanced upon a lifelike statue of a raven sitting on a bench? It was a first for me.

I went inside and learned that statue had been carved by Jim Eppler, an artist who specialized in ravens. Upstairs in the Manitou, I discovered a number of small raven statues and a few life-like statues of ravens also carved by Eppler.

I could not wait to show the raven on the bench to Dr. Powell. When she arrived at the conference, I walked with her to the gallery, and took some photos of her sitting with the raven. It looked just as lifelike as her, perching next to her on the bench.

The next morning while I was preparing to give my talk, I wondered if I should briefly mention at the end of my lecture my growing interest in ravens. I had been pondering the possibility that (1) ravens really could serve as messengers of spirit, and (2) if ravens can learn to speak, then (3) maybe ravens could serve as "mediums" and give verifiable information purportedly from spirit. (It turns out that ravens are extraordinarily intelligent and can learn to speak almost as well as the African Grey Parrot.) I even entertained the idea of adopting a raven and teaching it to speak in preparation for testing this admittedly novel yet possible hypothesis. Here I was, in Santa Fe, which was not only the home to many real ravens, but was also home to a remarkably lifelike raven sculpture sitting on a bench.

I had begun *The Afterlife Experiments* with a quote from the distinguished Harvard psychologist and physician Professor William James, which can be simplified and paraphrased from the original to read, "If you wish to upset the law that all crows are black, you need only find one white crow". (Crows, like ravens, are members of the Corvid family.)

The thought popped into my mind, *Given that there are albino crows, I wonder if there are any albino ravens?* I decided that if there were, I would briefly mention the raven communication hypothesis and surprise Dr. Powell by showing the audience the picture I had taken of her with the Eppler raven.

I searched online for "white ravens" and discovered that, sure enough, albino ravens appear from time to time, just as there are albino crows. I made the decision to end my talk with the photo of Dr. Powell with Eppler's raven. Dr. Powell was surprised and pleased, and the ending was a success.

What surprised me, however, was that as a result of offering this hypothesis, numerous people came up to me afterwards to tell me about their extraordinary raven spiritual synchronicity experiences.

I began to wonder, *was there something real about the relationship between raven and spirit? Furthermore, were ravens coming into my life at this particular time for some meaningful synchronistic purpose?* I could come to no firm conclusion one way or the other, but to honor the possibility that there was such a connection, I felt moved to purchase two of Eppler's raven statues. The small one, named Indy, sat on a stand to the right of the computer I was using to write the first draft of this book. The life-sized one, named Spenser, is visible in the living room to my left. (Indy currently sits on a rock in the living room, near Spenser.) I mention these facts because they will appear again as a startling synchronicity in this and the next set of supersynchronicities.

Ravens in Istanbul and Saint Petersburg

Two weeks later, I was scheduled to fly to Istanbul to speak about *The Afterlife Experiments* at an international conference on parapsychology. The invited speakers were from the US, England, Italy, Turkey, and Russia.

At the Tucson airport, I stopped in the bookstore and purchased a novel titled *Brimstone* by Douglas Preston and Lincoln Child. I had read a few novels by these authors before, and I had developed a fond appreciation for their recurring lead characters. I decided to save the new novel for my return trip from Istanbul. This turned out to be propitious, as we will see when we return to *Brimstone* soon.

The conference was well publicized; in fact, two of the speaker photos (one being mine) were published on the front page of Turkey's equivalent of *USA Today*.

The morning of the conference, I wondered if I should include a mention of the raven communication hypothesis in my talk. However, I had no idea if ravens carried any significance in Turkey. I explored a few websites, and to my great surprise, learned that the Turkish people have several sayings involving ravens.

One saying was, "Ravens see chicks as falcons". I had no idea what this could mean, but it inspired me to include the photo of

Dr. Powell with Eppler's raven in my talk. After my presentation, various audience members approached me with their own stories about ravens! I realized that either the raven-spirit illusion transcended cultures and languages, or something very real involving ravens was going on. This was Event #5.

That evening the speakers, along with the key members of the BILYAY Foundation who had invited us, held a private dinner at the hotel. The table was arranged in a square with approximately thirty people sitting around it, seven or eight people to a side. The seating was not prearranged. I ended up sitting at one corner, and to my right was a Turkish woman who was the Assistant Director of the Foundation. Sitting to her right was Dr. Konstantin Korotkoff, an invited speaker from Saint Petersburg, Russia.

I have known Dr. Korotkoff for over ten years, and we have become close friends. We see each other maybe once a year. He had arrived in Istanbul mid-afternoon that day, just in time to hear my presentation.

After Dr. Korotkoff sat down, he said, "Hi Gary, it's so good to see you again. I really enjoyed your talk, especially the part about the ravens."

Ravens? Did Dr. Korotkoff really say ravens?

"Thanks," I replied. "I appreciate your kind comments. But what was it about the ravens that you especially liked?"

Dr. Korotkoff said, "I know what you are talking about. I used to have a pet raven!" This was Event #6.

How many people do you know who have kept a raven as a pet? Up to this point, my count was at zero.

"You had a pet raven?" I asked incredulously. Dr. Korotkoff went on to describe in great detail how he had kept this pet raven during one of the years he was working on his PhD in physics.

I could spend pages describing his pet raven experiences, but something even more interesting happened next. Dr. Korotkoff sensed my great interest in ravens and asked, "Would you like to hear some Russian raven jokes?"

Russian raven jokes? He had to be joking.

Dr. Korotkoff went on to share a series of very humorous raven jokes. At this point, the entire table was listening in on our conversation, and I realized that him sharing these jokes constituted Event #7.

Then someone said, "We have raven sayings in Turkey."

"Yes," I said, "I recently learned about the saying 'Ravens see chicks as falcons.' Does anyone know what that means?"

The woman sitting to my right (between me and Dr. Korotkoff) said, "I think they mistranslated our saying. It should be 'Ravens see their chicks as falcons."'

Now I understood. If you have ever seen a baby raven, to many human eyes it looks more like a baby tarantula than a baby bird. However, apparently to a mother raven, it not only looks beautiful, but she also sees its great potential. At least, that is what the Turkish saying implies. The fact that the answer to my question came from the woman sitting between Dr. Korotkoff and me was Event #8.

As you can imagine, at this point I was in raven synchronicity shock. I was relieved that the dinner ended shortly after this conversation, and I sought a peaceful night's sleep.

However, the raven synchronicities were just revving up. The following morning, when I arrived at the Istanbul Convention Center, the woman who had sat next to me at dinner and explained the meaning of the "Ravens see chicks as falcons" saying handed me a folded piece of paper and said that I needed to read it.

I thanked her, placed the paper carefully inside the inner pocket of my sport jacket, and promptly forgot about it, as people were still coming up to me to share raven and spirit stories.

Lunch was served in a private dining room, once again at a square table. I arrived late, and there was only one seat available. And the person sitting to my left was none other than the woman who had given me the paper!

"Have you read it?" she asked. I apologized and said that I had not, then I took it out and examined it carefully. I could not believe what I was reading.

What she explained on the paper was that, on her drive home the previous night through her province to her hometown, she had thought about the English translation of the name of this town. The English translation was "Baby Raven." This became Event #9.

But I had had my fill of raven synchronicities in Turkey, and I was ready to return home.

Ravens in Brimstone

When I boarded the plane for my return flight to the United States, I yearned for some non-raven time. But apparently it was not meant to be.

I began reading my novel, *Brimstone.* The novel is one of a series involving two main characters: FBI Special Agent Aloysius X.L. Pendergast and Sergeant Vincent D'Agosta, a New York City policeman working for the Southampton Police Department on Long Island.

Early on in the novel, the authors write how Agent Pendergast, an independently wealthy man, takes Sergeant D'Agosta to his relative's estate outside of New York City. The estate was named "Ravenscry."

An estate named Ravenscry? I presumed it had to be a fluke.

Later on in the novel, the characters find themselves in Italy, and they are described as being "ravenously" hungry. "Ravenous" may be a more common word that the phrase "Ravenscry" as applied to an estate, but it is still a rare word in terms of the mystery and science fiction novels I read.

Toward the end of the novel, the characters are being chased by vicious dogs, and the authors describe their barking as sounding like "raven's cries." Dogs barking sounding like raven's cries? I had never read such a description before.

I began to wonder, *were these authors deliberately mentioning ravens in this novel?*

At the end of the novel, D'Agosta is alone, fearing that his friend and colleague Pendergast has been killed. The authors write how D'Agosta is looking out at a field and sees one lone raven.

At this point I had to seriously entertain the idea that the authors were intentionally including ravens in this novel. I later noticed that the cover of the novel included a drawing of what appeared to be a raven-like bird.

Four mentions of ravens, two in very unique ways, in the novel I seemingly chanced to read coming back from Turkey? I concluded that this deserved to be labeled as Event #10.

Coping with a Raven Supersynchronicity

As you will read in the next chapter, the combination of these ten raven synchronicities, all within the span of a month, was not only challenging for me, but was also philosophically and physically stressful.

Here is a review of the ten raven synchronicities:

1. A brilliant psychiatrist spending most of a shared meal confessing, unprompted, secret raven synchronicities.
2. The discovery that I had been collecting and living with ravens for years without knowing it.
3. Spending time the following day with a couple who were convinced that their deceased son was communicating with them via a raven, and who had photographic evidence consistent with this hypothesis.
4. Coming upon a lifelike raven statue on a bench in Santa Fe.
5. Going to Turkey and discovering that the country had sayings about ravens.
6. Learning that my Russian colleague and friend had once had a pet raven.
7. Hearing this colleague and friend tell his Russian raven jokes.
8. Sitting next to a woman who helped me to clarify the meaning of the Turkish saying, "Ravens see their chicks as falcons".
9. This very same woman realizing that the town she lived in was named "Baby Raven," and

10. The novel I had innocently purchased in Tucson and read on my return flight not only mentioning ravens, but also featuring an unusual usage of "raven's cries" and "Ravenscry."

And this was just the beginning. Many more raven synchronicities followed, though we will save them for a later book. The point here is not simply the realization that the conditional probability of all of these events occurring in sequence, if you tried to calculate it, being far beyond chance. The greater point is the possible meaning of this particular synchronicity implying that spirit was somehow involved with the orchestration of synchronicities, especially Type III Synchronicities.

Certain tribes in the Pacific Northwest believe that the raven actually brought the sun to humanity. The raven is often placed at the top of totem poles, and is sometimes carved with a sun in its mouth. In a sense, ravens are viewed as bringing "light" to humanity and the world.

Being a scientist and not a poet, I tended to view such beliefs as superstitions and myths. People have believed erroneous things throughout recorded history, even if the beliefs happen to be beautiful and inspiring.

However, the evidence I was accruing was now forcing me to wonder who held the erroneous beliefs—the Native American peoples whose art I so admired, or the mainstream scientists whose research I so admired?

Could some of these indigenous beliefs be true? Could some of these beliefs be verified, not merely through passive observational science, but also through more active scientific experiment as well?

I had no idea. I just knew that the collection of events was super-improbable, and that the implications challenged the foundation of my academic education.

I did not know what to do and promptly came down with the flu.

Chapter 6
Ravens in *The Doomsday Key* and Seattle: The Continuity of Encouragement

Lesson: Synchronicities Can Be Responsive to Our Intentions

Be careful what you ask for.
Author Unknown

If there is one lesson I have learned on this self-science synchronicity journey, it is to "be careful what you ask for". The phrase, "Ask and you will receive" may not only be true—sometimes—but it may be essential for understanding how synchronicity works.

The account of a Type III Synchronicity that occurred in May 2005, which you will soon read, represented a profound turning point for me. It provided the quantum leap of evidence that forced me to entertain the possibility that the occurrence and continuity of synchronicities—especially Type III Synchronicities—was a two-way street. In other words, the manifestation of complex Type III Synchronicities involves an interaction of the One Mind combined with our individual minds. It appears as if our individual attentions and intentions are an integral part of the occurrence and continuity of the process.

However, before revealing the evidence for this integrated process, I am going to skip ahead and share a more recent Type III Synchronicity that began one month before I wrote this chapter (in August 2009). The height of this particular string of synchronicities reached its peak ten minutes before I decided to write this chapter.

Since my experience is that "honoring the moment" sustains the continued appearance of synchronicities, I will "walk the talk" and share it with you now. Moreover, this particular Type III Synchronicity is valuable because it provides continued evidence for what will most likely evoke the greatest "I can't believe what I am reading" feeling some readers may have experienced thus far.

So while this present chapter is a spontaneous addition to the book, and briefly breaks the flow of the chronology of my awakening to synchronicity, it nonetheless provides a meaningful preamble for you to better understand and interpret the evidence discussed in the next chapter.

And it gives me the excuse to share a little more about ravens.

Honoring the Moment: The Latest Novel Plus True-Life Raven Synchronicities

On a Tuesday afternoon, August 4, 2009, Rhonda and I were flying to Seattle. I was scheduled to present a scientific paper on August 7 at the Parapsychology Association meeting, which was being held at the University of Washington. Rhonda had lived in Seattle for twelve years, and we were married in Seattle as well. Our plan was to spend two days visiting some of our friends and favorite places before attending the conference.

On the morning of August 4, Rhonda saw a raven flying near our house. We see a raven flying near our house maybe twice a month during the summer. By itself, this raven sighting was insignificant and unimportant. However, given my continuing history with ravens, I include this sighting as Event #1. From a conditional probability point of view, this event would be given a 1/14 probability.

We arrived at the airport and decided to have lunch. After ordering and before the meal was served, I felt the urge to leave the table and visit the airport bookstore. I intuitively sensed that there was a novel I needed to read, and I discovered that the James Rollins novel *The Doomsday Key* had just been published. I bought it without opening it, and looked forward to reading it on the flight to Seattle.

We were flying Alaska Airlines. I used my frequent-flyer miles, and we flew first class—something we rarely do. Why I felt the urge to fly first class on that particular trip became startlingly clear to me once we were airborne.

As the airplane reached its altitude, Rhonda and I talked about which places we should visit first in Seattle, as we had not visited in over two years. Our first stop would be the Northwest Tribal Art store at Pike Place Market, with the goal of adding another Native American raven mask to our collection. Though I did not realize this at that precise moment, the propitious timing of this conversation turned out to be Event #2.

In terms of the type of conversations Rhonda and I have, at that time we had probably mentioned ravens once every 20 to 50 conversations—we have amassed an extensive collection of raven art together and enjoy it immensely. A conservative probability might be 1/20 or, more accurately, 1/50.

After talking about our plan to purchase a special raven mask to honor this trip, I opened the Rollins novel and began reading it. I always kept a pen handy, because I track synchronicities as they occur. I also carried a digital camera and digital tape recorder to record events as they happened (today I use a smart phone and digital tablet).

On page one of the novel, in the very first line, the author wrote: “The ravens were the first sign”.

The ravens were the first sign? Of all the novels I have read, none has begun with a sentence about ravens, let alone about ravens being “signs.” I circled the sentence.

The next paragraph was chilling. The author wrote:

"As the horse-drawn wagon traveled down the rutted track between rolling fields of barley, a flock of ravens rose up in a black wash. They hurled themselves into the blue of the morning and swept high in a panicked rout, but this was more than the usual startled flight. The ravens wheeled and swooped, tumbled and flapped. Over the road, they crashed into each other and rained down out of the skies. Small bodies struck the road, breaking wing and beak. They twitched in the ruts. Wings fluttered weakly".

The words took my breath away. This was clearly an ominous sign for the novel, but was it possibly a welcoming sign for me? Event #4.

I estimated that the probability of the novels I have read mentioning ravens somewhere in the text as being conservatively 1/50, and more accurately probably 1/100. In terms of mentioning ravens in the first sentence, I have read at least 1000 novels over 40 years, so 1/1000.

I shared the first sentence and paragraph with Rhonda.

As it turned out, first class was serving drinks and lunch. We decided to live it up, and ordered complimentary champagne.

A flight attendant came with our drinks and napkins, and when I glanced at the napkins, I could not believe what I was seeing. The pattern on the napkins was a Pacific Northwest Coast design, and the animal featured was a raven.

I had traveled by airplane 6 to 12 times a year for at least 30 years. This comes out to approximately 270 flights. To the best of my knowledge, none of these flights had ever included a Pacific Northwest Coast image of a raven.

I asked Rhonda if I could keep her napkin, and I kept mine as well. I wrote on my napkin "8.4.09 Sync #4" and inserted it as a bookmark on page 1 of the novel.

Lunch was then served, on placemats. The placemats also happened to have Pacific Northwest Coast images—again of a raven. Rhonda gave me her placemat, and I placed the two of them in my computer case. This was Event #5. To be conservative, I will give it a 1/1 probability, since placemats often match napkins. In other words, it will not add to the final conditional probability.

However, what happened next was truly improbable, and very odd. Another flight attendant noticed that we had neither napkins nor placemats, and was concerned about why this was the case. For some reason, I decided to share with him our affection for ravens and the synchronicity of the moment. He asked us if we would like some extra napkins. I could not resist. He went off and came back with an inch and a half stack of raven napkins.

He then shared with us that he was from Alaska, and had a special association with ravens. His father was a member of the Raven Clan. I have never met someone from the Raven Clan—at least no one has ever revealed this aspect of their personal history to me. He allowed me to take his photograph. This was Event #6.

What would you estimate to be the probability of spontaneously meeting someone from the Raven Clan? Would you say 1 in 100, 1 in 1000, 1 in 10,000, 1 in 100,000, 1 in 1,000,000?

Of course, on Alaska Airlines traveling to Seattle, the probability is probably closer to 1 in a 100 than 1 in 100,000.

On the other hand, of the estimated 270 flights I have taken, we can ask, "How many have been on Alaska Airlines?" The answer is 2.

The point here is that the probability is very low by normal standards of meeting someone and learning that they are from the Raven Clan.

Rhonda suggested that this might be our "Raven Trip." She turned out to be correct, in spades.

For example, when we arrived in Seattle and were walking toward the baggage claim area, Rhonda spotted a mural of a seven-foot high raven wearing a crown.

I had never seen such a large raven painting, ever. This includes airports, museums, and galleries. This was Event #7.

Rhonda continued on to baggage claim while I entered the establishment to photograph the raven and learn of its history. The store was relatively new. The company is called Butter LONDON, and it was founded in 2005. Their logo is a raven wearing a crown.

They allowed me to take some photos, and I purchased two clear glass coffee cups adorned with the raven logo as mementos.

To keep this relatively brief, I will not share the complete wealth of subsequent raven synchronicities that happened on this trip. However, I will highlight three, because they are directly related to the seven that started the synchronicity string.

First, we did purchase a raven mask at Northwest Tribal Art on Wednesday, August 5, the day after we arrived in Seattle. However, we asked the sales woman to hold it for us while we had lunch. We wanted to make sure it was the "right one" for our collection.

The mask is a little over a foot and a half tall and rests on a wooden stand that sets it approximately two feet high in the air. Its cedar bark hair trails almost a foot and a half.

When we returned, I noticed that a couple was admiring the raven mask. I asked them about their interest in the piece, and the woman explained that she was originally from Alaska and that her father was a member of the Raven Clan. I kid you not. Event #8.

For the record, I have visited hundreds of Pacific Northwest Coast art stores over the past 30 years, and never has someone spontaneously told me that they (or any of their relatives) were a member of the Raven Clan. Of course, we would expect it to be more likely to meet people associated with the Raven Clan in Pacific Northwest Coast art galleries in Washington State and British Columbia, Canada than in modern art galleries in New York and Massachusetts, or even Southwest Native American art galleries in Arizona and New Mexico. (Ravens are not nearly as prominent in Southwest Native American art as in Pacific Northwest Coast art). Hence, the estimated probability of meeting someone from the Raven Clan in a Pacific Northwest Coast art gallery is closer to 1 in a 100 than 1 in 100,000.

Second, on Saturday, August 8, we arranged to have lunch with a friend and walked across the University of Washington campus to one of Rhonda's favorite local restaurants. Our friend noticed some black feathers on the lawn. Some were raven feathers, and the majority were probably crow feathers.

I have occasionally come upon an isolated raven feather on the ground. However, we were literally looking out at what Rhonda called a vast "feather field." On our walk to the restaurant, we picked up approximately 200 raven and crow feathers. Our collection of black feathers filled a large shoebox.

As we were picking up the feathers, I was reminded of the dramatic first paragraph from Rollins' book about the ravens falling to the ground. Event #9.

How many times have I been in a place strewn with raven and crow feathers? Never. How do we estimate this probability—or more appropriately, improbability?

Third, that night we decided to take a ride in the evening and drive past a street called "Ravenna," which I had discovered a few years ago near the University (although I did not include this as a synchronous event).

As we headed back, we spontaneously passed a pub called *The Rat and Raven.* It had ravens painted on its outdoor signs, and even black raven statues on its roof. I had never seen a pub named after a raven before.

I stopped the car and took multiple photos of the building's exterior. I then parked and we went inside. It turned out that the pub had just opened the previous Saturday. The establishment was named after a rock band that had produced an album with a raven on the cover.

On the back wall of the stage for live bands was a painting of a seven-foot tall raven! No, it was not wearing a crown (like the one in the airport), but it was huge. I took some photos of Rhonda standing next to the painting. Event #10.

How often have you seen a pub named after a raven? How often have you seen a seven-foot raven painted on the wall of a bar or restaurant? For me, the answer (up to that point) was never.

Yes, I look for ravens, and hence I am more likely to find them. However, we are not talking about looking for VW bugs and finding them because they are there. We are talking about highly improbable events that occur in sequence in an apparently nonrandom and potentially meaningful pattern.

It is important to understand that I was not looking for the raven that flew over our house; Rhonda saw it.

I was not looking for a novel that had ravens in it; I just found it, apparently by following my intuition.

I was not looking for raven napkins and placemats; they were just given to us.

I was not looking for a man to be a member of the Raven Clan, and spontaneously share it; he just revealed it.

I was not looking for a seven-foot high painting of a raven wearing a crown in the airport; Rhonda spotted it.

I was not looking for a woman to admire a raven mask and spontaneously share with me that her father was a member of the Raven Clan; she was just there, and she shared it.

I was not looking for lawns strewn with raven and crow feathers; Rhonda's friend discovered them.

I was not looking for a raven-themed pub with a seven-foot raven painted over the stage; I just drove past it.

Yes, I was consciously seeking to purchase a raven mask. And yes, I decided to visit the Ravenna street to celebrate "The Raven Trip." Though I included Rhonda's and my discussing the planned raven mask purchase because of its uncannily precise timing with my reading about ravens in the introduction to Rollins' novel, I did not include the spontaneous decision to visit the Ravenna street as a synchronicity.

I will leave it to you to calculate, if you wish, an estimated conditional probability of these ten events happening in the span of a few days. The take-home message should be obvious—it is super-improbable.

The Ten-Minute Lesson

The reason I decided to include the above data was because of the precise timing of what transpired in a propitious ten-minute period. (In fact, the data would hold up in a court of law, because they were carefully observed with handwritten and digital notes, photographed, witnessed by various people, and so forth.)

Here is what happened. I had just finished writing the end of Chapter 4, and had typed a paragraph that I repeat below:

Certain tribes in the Pacific Northwest believe that the raven actually brought the sun to humanity. The raven is often placed at the top of totem poles, and is sometimes carved with a sun in his mouth. In a sense, ravens are viewed as bringing "light" to humanity and the world.

I had never written about ravens and the sun before. This was a first for me.

I finished the chapter, and then took a break and decided to read a few pages from *The Doomsday Key.* I had stopped reading it because when I arrived home, a pre-publication copy of William Gladstone's *The Twelve* had arrived in the mail and I sensed I should read it first.

Returning to *The Doomsday Key,* I was at that point on page 398, and doing my usual charting of historic and current synchronicity tracking. I then read the following paragraph:

Wallace ran a finger through the dust. "'Here lies Meritaten, daughter of King Akhenaten and Queen Nefertiti. She who crossed the seas and brought the sun god Ra to these cold lands.'"

What caught my attention was mention of a queen who "brought the sun god Ra".

I had just ten minutes earlier written about a raven bringing the sun to the earth, and now I was reading about a queen bringing the sun god Ra to the earth. What also struck me was that the name of the sun god "Ra" has the same letters as the first two letters of "raven."

Obviously, this is a creative stretch. By itself it is a Type I Synchronicity, and could simply be a coincidence.

However, this was the same novel that began with the phrase, "The ravens were the first sign". This was the same novel that wrote about ravens raining down from the sky. This was the same novel that heralded the then-current reappearance of Type III raven synchronicities in my life. And I read the "sun god Ra" paragraph virtually immediately after writing about the myth of how the raven brought the sun to humanity and the rest of the earth.

Out of context, the sun god Ra / raven sun connection would appropriately be labeled as a coincidence, if not "loose associational thinking."

However, in context, the sun god Ra / raven sun connection is no less bizarre, strange, or unbelievable than the photographing of not one but two different seven-foot ravens, meeting not one but two different people whose fathers were members of the Raven Clan, and coming upon not one or even two black raven or crow feathers, but hundreds of apparent raven feathers and possibly thousands of crow feathers.

If you are wondering how is it possible that the writing of a novel could be connected, somehow, to a scientist doing self-science research on the apparent reality and possible meaning of synchronicities—especially Type III supersynchronicities—then welcome to the club.

Is it in any manner conceivable—and ultimately reasonable—that such apparent non-random connections could exist and actually be orchestrated?

The easy way out is to say, "It's crazy. It can't be true. It's coincidental. It's anomalous," and forget about it. Not only do I understand this instinct, I probably experience it more often than most people, because I actively seek and chart such startling apparent synchronicities, and so I understand the desire to ignore the deep implications about their reality.

Real gold, or fool's gold? Evidence for the existence of a creative One Mind whose intelligence we cannot begin to fathom—save for using words like "infinite intelligence"? Or evidence of the human folly to seek patterns and meaning where none exist?

Does the universe provide us with what Rhonda calls "the continuity of encouragement" to keep us seeking, expanding, growing, and awakening? Or are the wealth of people from all walks of life who are discovering ever more complex Type II and Type

III Synchronicities in their lives succumbing to a mass delusion, or what might be called a "logic deficiency disorder"?

We are now ready to return to my post-Istanbul flu and explore what happened in response to my angry ultimatum to the universe. But first, let's take a break and consider a brief Interlude.

Interlude – A Supersynchronicity Involving a "Raven Eleven" Celebrity

Their flight paths formed an 11!
Phil Hellmuth

The following Interlude presents a novel true-life supersynchronicity involving the number eleven, including a pair of ravens. It was written for this book by Phil Hellmuth shortly after winning his eleventh World Series of Poker championship. Eleven was the record for the number of World Series of Poker championships won by a single individual. Phil went on to beat his own record. By the time *Super Synchronicity* had gone to press, Phil had increased his total to fourteen. Phil is known as the "Poker Brat" and he often appears that way on TV. However, in real life he is known to be kind, thoughtful, a caring family man, and fun to be with.

His synchronicity account speaks for itself. I have included it partly as additional evidence of real-life synchronicities involving the number eleven (including a pair of ravens), and also because it was a meaningful and memorable moment for the three of us (Phil, his wife, and me).

Save for some minor corrections in content and a few explanations (indicated in the text as [Additions]), plus my labeling the synchronicities [Event #], the words below are Phil's exactly as he emailed them to me.

I was at the world famous Canyon Ranch health spa with my wife for a week. We arrived on a Monday, and now it was Wednesday morning at breakfast, when the director of our section made a few announcements regarding the day's activities ending with, "Tonight at eight o clock, Gary Schwartz will be doing a presentation on sound and energy healing in the Pavilion."

I told my wife (who happens to be a physician) that I wanted to attend and she said, "OK, but you're on your own, as I already saw him last time I was here." I showed up a few minutes late, after a two-hour massage, and was surprised and happy to see my wife was there.

After a few minutes, Gary was going on about our ability to be antenna's for a television set, and how he had discovered that ability when he was young, with his old black and white television set. Way back in the nineteen fifties Gary would unplug the antenna connected to the back of his parents' television set, and then put his finger in the connection instead, and the picture would come back online.

He went on to say, "In fact, we have signals going through us right now including: cell phone, television satellite, radio, and God knows what else. Anyone care to guess how many cell phone signals are going through us right now?"

I thought to myself that it must be over ten thousand. So after someone else guessed 8,000, I said, "Eleven thousand."

Gary stared at me a moment, and then went on with his lecture.

[Addition/Comment: In the hundreds of lectures I have given to many thousands of people where I have asked the audience to guess how many cell phone calls were reaching them at that moment, only one person has spontaneously said 11,000 – or eleven anything, for that matter—hence my synchronicity antenna went on alert when the Canyon Ranch guest, who I later learned was Phil Hellmuth, said that number]

By then, I had made up my mind that I was going to stay behind and chat with him about his work where he measures the energy that came out of us through our hands. After all, I'm the one that said (on ESPN), "Sometimes I feels like fire comes out of my hands."

ESPN took that line and turned it into a clever little three-part dramatization where they first showed me saying, "I wanna be at full power," (as I lifted my hands up to my head level and held them face down) and then they made it look like I was causing an earthquake.

The second part showed me raising my arms up in the air even higher and I said (a little bit louder than the last time), "Full power," and then they cut in lightning bolts coming out of my hands.

Then in the third part they showed me saying the fire line (above) and cut in fire coming out of my hands and filling the television screen. The whole dramatization lasted about 12 seconds, but my wife, kids, and I thought that it was so cool, that we played over-and-over five or six times. You can watch it at youtube.com.

Gary was now going on about the fact that the number "11" had led him away from the path of being the youngest professor in the history of Yale.

[Addition/Correction: I was one of the youngest tenured faculty members in the history of the Department of Psychology at Yale].

The number 11 had had a profound impact on his life, and led him towards the path of "Synchronicity." Another synchronistic theme from Gary's lecture was "Ravens." He had a slide with "Raven Software" on it, and in the crowd was a young woman who was doing her PhD on ravens, and was living with them and teaching them to save human beings from dangers like the ocean.

[Addition/Correction: Emily Cory was then working on her MA degree investigating the possibility of using ravens for search and rescue and she was living with a single raven. At the time *Super Synchronicity* was published, Emily had successfully completed her PhD].

Near the end of the lecture I told my wife that I was staying around to chat with Gary. I rarely stick around after a seminar or lecture to chat with the lecturer, as it seems a bit needy to me, but in this case I felt compelled to stay.

Right as the lecture ended Gary came up to me and said, "Do I know you from somewhere? Your face looks familiar."

I said, "I'll tell you in a minute." I was waiting for the class to clear and then I said, "You probably see me on TV a lot, and I have a great '11' story for you as well."

First I told Gary about the fact that I had won 11 World Series of Poker bracelets (titles) [Event #1].

Then I mentioned that my sister Molly was born on 11/11/71, and that she had been promised my eleventh bracelet years before [Event #2].

Finally, I mentioned that I won that bracelet on June 11, 2007 [Event #3]. Gary was pretty excited and we agreed to meet for lunch on Saturday.

When we later met at our suite, my wife immediately told Gary that we live at 1101 XXXX Ave [Event #4].

As we were chatting, about 100 yards in the distance two ravens flew from left to right, and Gary interrupted me, apologizing profusely as he ran over to the edge of our perimeter to watch them.

Gary said, "This is extraordinary! In 18 years I have never seen a raven on this property, never mind two of them!" [Flying as an "11" pair, see below, Event #5].

[Addition/Comment: Over the subsequent fifteen years, I have noticed a few more single ravens – I am at the Ranch approximately 4 – 8 times a month – but they are very rare, and have never flown directly over my head].

About five minutes later, the pair of ravens flew right over us. One flew to the right of us, and the other flew to the left of us. ["11" pair again, Event #6].

Now Gary was absolutely beside himself, and my wife and I were pretty stunned as well.

[Addition/Comment: I was startled by the pair of ravens flying directly overhead; I had not made the connection to the two of them being like an 11.]

Then I said, "Their flight paths formed an 11!" As we continued our dialogue--on both Saturday and Sunday--other synchronistic ties were revealed, but nothing as out of the ordinary, or as immediate as the elevens and the pair of ravens.

Of course, I have a publishing company, and Gary is an author. A few days later I decided to name a division of my publishing company "Raven Eleven Publishing." Of course, "Raven Eleven" has 11 letters in it, and I knew that Gary would love that!

[Addition: as far as I know, Raven Eleven Publishing has yet to be formed]

Chapter 7
Asking the Universe for Proof: The Rose Killer
Lesson: The Universe Can Reveal that It is the Higher Source of Synchronicity

Truth and roses have thorns about them.
Henry David Thoreau

This is probably the most challenging chapter I have ever written. The reason will become clear as you read it. It confesses an experience that is as real as steel, yet as bizarre as a caviar star.

I obviously made up the image of a star made from caviar. I did not make up what you are about to read—any of it.

The previous Chapter 6 sets the stage for returning to the time surrounding my bout of the flu and my state of mind at that time.

We are about to test the universe, so to speak, and have a close encounter of an unimagined kind.

Setting the Stage: Emerging Fury at the Universe

I returned from Istanbul fatigued, confused, and stressed. I was scheduled to fly to California to participate in a small invitation-only group working on the topic of life after death. However, I came down with an awful flu, and was restricted to bed for almost a week.

My fever persisted at 100 to 101 Fahrenheit. I had chills, aches, a terrible cough, the whole nine yards. I was so ill that I could not even watch television. I have experienced such a debilitating flu maybe once every 5 to 10 years.

At times like this, the only thing I am able to do is reread old mystery novels, especially those written by Robert B. Parker.

I read Parker's first novel when it was initially released in 1973. Titled *The Godwulf Manuscript,* the novel introduced a private detective named Spenser who became something of a fictional hero to me. At that time I was a young assistant professor at Harvard, and I read mysteries for entertainment and fun.

I have read—and reread—every Spenser novel Parker has written. I read them primarily for Parker's clever dialogue and complex plotting, as well as the myriad of psychological and ethical insights interwoven into the stories. I rarely remember the titles, the details of the plots, or the endings. Part of the reason for this is that I tend to only reread them when I am sick, which does not happen too often. Hence, I can read them over and over and continue to enjoy them anew.

Spenser is a complex character. He is a romantic, logician, gourmet cook, philosopher, psychologist, protector, fitness (and sexual) aficionado, poet, "do the right thing" kind of person, and thug. His girlfriend, Susan Silverman, is a black-haired beauty with a PhD in clinical psychology from Harvard. His close colleague and friend is a super tough and loyal African-American "bad guy" named Hawk.

Returning to my flu, I had randomly grabbed a Spenser novel to read. To my chagrin, despite my cloudy mind I was still noticing apparent synchronicities in my life. I began to feel as if I could not escape the presence of synchronicities, and I really needed a break.

I was convinced at that time that I could not prove, ultimately, whether what I and others like me, such as Dr. Powell, were experiencing was somehow mediated by a higher power or intelligence. Being a scientist through and through, if I could not somehow make sense of what was transpiring and help others do the same, then I had no need for such a distraction in my life. In fact, although I was doing personal self-science on synchronicity, this was not part of my academic life at that time. It was not part of my university laboratory research. It was extracurricular, and it was becoming a serious distraction.

Angered and frustrated by my raven experiences in Istanbul, especially in the novel that I read on my return flight, I realized that I either had to figure out how to take the work to the next level and make sense of it, or I wanted out.

After finishing a Parker novel filled with synchronicities—I do not recall exactly which one—I reached such a point of fury inside that I said in my head, *Universe, if you are here, and you hear me, either show me a way to prove that you are responsible for what is going on, or leave me the f*** alone.* I rarely use coarse language, but I was sick, exhausted, fed up, and furious.

In response to my spontaneous and furious question, I heard the following calm response in my mind as clear as a bell:

Why don't you ask me to pick a book?

What? Did I hear correctly? Ask the universe to pick a book? What a crazy—yet—creative idea.

I realized that if I asked the universe to pick a book, and if the information in the book purportedly selected by the universe was somehow expressly related to its supposed role in all this, then this information would be interesting indeed, if not importantly evidential.

For the record, I have no idea:

- whether the "universe" actually answered me,
- whether the idea came from some other spiritual source,
- whether the idea came from Jung's collective unconscious,
- whether the idea came from someone else's unconscious, or
- whether the idea came from my own unconscious.

All I know for sure is that, in my mind, I directed a question to the universe, and I heard a series of words back in my mind.

Probably thanks to the fever, my inhibitions were decreased, and I decided to follow the suggestion as I heard it.

I said in my mind, *Okay, universe, why don't you pick a book?*

Almost immediately, I heard the words, *Please read Crimson Joy.*

A novel titled *Crimson Joy*? Remember, I had not put to memory the titles of all the Spenser novels I had read. At that moment, I could not recall if Parker had written a book with that title. However, *Crimson Joy* is what I heard. I got out of bed, went to the shelf in my closet where I stored Parker's books at that time, and scanned the book spines for the title *Crimson Joy.*

The Parker books were stacked in piles, not organized upright on the shelf. Toward the bottom of one pile I found a book titled *Crimson Joy.*

I thought, *Oh boy, here we go.* I got back into bed, shaking and sweating with the flu, and began reading the book.

I read a good two thirds of *Crimson Joy,* and I could not believe what was happening. What was happening was "nothing," and I mean *nothing.* Here I was, searching for synchronicities, and I could not find anything of note.

Talk about a failure. Yes, there were a few minor "stretches," but nothing like my history of 11s or dragonflies or ravens. Whereas the previous Parker novel had presented a slew of synchronicities, this one had virtually none.

Though I was sick, I could still reason somewhat, and I realized that this finding was most curious.

If my unconscious mind had picked the book—and this was a possibility—and the book had contained information that I previously knew that might relate to my current life, then the experiment should have worked.

Instead, my "experiment" had been an utter flop. The experiment not only failed to support the purported "universe's" explanation, it also failed to support a simple "psychological" (and skeptical) explanation as well.

What was even weirder was that in the previous books that had revealed synchronicities to me, I had not been looking for specific synchronicities. *Crimson Joy* was the first book I read where I consciously looked for any and every possible synchronicity in the text. And instead of finding a flock of them, I found virtually none.

Then the most bizarre set of events transpired. I will take you through them slowly, so that you can appreciate how much I was trying to be a "detective," as I was in the process of reading a detective story featuring my fictional detective hero.

You may want to consider putting on a second set of metaphorical seatbelts.

I began paying closer attention to the plot of the novel, and realized that Spenser was thoroughly confused about the symbol that the serial killer had been leaving at the scenes of the crimes. The killer was called "The Rose Killer," because he left a single red rose with the body of each of the women he murdered.

Why a single red rose? What could it mean? Spenser discussed this with Susan, his brilliant and beautiful psychotherapist girlfriend. Susan's analysis stunned me.

The gist of what Susan said is that you cannot understand the meaning of a symbol without understanding the mind of the person who is using the symbol.

Let's repeat this statement, because it held the key to the mystery I was currently facing: *To understand the meaning of a symbol, we must first understand the mind of the person using the symbol.*

I went back to the beginning of the book, and reread it slowly. As I read, I realized that the word "rose" was being used repeatedly. I searched for connections to my own life, and I found none. And then it struck me like a lightning bolt: if the universe really chose this book for me, and it held some key to understanding its role in producing synchronicities (particularly, Type III Synchronicities), then maybe what I had to do was attempt to understand its Mind—the universe's Mind—in order to understand why it might have picked this specific book.

What was I reading about in *Crimson joy?* Roses and secret symbols.

Roses meant nothing to me personally. Sure, I thought of Valentine's Day and birthdays. My mother had always kept rose bushes, and I had an aunt named Rose. So what? These associations had no obvious connection to my present life, nor to my understanding of the universe.

And then I remembered something I had read in a book on the history of religion about a group called the Rosicrucians. I vaguely remembered that Rosicrucianism had something to do with roses and crosses. I got out of bed, went to my bookshelf in my study, and pulled out the book in question. I went to the index and located the section on Rosicrucianism, but there was no discussion of the origin of its name or its significance.

I then went online and searched for any significant relationship between roses and the universe. I typed in the keywords "Roses" and "God."

My fever was 101 plus. I was as sick as I could ever remember being. The last thing I wanted to do was make a discovery. But I did, and I could not believe what I was reading.

Unbeknownst to me, the rose had a long-standing relationship to the Divine, God, the Virgin Mary, Jesus, Allah, the Rosicrucians, and on and on. In a deep sense, one could say that the rose was as much a symbol for our spiritual ideas about God and religion as was the six-pointed star, the cross, the sun, or the moon.

The rose was a sacred symbol.

I have since asked many people how aware they are of this historical fact. Most of the people I have asked have no idea of this, save for specific references to Mary or Jesus being shown in images with roses, for example. The scope of the rose-God connection apparently is not widely known and appreciated.

I went back to bed, shocked and more confused than ever.

If this discovery—from the selection of *Crimson Joy* to the deep meaning of secret symbols, the mind of the symbol user, and the sacred history of the rose—came from my personal unconscious, then I was quite impressed with it!

If this was just a chance connection, then I would have to develop a profound new respect for the power of random coincidence.

However, if this was actually the handiwork of the universe, and the Divine was indeed guiding me to make this discovery, then I was going to need more proof. Much more proof. I was going to have to see evidence of roses now appear in my life in ways that would defy anything I could imagine.

I decided to wait until my flu had subsided to see what transpired next. What unfolded made my previous experiences with 11s, dragonflies, and ravens seem like essential baby steps on the path to envisioning an unfathomable—yet in some sense, ultimately knowable—greater reality.

The Power of Integrating Reason and Intuition: The Raven Mask and the Rose-God Mezuzah

At this point, I was attempting to make sense of a seemingly extraordinary pair of super-improbable synchronicities involving roses. Event #1 was my observation of the repeated use of the word "rose" in *Crimson Joy* (employed over 120 times in the book). I was aware of only one other novel that I had read that mentioned the rose with this frequency, and that was Umberto Eco's bestselling mystery *The Name of the Rose.* In terms of probabilities, 1/500 is a fair estimate.

Event #2 was my discovery that the symbol of the rose had a longstanding historical connection to God. It is difficult to place a probability on this event: for example, would we look up every major flower and see how frequently it was historically associated with the Divine across the major religions? Also, Parker could have picked other symbols to have the killer leave at the scene of the crime, such as brandings of crosses in circles—the symbol used in *The Doomsday Key.* What is important here is to recognize that the probability is quite small.

In addition, we must remember that the rose-God connection was discovered due to my asking the universe to prove whether it was playing a role in the synchronicity process, and its purported choice of the novel *Crimson Joy.*

Though I had not yet formulated the three categories of synchronicities, I was well aware that I needed many more replications of highly improbable rose-related events before I could come to the conclusion that it was a genuine synchronicity. What unfolded next was the evolution of a highly improbable Type I Synchronicity into an even more improbable Type II Synchronicity, and then a super-improbable Type III Synchronicity.

As we examine this discovery process, you will notice the emerging integration of reasoning on the one hand, and intuition on the other (an extremely important topic that is the focus of the pioneering multidisciplinary anthology titled *The Beacon of Mind: Reason and Intuition in the Ancient and Modern World,* published by Param Media in 2015).

Just as it is easier, quicker, and more effective to type with two hands than one, it turns out to be much more expedient to discover synchronicities if you combine reason with intuition, rather than restricting your synchronicity detecting to either one alone.

Here is what transpired.

First, when my fever finally broke and it became safe for me to drive, I felt the urge to visit a small art gallery approximately 3 miles from my home to see if they had a rose memento I might purchase. I had previously visited this gallery maybe 3 times. I picked it, at least consciously, because it was the closest gallery to my home.

I did not interpret my seeking a rose as a synchronicity itself, since I was consciously looking to purchase a memento of a rose. However, my intuitive sense was that this gallery would have something both meaningful and affordable involving a rose.

I was still feeling weak and tired, yet excited to look for a rose to take home with me. I got to the gallery, and searched everywhere. No roses. No rose paintings, no rose cups, no rose statues. Nothing. Another failed experiment?

Curiously, they happened to have paintings of ravens—which they have not featured at the gallery since—but I was not looking for ravens then. I dismissed this observation (although it will turn out to be meaningful shortly).

Finally, I asked the salesperson if the gallery carried any items featuring roses, and she said no.

Nonetheless, a feeling persisted that if I looked hard enough, I would find the rose I was looking for. I left the gallery, and stood outside staring at the display window. I noticed that it featured two tall, red metal flowers with long stems.

I went inside and asked the salesperson what kind of metal flowers were in the window. She did not know, so she retrieved the flowers, and they turned out to be roses. They were inexpensive, and could be kept outside. The pair reminded me of the number 11; I had been looking for one rose, and ended up finding a pair. I decided I would place them under my finch feeder as a reminder.

I have visited this gallery a number of times since this incident, and roses are still not their thing.

Would this gallery visit count as Event #3? I did not list it as such, even though it turned out to be improbable and meaningful, especially in light of what happened next.

After a major flu, one's energy is depleted and it is wise to resume one's normal activities gradually. I knew I should return home, but I felt the urge to drive a few more miles and visit a small plaza that had a Southwest Native American gallery (the gallery has since moved to New Mexico). Though I was well aware that Native Americans, at least in the Southwest, rarely paint or carve roses, I felt the urge to visit the store, and so I did. I had not been there for a least a year.

When I arrived at the gallery, I learned they were having their annual sale. I looked through the beautiful pieces on display and discovered in the back a huge Pacific Northwest Coast mask of a raven on a tall metal stand. The mask was thirty-two inches tall, and on its stand stood over five feet high. I had never seen such a mask in Tucson—or in Phoenix, Flagstaff, or Santa Fe, for that matter. Southwest Native American galleries do not, as a rule, include large and expensive Pacific Northwest Coast carvings.

Remember, I was not looking for ravens. However, it was my Type III Synchronicity with ravens, ending with my reading about "Ravenscry" in *Brimstone,* that had pushed me over the edge, leading me to the rose discovery.

Though at that point I was not in the habit of purchasing such expensive pieces of art, the presence and timing of the mask seemed propitious, and I was tempted, especially because of the annual sale.

But there were no roses!

One of the galleries in the plaza featured contemporary art, and I had a gift certificate for $100. I had also not visited that gallery in over a year, and so I thought to myself, *I am going to go there and see if they have any rose mementos. If they have one, if it is meaningful, and if it can be purchased with my gift certificate, then I will purchase the rose token, then go back to the Native American gallery and purchase the raven mask as well.*

Although my post-flu fatigue was mounting, I was on a mission. As my former writing partner, William Simon, proposed in *The Afterlife Experiments,* "We do not find a mission, a mission finds us." That was how I felt as I entered the contemporary art gallery and began searching for a meaningful rose.

I was beginning to feel that we do not find synchronicities; rather, they find us.

I looked everywhere in that gallery for something involving a rose. There was nothing. No paintings, carvings, trinkets—nothing. I thought to myself, *Another failed experiment?* If I were to honor the agreement I had made with myself, this meant that I should not purchase the raven mask.

I asked the salesperson if they had any artwork with a rose. He thought for a while, looked around the gallery, and then told me he was not aware of any pieces with roses.

It turned out that a small display case in this sizable gallery featured artwork from Israel. In terms of floor space, Jewish artwork in this gallery represented maybe one one-thousandth of their art. I had not paid much attention to this case, partly because I do not collect Jewish art, and partly because Jewish art rarely depicts roses.

I scanned the shelves, exploring the various pieces, when I noticed something absolutely unique (at least to me). Among their beautifully handcrafted collection of at least a dozen painted "mezuzahs" was one that featured a symbolic representation of the hand of God. And placed within God's hand was a single red rose.

As described in the Oxford Dictionaries, a mezuzah is "a parchment inscribed with religious texts and attached in a case to the doorpost of a Jewish house as a sign of faith". I have probably seen hundreds of mezuzahs in my life. I could not remember seeing one that included a red rose (though I later learned that they sometimes do).

It's one thing to find a rose when you are looking for it; it is another to find it hidden within a religious object that speaks directly to the rose-God connection.

I was dumbstruck. If I was looking for a meaningful rose gift, in addition to my "11" pair of outdoor metal roses (which the salesperson had not remembered were there), I was now staring at a religious symbol directly connecting the rose with God (which this salesperson also had not remembered was there).

And thanks to my discovery of the rose-God mezuzah, I now had the excuse to purchase a beautiful, one of a kind Pacific Northwest Coast raven mask.

It was mindboggling to me to think that I had intuitively sensed that I should visit this Native American art gallery, where I not only discovered the raven mask, but also did so when they were holding their annual sale. It was even more mindboggling to think that I reasoned I should only purchase the mask if I could find a meaningful rose token—the original intent of my journey—and after diligently searching, I found not only a rose memento, but one that directly addressed the rose-God connection.

Whereas the pair of inexpensive metal roses can be conservatively treated as a non-synchronicity, the discovery of the finely crafted rose-God mezuzah, especially combined with the raven mask, deserves being counted as Event #3.

I purchased the mask and placed it prominently in the entryway to my home (today it sits proudly on a smaller stand in the center of our dining room table). I placed the mezuzah on my desk near my computer. I was exhausted, both physically and psychologically, and spent the rest of the day rereading another Parker novel. I purposely did not allow myself to pay attention to any possible synchronicities. I needed a break.

But the rose synchronicity journey was just beginning.

A Conflict: Mount Lemmon or the San Xavier Mission?

The next day, with renewed energy, I decided I wanted to take a longer drive. It was the Sunday of Memorial Day weekend, and I felt torn between driving to the San Xavier Mission or the top of Mount Lemmon. I had not been to either of these places in over a year. Each holds a special beauty and meaning to me. Mount Lemmon required me to drive north and east; San Xavier was south and west. Either one was an hour's drive each way. I got in the car, undecided as to which way I should go. Intuitively, I found myself being pulled more toward Mount Lemmon, so I decided to save San Xavier for Monday.

I had no idea why I was driving to Mount Lemmon. One can have a simple breakfast at the top of the mountain, and there are a couple of quaint gift shops at the summit. Neither seemed synchronistic to me, but I sensed I should "go with the flow," and so I did.

As I was driving up the mountain, I noticed a street sign that I had probably seen many times before, but had never registered. The sign read, "Rose Canyon."

Rose Canyon? How odd. I tried thinking of all the canyon names I knew, and realized that Rose Canyon was not one of them.

Was this my unconscious mind at work, leading me up the mountain? Or was there something more? At that moment, I was skeptical as to whether the Rose Canyon appearance was important.

I continued up the road, and then noticed another street sign that took my breath away. The sign read "Spencer Canyon."

Spencer Canyon? How very odd. Though spelled slightly differently than Parker's Spenser, the similarity was too great to ignore. I realized that if you asked to list the Canyons I knew, Spencer Canyon would not be one of them either.

First Rose Canyon, then Spencer Canyon. Even if my unconscious mind had previously registered both street signs and had then made the Spenser–Rose Killer–God connection, the fact remained that my intuition to drive to Mount Lemmon was propitious, to say the least. I drove the rest of way up to the summit, enjoying the exquisite timing of this event, which became Event #4.

On the Monday morning of Memorial Day, I was eager to make my excursion to the San Xavier Mission. It is located on the Tohono O'odham Reservation, and they have a few Native American gift shops close to the Mission.

However, before leaving home I received a phone call from a woman I will call Dr. Smith (not her real name) who counsels professionals regarding psychological and spiritual matters. Dr. Smith held two PhDs, one in theology, the other in family counseling. She was in her mid-seventies and she had the wisdom of both higher education and accumulated life experience. Dr. Smith had called to remind me that we had our monthly appointment scheduled for that day.

I asked her, "You made our appointment on Memorial Day?" She reminded me that it was actually due to the limitations of my busy schedule that had led us to pick the holiday Monday. I asked her if she was counseling anyone else that day, and she said no.

I apologized and suggested that we postpone our meeting. To my surprise, she felt it was important that we keep the appointment. This struck me as odd, because I was, after all, seeing her voluntarily, and she did not charge for her services. We mostly had lively philosophical and spiritual discussions, and I experienced my time spent with her as a gift in multiple ways.

It dawned on me that maybe Dr. Smith was unwittingly giving me a perfectly timed opportunity to discuss with an expert the synchronicities that were unfolding in my life. Here I was, struggling with the possibility that I was witnessing the emergence of compelling evidence indicating that the universe was involved in complex synchronicities, and now I was being given the opportunity to gain some professional advice about all of it. Remember: if Dr. Smith had not called me that morning, I would have taken off for the San Xavier Mission and missed our appointment!

We greeted each other with a hug and settled into our respective chairs. I told Dr. Smith that I was having some potentially meaningful experiences, but before I could share them, I needed to ask her a basic question.

I asked her, keeping my question intentionally vague, "When you think about the rose, what comes to mind, and what does it mean to you, psychologically and spiritually?"

The first thing she said was that she was reminded of the novel *The Name of the Rose.* This made me smile, as it was the one novel I had read that prominently featured the rose prior to *Crimson Joy.*

She then said, "A rose by any other name". I vaguely remembered the phrase, but did not know what it meant. (I later learned that it was from Shakespeare's *Romeo and Juliet.)*

Then she said, "You know that Mother Mary was often depicted with a rose?" I confessed that I was aware of this fact, but had only learned it a few days prior.

And then Dr. Smith said something that shook me to my core. She said, "And you probably know that roses were part of the miracle of Our Lady of Guadalupe."

I had not been aware of the story of Our Lady of Guadalupe. The only thing I knew about her was that she was apparently a Mexican saint and that the San Xavier Mission had a special relationship with her. In fact, they had a tribute to her in a cave-like structure in a small hill adjacent to the Mission.

Roses were connected to the San Xavier Mission? With great trepidation, I asked Dr. Smith if she would explain.

Her explanation went beyond anything I could have imagined. This became Event #5.

Before I share the story associated with Our Lady of Guadalupe, we should consider what makes Event #5 so improbable and revealing:

- If I had not had the urge to revisit San Xavier at that moment, the timing of the Our Lady of Guadalupe event would not have occurred.

- If I had not scheduled a meeting with Dr. Smith for Memorial Day, and if I had not had the rose-God synchronicities a few days before Memorial Day, the timing of the Our Lady of Guadalupe event would not have occurred.
- If Dr. Smith had not thought to call to remind me of our appointment, and she had not been persistent in wanting to keep the appointment, the timing of the Our Lady of Guadalupe event would not have occurred.
- If I had not thought to ask Dr. Smith about roses, the timing of the Our Lady of Guadalupe event would not have occurred.
- And if she had not spontaneously mentioned Our Lady of Guadalupe, the timing of the Our Lady of Guadalupe event would not have occurred.

In other words, a complex chain of events had to occur in order for me to have observed the unfolding of the Our Lady of Guadalupe lesson as I did. We should not lose sight of the fact that synchronicity is all about timing.

The nature of the Our Lady of Guadalupe story, combined with its timing, evoked in me Dr. Pearsall's 11th emotion—AWE. Words cannot do justice to what I experienced as Dr. Smith revealed the purported miracle of Our Lady of Guadalupe with the roses.

Please note: it is not important here whether this purported miracle involving roses actually happened. I have no idea about the veracity of this religious story. What matters to our discussion is the intricate and precise timing of how this rose-God story came to my attention in the context of the emerging rose-God Type III Synchronicity.

Here is the gist of the story as relayed by Dr. Smith, taken from my notes of that session, mixed with further details I read about later:

It was the dead of the winter, and a poor farmer was walking along the road when he met a young woman surrounded by light, whom he believed to be the Virgin Mary. She beseeched him to go to the local Spanish bishop and convince him to build a church there in her honor. He felt privileged to serve her, and so he went to the church in Mexico City and begged to see the bishop. He was granted an audience with the bishop, but unfortunately, the poor farmer had no evidence that he had met the Virgin Mother, and the Bishop dismissed the purported holy message. The farmer left dejected, feeling he had failed the Virgin Mother.

Walking back to his village, he came upon Mary again. She asked what had happened, and he humbly explained his failure. What happened next was the essence of the miracle. She removed from her cloak a bunch of perfectly fresh roses. (Or, in another version, she sent him to the top of the hill to gather Castilian roses, which came from the Spanish bishop's native home). She then requested that the farmer present them to the bishop. Since this was in the sixteenth century, and it was winter, there would be no fresh roses to be had.

Armed with his miraculous evidence, the farmer returned to the church, and again begged to see the bishop. When the bishop saw the roses, he knew that what the farmer claimed was true. (Apparently, the image of the Virgin also then appeared on the farmer's cloak.) Not only was the church built, but the legend of Our Lady of Guadalupe was born.

What amazed me as I heard this story was the "miraculous nature" of the meaning of the roses in the story. This was not just any old rose story; it was an inspiring and meaningful one, even if it was a bit fanciful. And it fit the rose-God synchronicity string to a tee.

It is hard for most logical and reasonable people to believe the Our Lady of Guadalupe story. I fall squarely within this camp myself.

Similarly, I realize that it is hard for most logical and reasonable people to believe my rose-God synchronicity story. And the truth is, I again fall squarely within this camp, even though I experienced this story directly, and have the evidence to prove it.

You will recall in Chapter 3 what I termed "Discovery Principle 4" in science in general, and self-science in particular: *Some data are extraordinarily surprising and seem unbelievable, if not impossible.*

Just because something seems impossible does not necessarily mean that it is untrue.

Just because something strikes us as bizarre, crazy, and unimaginable, does not necessarily mean that it is false.

The key is to discern the difference, to distinguish fool's gold from real gold. This is our greatest challenge: to discern what is unreal, and what is real.

It is prudent to remind ourselves that the discovery and evolution of quantum physics—which is the most successful theory in the history of science and technology—includes a core set of observations and premises that challenge common sense and, in fact, turns it on its head. More importantly, quantum physics challenges the brightest minds (Einstein's included) to go beyond anything they could have previously imagined.

The truth is, many physicists admit that they do not really understand quantum physics. Here is what Dr. Richard Feynman, an acknowledged genius in science, said about quantum physics during his 1996 Nobel Lecture:

"What I am going to tell you about is what we teach our physics students in the third or fourth year of graduate school.... It is my task to convince you not to turn away because you don't understand it. You see my physics students don't understand it.... That is because I don't understand it. Nobody does".

Dr. Feynman does not mean that we can't describe the mathematics of quantum physics, or that we can't make accurate predictions that can be confirmed in experiments; we can do both extraordinarily well. What most of us do struggle with is trying to make sense of how and why quantum physics works in the deepest sense, because the nature of what we observe and predict goes beyond what our minds are, at least presently, able to grasp.

However, Dr. John H Spencer's recent book, *The Eternal Law: Ancient Greek Philosophy, Modern Physics, and Ultimate Reality,* does provide a novel way of understanding these deep conceptual difficulties in quantum physics. But, as Dr. Spencer makes clear, in order to achieve this understanding, we need to reject the outdated and overly simplistic view of reality known as "materialism," which claims that only material (or physical) things are real. A scientist who clings to the assumptions of materialism will never be able to understand the depths of quantum physics.

Type III Synchronicities are like quantum phenomena: we can observe them, chart them, and even glean some of their potential meaning. But when we examine them closely and carefully, they appear utterly bizarre, if not crazy, in comparison with everyday common sense. But by questioning the assumptions of common sense (which usually comes down to a form of materialism in this context), we can open the way to embracing a non-materialistic philosophy, which can help us to understand the reality of synchronicities.

Returning to the rose-God synchronicities, I would invite you to imagine, for the moment, that what I had been experiencing and charting was actually evidence of the universe playing an active and intelligent role in my education—my discovery process.

Please imagine, for the moment, that the One Mind was actually revealing itself through the rose-God string of synchronicities.

If this is true—and I underscore *if*—then shouldn't we be grateful to have received this information? Shouldn't we be gracious about the gift of this knowledge? Shouldn't we be humbled not only by the emerging presence of the universe in our individual and collective lives, but also by the power of our own super minds to make such discoveries and awaken to such possibilities in the first place?

Event #6: Another Improbable Rose

As I reviewed the unfolding sequence of rose-God synchronicities, it occurred to me that there was a Southwest Native American gallery in Tucson that sometimes had a few Pacific Northwest Coast pieces. I wondered whether they might have a raven mask too, as it would be more probable to find such a mask in Tucson. If they did, I would reevaluate the significance of the raven mask I had purchased in the context of the rose in the Hand of God mezuzah.

The next day I made a special trip to this particular gallery, which I had not visited in at least a year. Sure enough, they had some Pacific Northwest Coast pieces of art, but none of them depicted a raven. I remember one of a bear, another of an eagle, a third one of a wolf, but no ravens.

I also looked through the store, searching for any sculptures or paintings involving roses. As I expected, there were none. Southwest Native American art rarely portrays ravens, and virtually never depicts roses.

On a lark, I decided to look at their Native American jewelry. At one point in my life (my Harvard and Yale years), I habitually wore primarily Native American jewelry (including watch bands). However, when I moved to the University of Arizona, I reverted to conventional watchbands and rings.

There I was perusing the jewelry when I discovered, to my amazement, a small collection of pendants, rings, and a belt buckle all featuring roses. At first I thought I was having a hallucination, or at least needed to get my glasses checked. I asked the salesperson to show me the jewelry. Sure enough, a Native American artist had recently begun a series of pieces featuring roses.

The salesperson explained that she had been involved with Native American art for more than twenty years, and that this was the only Native American artist she knew of who featured roses in their work.

This was Event #6. I went to the store looking for ravens, and what did I find but roses!

I quickly calculated the odds, and realized they were off the charts. I had visited hundreds of Native American art and jewelry stores over my forty years of collecting, and I had looked at many thousands of pieces of Native American jewelry in my life. And now, the first time I saw Native American jewelry depicting roses was occurring a few days after undergoing the most startling and spiritual experience of my life—the rose-God synchronicities.

The Rose-God Journey Blooms

I could probably write a whole book about the host of rose-related synchronicities that have continued and expanded in my life. Probably the most profound relate to my meeting Rhonda and the rose-God synchronicities that connected us.

Rhonda and I do not describe ourselves as a couple; we experience ourselves as a tripartite relationship between her, me, and Divinity. If you find my initial rose-God encounter hard to believe, you will find the synchronicities that brought us together even more unbelievable.

In Part III of Rhonda's book, *Love Eternal,* she presents examples of our respective blooming more poetically and gracefully than I ever could. The original subtitle to her inspiring book was *Personal and Scientific Reasons to Believe in Life After Death: A Memoir.*

In one sense, what you are reading is a "memoir," in that much of the evidence I have collected is presented in the form of accounts of my personal self-science journey as it unfolded, and not as tables of words and numbers accompanied by bar graphs. I chose to present most of the evidence descriptively in part to convey the actual process of exploration and analysis, but also to illustrate the dynamic nature of awakening and accepting, and finally, to express the sense of fun inherent in the mystery of discovery.

Indeed, the more we discover and learn about synchronicity, the more we realize how reasonable it is to hypothesize what I have termed the "Synchronizing Intelligence Agency (SIA)."

Because we are an integral part of this grand SIA process, the process itself is at least as complex as all of us—every being in the universe—put together. If there is a Grand Script or Plot at work here, we each are serving as co-writers of the emerging Play, whether we are aware of this fact or not.

At this point, after postulating the reality of the SIA, I began to entertain the hypothesis that we were each part of a universal super mind or One Mind, and that we each had individual yet interconnected super mind capabilities. But even though the concept of the One Mind can greatly further our scientific and personal understanding of reality, it also opens the way to exploring ever greater mystery.

Returning to *Crimson Joy*, the rose-God mezuzah, the raven mask, and the rose belt buckle, I now had a few tangible (and beautiful) reminders of this "turning point" Type III Synchronicity. I also had some photographs, notes, and even an enlightening conversation with an expert with two PhDs.

However, even though I had now amassed substantial and meaningful evidence, I still could not accept it. The more I observed, the more I could not believe.

I knew I had to keep searching, questioning, testing, and learning if I was ever going to accept what was apparently happening around me.

As you will read in the next chapter, the universe seemed to have sensed that I was prepared to move forward, and it raised the bar concerning what I was ready to discover next.

It was time to integrate this new information and start putting it all together.

Chapter 8
Levels and Subplots of Type III Synchronicities
Lesson: Never Underestimate the Genius of the One Mind

My life has a superb cast but I can't figure out the plot.
Ashleigh Brilliant

It is one thing to notice the appearance and reappearance of 11s, dragonflies, ravens, or roses, and attempt to calculate their frequencies and conditional probabilities. It is quite another to figure out how complex events are interconnected and determine whether there is a pattern, or even a plot, to be found there.

Before we can address the question of plot, we need to determine if there is enough complexity of content and timing to warrant positing one. What you are about to read is an account of the first time I experienced, within a twenty-four hour period, a complex super combination of previous supersynchronicities.

A common characteristic of complex novels involves the author carefully crafting levels and subplots within the grand plot of the story. If the One Mind is at least partly involved with the manifestation and orchestration of synchronicities that connect people, animals, and other events in nature, we would expect to see evidence of even more complex levels and subplots going on in our world, even if we were not intelligent enough to figure out what the grand plot was.

What follows is an account of the first instance where I experienced the intertwining of multiple Type III Synchronicities within a twenty-four hour period. As this complex combination of multiple categories of synchronicities was unfolding, I could not believe it. If you find yourself feeling like you are reading a novel rather than a non-fiction book, you are not alone.

This extraordinary Type III Synchronicity involved a propitious weekend with a special family whom I will call the Baxters. To protect their privacy, I have changed their names and a few incidental details about them. I thank the leaders of the former company Zunani Experiences, Inc.—Charlie and Rhys—for giving me permission to reveal their active participation in these events. Apparently, these individuals were meant to enable me to have these unique experiences in the first place, to help me witness and verify them, and finally, to inspire me to share them with you.

A Bit of History: Celebrating a Special Forty-Fifth Birthday

Emily Baxter, a gifted painter and paramedic, was celebrating her forty-fifth birthday. Emily is a deeply spiritual person who has a special interest in Native American culture. She and her husband, Joe Baxter, MD, had never experienced a sweat lodge and had decided to have one with their family for her birthday.

For over twenty years, Joe had held a senior position at a Tucson medical center. Joe shares academic as well as personal interests with me. I met Emily and Joe in 1989, shortly after arriving in Tucson, and we quickly became close friends. I also became the godfather of their children, Erik and Kathy.

Emily had recently learned about Charlie Onehorse Hill, who was then Director of Zunani Experiences, a team of individuals (including Rhys Davies, a skilled wilderness instructor from Wales) who together provided Native American healing experiences and ceremonies for individuals and groups. Charlie is half Yaqui Indian, and grew up in Mexico, where his grandmother was a local medicine woman. For years, Charlie worked as a mental health professional.

Emily had heard about Charlie from her son Erik, aged fifteen at the time, who had experienced a sweat lodge with Charlie as part of his training at a private boarding school in southern Arizona.

When Emily invited me to join the family and drive with them from Tucson to Tombstone, so that I could experience the twenty-four hour set of Native American and healing ceremonies with them (save for time spent resting at the historic Gadsden Hotel in Douglas), I could not say no. I knew this would be a special moment for Emily and her family, and I felt honored to be invited to share it with them. Though I decided not to partake of the actual hour and a half sweat lodge ceremony itself—primarily so that the family could experience it un-distracted by their scientist godparent—I agreed to share the majority of the events with them.

I never could have guessed what would unfold that day, and the next.

Five Type III Synchronicities

Four primary Type III Synchronicities that we have previously discussed occurred during this period, and a fifth that we have not yet reviewed. They are synchronicities involving:

1. the number 11;
2. dragonflies and the movie *Dragonfly;*
3. ravens;
4. roses and God; and,
5. the integration of truth, planning, sanity, and survival.

As I describe each emerging synchronicity from these two days, I will briefly illustrate how the event speaks to one or more of the five synchronicities. Because this unfolding of synchronicities is complex—there are a total of 29 events—I will notate **in bold** each synchronicity as it occurred and number it accordingly. As you read along, you will see that the synchronicities become more remarkable and improbable as time went on, especially when viewed in the context of the fact that they occurred collectively at this precise and meaningful moment.

Given the complexity of this account, though I indicate which category applies to each of the synchronicities in question, I have not sorted and numbered the synchronicities into discrete content categories, as the key here is readability.

It Begins with Mother Mary?

The night before I packed to leave with the Baxters, I was reading two books. One was a non-fiction book titled *The Jesus Mysteries* (by Timothy Freke and Peter Gandy), which discusses the similarity between Christian claims for Jesus and the history of pagan claims for the Greek Mysteries of Dionysus and the Egyptian Mysteries of Osiris. (Parenthetically, it was only during the process of the editing of *Super Synchronicity* in the summer of 2015, after having checked the spelling of Preston and Child's FBI character, that I realized that his first name was "Dionysus" as well. Was this a random coincidence, or is it part of a greater "Super Plot"?)

The other was a novel by Clive Cussler, a fiction book titled *Trojan Odyssey* about Pitt Kirk and Al Giordino, the effects of Hurricane Lizzie, a mysterious brown tide infesting international waters, and a secret company plotting to produce worldwide climate changes. (I often read a few books at a time, switching from one to the other as the mood moves me.)

I was pondering the historic meaning of the virgin birth and the rose attached to Mother Mary *(The Jesus Mysteries),* as well as the Celtic stories and the number 11 *(Trojan Odyssey)* silently to myself as the Baxters and I made our way to Tombstone. These topics remained in the back of my mind as Charlie and Rhys took the Baxters and me on the first leg of our journey in their van, from the town of Tombstone to the rocks and mountains of Cochise County, where we would hike up to the so-called Counsel Rocks, where Cochise and other chiefs supposedly used to gather.

As we approached the parking lot, Charlie pointed out a remarkable natural rock formation in the distance. At least 30 feet tall, toward the top of the mountain, was what appeared to be a sculpture of the Virgin Mary looking down over the valley.

I had never seen a natural rock formation that looked as if it were carefully sculpted by human hands. **I gazed at the Mother Mary look-alike and silently said to myself, *That's weird.*** [**Event #1:** the connection to Mother Mary was meaningful in light of the previous chapter]. Of course, I didn't say anything, at least not then; I simply noted it quietly to myself. The coincidence of seeing this sculpture out in the desert, timed with my reading and pondering about Mother Mary and my prior Our Lady of Guadalupe adventure, was curious to say the least.

We hiked up to Counsel Rocks and then beyond them to a low-level mountain peak, where it was possible to scan the surrounding area a full 360 degrees. We were each given a piece of paper with an empty medicine man shield, and were invited to draw things that symbolized our strengths and values. We were to split up and find a private space. Emily, Joe, Erik, and Kathy went their separate ways, and I found myself moving in a direction that would afford me a clear view of the Mother Mary formation, which was about a mile away.

For reasons that you can appreciate, I ended up drawing a five-petaled rose on my shield, as well as a sun emanating 11 distinct rays. I considered drawing a raven, then decided against it. My drawings were not a synchronicity, obviously; they simply reflected my conscious intention to honor their history.

After completing my drawings, I found Charlie and Rhys sitting next to a small pool of recently-accumulated rainwater. I handed over my drawing, and then began walking in the opposite direction, looking out across the distant mountains.

As I sat down, I noticed a large boulder in front of me, at least eight feet in diameter. **On the boulder was a natural rock formation that appeared to be in the precise shape of a rose! [Event #2]**. The rose measured about two feet across. I couldn't believe my eyes. I took pictures of the apparent rose figure, then turned around and saw that **the Mother Mary sculpture was clearly visible from where I stood, as if the rose were in her line of vision—and it should be noted that in many places in that same area, the sculpture was blocked by boulders and trees and so could not be seen [Event #3]**. I took a picture of her, too.

I said to myself: *What is the probability of seeing a natural Mother Mary figure, and a natural rose figure, both facing each other, and precisely at this moment in my life?* Thinking about my emerging synchronicity journey—and particularly my raven and rose-God Type III Synchronicities—I said to myself, *If this is really a synchronicity, and is meant to have meaning for me, then could you affirm this for me by having a raven appear now?*

Almost immediately after making this silent request, I heard a clear cawing sound coming from the direction of the Mother Mary formation. I said to myself, *Could this possibility be a raven—or a crow?* **I turned my head in the direction of the sound and saw a large black bird flying by [Event #4]**. However, given the distance I could not tell for certain if it was a raven or a crow (but I was soon to receive confirmation).

I asked silently in my head, *If this is really a raven, could one appear closer to me?* Within ten to fifteen seconds, I heard a second cawing sound, this time coming from the rose rock area. **Seemingly out of the blue, a large raven appeared [Event #5],** then began flying away from me.

I asked in my head, *Please, raven, if you are meant to be a sign for me, please don't go away.* **The raven then circled around, flying directly over my head [Event #6]**, and then caught up to the first raven in the distance.

I was shocked. I returned to Charlie and Rhys. Charlie said, quite spontaneously, "Gary, did you see the raven? He flew over your head. He was there for you."

I briefly shared my interest in ravens with Charlie and Rhys, and also mentioned the rose rock. **Rhys then told me a remarkable story about the "true beauty of the rose" which had come to him intuitively [Event #7]**. This story was very meaningful for him.

Because his story is complex, and I do not recall all of its details, I will not attempt to relate it here.

The coincidence of Rhys' profound insight about the "true beauty of the rose" and my recent rose-God synchronicity led me to ask Rhys if I could interview him about his experience for a possible future book about synchronicity. Rhys was "blown away," not only because I understood his rose story, but because he was currently reading a book about intuition and synchronicities—*The Celestine Prophecy*.

Rhys told me his ancestry was 100% Celtic [Event #8]. I was quite surprised, because the mystery novel I was reading, *Trojan Odyssey*, involved the Celts! I could not recall either having read a novel about the Celts, or having met someone who told me he was 100% Celtic.

I shared with Rhys that I was struck by this synchronicity, and that I was planning to write a book about the science of synchronicity. Rhys then told me that **he was currently reading a book that focused on what the author called "intuitive synchronicity" [Event #9]**.

Rhys and Charlie then mentioned in passing that **for the past ten minutes, they had been watching two dragonflies, coupled, dipping in and out of the water [Event #10].** These dragonflies were observed during the same time that the ravens had appeared. Rhys and Charlie did not know that dragonflies were also central to my awakening to synchronicity.

Meanwhile, I wondered whether the appearance of the ravens had been a genuine synchronicity. I resisted drawing any conclusions, and decided I would see if other ravens spontaneously appeared over the twenty-four period [it turns out that they did not]. Only if this was a unique event, precisely timed to my silent request for the appearance of a raven, would I conclude that it might well be a meaningful synchronicity.

I also decided to reserve judgment about whether the dragonfly observation was truly a synchronicity or not, waiting to determine how common dragonflies were in the area, and if they did appear, when they did so [as you will read below, I observed only one other dragonfly in the twenty-four hour period, and its timing was propitious].

I said nothing of any of this to the Baxters. We finally gathered together, and followed Charlie and Rhys to a rock where they took us through a Native American pipe-smoking ceremony.

We were each to present our shield drawings and discuss their symbolism. The order of presentation was Emily, Kathy, Erik, Joe, and then me. Both Emily and Kathy had drawn hearts; they focused their symbolism on love and truth [two meanings of the rose]. Emily had drawn the sun, as well. Erik's shield featured trees and rocks, plus a fire symbol. He made a point of drawing 11 branches on his tree, plus 11 rocks [Erik has had a fascination with the number 11 since childhood; he did not then know about my fascination with the number 11.] Joe had also drawn a tree. Erik was touched when I showed him that my sun had 11 rays. Erik spells his name with a K (rather than Eric) partly because K is the eleventh letter of the alphabet. There was an obvious psychological reason for the presence of 11s between Erik and me. Hence, I did not classify any of the above as synchronicities.

However, Rhys then asked me if I had an 11 connection, and I said yes, and so did Erik. **Rhys then went on to share that over the previous two weeks, he had seen a total of 11 different coyotes, more than he had ever seen in his life [Event #11].**

Then, to add metaphorical insult to injury, Charlie asked me if I knew what the Yaqui meaning of 11 was. I said, "What? The Yaqui have a history with the number 11?" Charlie explained that his grandmother was a local medicine woman, and that he was a twin whose brother had died. **Charlie's grandmother used the number 11 to symbolize how humans have both a "light" and "dark" nature (the latter called "shadow" by Carl Jung), and that it was the successful integration of the light and the dark that turned the number 11 into a unified one [Event #12]**.

At this point, I was seeing an emerging pattern. From the Mother Mary look-alike and the Rock Rose carving, through the two ravens, the "true beauty of the rose," through two dragonflies,

11 coyotes, and the Yaqui meaning of the number 11, something highly synchronistic was occurring.

After hearing Charlie's story, I looked up and saw a huge heart-shaped cloud over Kathy's and Erik's heads. **Here Emily and Kathy had just shown their drawings of multiple hearts, one of the deep symbols of the rose is the heart, and then there is an almost perfectly heart-shaped cloud above their heads [Event #13].**

As you now understand, because I am a scientist, I do not simply accept such coincidences as synchronicities. For something to be a potential synchronicity—particularly a strong one—it must be unique, if not rare, meaningful, and precisely timed.

If I had not been pondering the meaning of Mother Mary (something I rarely did in the past), and then had seen a Mother Mary look-alike in, of all places, the desert, I would not have interpreted the Mother Mary natural carving as a potential synchronicity.

If I had not just drawn a rose, and also thought about the rose connection to Mother Mary, and then seen a rose figure naturally carved in a rock, I would not have interpreted the rose carving as a potential synchronicity.

If I had not specifically asked to see a raven, and then heard and seen one, then asked for confirmation, and seen a second one, and then asked that it not fly away from me, and had it fly right over me, I would not have interpreted these three raven events as potential synchronicities.

If I had not been reading a novel that emphasized Celts, and then met a person who spontaneously told me he was 100% Celtic, I would not have interpreted my reading about Celts and meeting a Celt as a potential synchronicity (especially when this person was part of this unfolding Type III Synchronicity).

If I had not been thinking about writing a book about synchronicity, and Rhys had not recently been reading a book about synchronicity, I would not have interpreted his book as a potential synchronicity.

If I had not experienced my previous dragonfly synchronicities—including receiving a dragonfly sculpture from the Baxters for my sixty-first birthday—and if Charlie had not specifically commented on the raven flying over my head (which had happened while he saw two dragonflies), I would not have interpreted the appearance of the two dragonflies spending time with Charlie and Rhys as a potential synchronicity.

If I had not experienced the Mother Mary / Rose Rock connection, I would not have interpreted the presence of Rhys and his story about the "true beauty of the rose" as a potential synchronicity.

If Erik and I had not both included symbolisms of 11 in our respective drawings, and then heard Rhys' anomaly of seeing 11 coyotes, followed by learning that Charlie had a grandmother who taught him the Yaqui meaning of the number 11, I would not have interpreted these rare events as potential synchronicities.

Finally, if Emily and Kathy had not drawn multiple hearts, and I had not been pondering the presence of the rose symbol out in the desert—in a rock formation and also with Rhys—I would not have interpreted the precise timing of the presence of a heart-shaped cloud overhead as being a potential synchronicity.

You may be wondering how common it is for clouds to appear in an almost perfect heart-shaped formation. As you can probably guess, I looked at numerous clouds that afternoon and the following morning, to see how many individual heart-shaped clouds I could find. The only one I found was the one that appeared at the end of our special pipe ceremony.

If you are like me, then you are probably not convinced at this point. Was there really a pattern to these apparent synchronicities? Was this really an important integrative moment to ponder?

As we hiked back down to the Zunani van, I asked myself these fundamental questions. To my surprise, the apparent synchronicities continued unabated. By late the next morning, I was suffering from a strong case of hyper-synchronicity. When I told Emily a few days after our trip that I was feeling stressed by the totality of the experiences, she commented that I was suffering from "synchronicity overload."

Continuation of the Apparent Synchronicities

If I listed in this chapter every one of the apparent synchronicities I witnessed during this period, you might experience a case of synchronicity overload yourself, or perhaps interpret the totality of the evidence as a case of synchronicity overkill. So I will share only a few of the more exceptionally memorable synchronous events to illustrate why this twenty-four hour period could be described as a hyper-synchronicity moment.

Consider the historic Gadsden Hotel. Though I noticed that it was located at 1046 G Avenue (and the numbers added up to 11), for some reason (possibly a symptom of synchronicity overload to the number 11?) I did not think to classify it as a synchronicity at the time.

However, the sign over the table where Joe and Kathy were sitting at 9:45 pm was unusual and meaningful. The hotel restaurant closed at 10 pm, and Kathy and Joe were sitting at a two-person table for dinner. They did not know I would be joining them. I raced down to the restaurant, and to my surprise, I saw that **over their heads was a sign that read "The Special Rose" [Event #14].** Given the significance of the rose and rose synchronicities in the previous chapter, as well what was happening on this day, being reminded of the rose again, this time in a restaurant, was awe-inspiring. How many restaurants do you know that have tables with signs that say "The Special Rose"?

The next morning when I went to shower, I was dumbstruck to discover that **the soap used in the hotel was called "Rosa Venus" and featured an image of a single reddish rose [Event #15]!**

Meanwhile, after dinner I continued where I had left off in *Trojan Odyssey.* **A woman was introduced in the story who had "raven" colored hair [Event #16].** How often does the word "raven" appear in a novel, immediately following the sighting of two ravens under very special circumstances? This was followed by another discussion of Celts in the book [which I did not count as a synchronicity, since I had previously read about Celts in the same book].

However, when I awoke the next morning, before taking my shower I read another couple of pages. **The main characters had just rented a boat called "Dear Heart" [Event #17].** A boat called "Dear Heart"? I was aware that this was not a common name for a boat, and I had read these words the morning after witnessing a novel "heart cloud." As you will read below, both "dear" and "heart" would appear again, in two very curiously timed events.

Before leaving the hotel for breakfast, I listed the events on a yellow sheet of paper, and briefly shared with Charlie, Rhys, and the Baxters the apparent avalanche of synchronicities that were unfolding. Everyone was now aware that something special seemed to be happening. I told them that perhaps this collection of events would be a meaningful way to introduce the concept of synchronicity to the wider public.

Charlie drove us over the border to a Mexican restaurant, which was selected because they offered a Mexican buffet, a preference of the Baxters.

The synchronicities I will share here involved ravens and dear/deer. When we sat down for breakfast, I was seated at the head of the table. Erik sat to my right, with Charlie to my left. It wasn't long before Erik turned around and called out to me, asking me to look at what was hanging on the wall. What I saw made my jaw drop to the floor. **The artwork was a taxidermy that included a cougar-like animal and, yes, a real stuffed raven [Event #18]!** I have eaten at countless restaurants; I do not recall ever having eaten at a restaurant with a real stuffed raven on the wall. Have you?

I showed Erik some of the novel raven connected pictures I had stored in my cell phone. One was a picture of dog named Raven (a great story, although not essential here). I asked everyone at the table if they knew of any dogs named "Raven." None did. **But Erik then said, "I know a horse named Raven" [Event #19].** A horse named Raven? I asked everyone at the table if they had ever heard of a horse named Raven; none did, including Charlie, who has raised horses for years.

However, Charlie told me that a dear friend of his, who he had told me earlier died the previous year in motorcycle accident, had a girlfriend for nine years whose nickname was "Raven" [Event #20]. A girlfriend named Raven, who was the friend of the person sitting next to me? I asked everyone at the table, did they know anyone, male or female, who had the nickname Raven? None did.

Then Charlie said, somewhat sheepishly, that he also had a "Raven" girlfriend whose name was "Laughing Raven" [Event #21]! I could not believe what he was telling me. Was this a joke? Or was there really a raven connection taking place here—in the desert, in the restaurant, in Erik's life, and in Charlie's life?

Kathy then noticed something that I will include here as a tentative synchronicity. Remember, Kathy had drawn multiple hearts on her shield the day before. I had told everyone about the "Dear Heart" boat name before we went to the restaurant. Kathy said, "Gary, look on the wall!" **As you may have guessed, further down the wall, along with the cougar and the raven, was the head of an antlered deer [Event #22].**

I am including this as a tentative synchronicity, because the deer had antlers. I trust you are sitting down. It turns out that the man who had died in the motorcycle accident, whose girlfriend was nicknamed Raven, had died in a freak accident involving an elk (a member of the deer family) and his antlers.

The elk had apparently jumped across his path, and Charlie's friend had hit the elk with his bike. As unbelievable as this may sound, according to Charlie, the elk's antler then pierced his friend's brain and killed him. The elk then separated himself, and ran away. Charlie was with his friend when he died.

Because of what had happened in the restaurant involving ravens, as I was leaving, I asked the cashier for a business card. The writing on the card was in Spanish, and it read, "Magdalena Machado Eltas." **I just realized that** Magdalena **is a** name **sometimes attached to Mother Mary, or to a woman close to Jesus and associated with his mother [Event #23]**.

Also, upon looking at the address on the card, I realized that it is "650" Col. Centro Aqua Preta. **The numbers 6+5 add up to 11 [Event #24].** Given that (1) the historic Gadsden Hotel address added up to 11, and (2) this hotel had significant synchronicities, and (3) the restaurant address added up to 11, and (4) that this restaurant had a few additional remarkable synchronicities described below, it seemed appropriate to include the restaurant address as a synchronicity and therefore classify the **hotel 11 address as a synchronicity as well [Event #25].**

By now you may have a better sense of what I mean by hyper-synchronicity, and understand why I was experiencing synchronicity overload. I will now share four more apparent synchronicities to honor the totality of the experience.

After breakfast, we crossed the border back into the US and went to the site of Charlie's sweat lodge. The family's task was to combine our five individual drawings into one integrative shield. I let the family do this alone, and they placed all of the symbols inside a huge heart. **Rhys then noticed that in the center of the leather of the drum the family had made was a naturally occurring pattern that looked very much like a heart [Event #26].** Everyone could see the heart once it was pointed out to them, and we all had chills.

The chills continued when Charlie said that we could each bring a "grandfather" home. The term "grandfather" is used to refer to rocks that are heated and then placed inside the sweat lodge. You will recall that I did not go in the sweat lodge the previous night; I had stayed outside with Gabriel, the fire keeper, and Rhys.

As Gabriel was retrieving the first few "grandfathers," they literally cracked. He was visibly shaken, and he explained to me, quietly, that grandfathers almost never crack outside, although they sometimes crack inside the sweat lodge. A total of three grandfathers cracked outside. Gabriel then whispered in my ear that "The fire spoke to him, and the cracks symbolized spirits leaving the rocks to help the family with their healing." As a scientist, I listened and drew no conclusions of my own.

However, when Charlie said that we could pick a grandfather, I bent down to select one of the rocks that had cracked. **I picked up a grandfather and discovered it had cracked in the shape of a heart [Event #27**]! The heart shape was almost perfect.

As we stood in a circle sharing our experiences to end the twenty-four hour set of events and ceremonies, Emily spoke about how this was the most meaningful and memorable birthday she ever had. **As I watched her, a dragonfly flew up to her, circled her head, and then departed [Event #28]**. It was the only dragonfly I observed over the twenty-four hours. You will recall that Emily had given me a dragonfly sculpture for my sixty-first birthday. The timing could not have been more propitious.

As I was putting away the Magdalena restaurant business card, I noticed in the upper left-hand corner an insignia for the "Hotel Plaza," which houses the restaurant. **Bcncath thc namc is a small flying insect with four wings that looks very much like a dragonfly [Event #29]**. How many restaurant business cards have you seen that contain a dragonfly-like insect?

Supersynchronicity, or Supersynchronicity Illusion?

If one is going to conduct synchronicity self-science, one has to record events as they happen, and then later attempt to analyze them in context. It is easy to get carried away as a "believer" and see virtually "everything" as a synchronicity. It is also easy to get carried away as a "disbeliever" and see most "everything" as being misinterpreted coincidence.

If you find yourself leaning toward immediately accepting everything I wrote above as being meaningful synchronicities, you may be erring on the "carried-away believer" side.

If you find yourself immediately rejecting everything I wrote above as being misinterpreted coincidences, you may be erring on the "carried-away disbeliever" side.

Though I have come to accept the existence of Type I, Type II, and Type III Synchronicities—especially in light of all the evidence you will read about in the rest of this book—I nonetheless try to step back after collecting the data and discern what is a non-random synchronicity versus a chance coincidence.

If you are highly skeptical, your instinct may be to focus on an event that might well be a coincidence, and then use that as the reason—or excuse—to reject the rest of them, regardless of the degree of their apparent synchronistic significance. If you find yourself "throwing the baby out with the bathwater," this would be unfortunate. *It would also be thoroughly unscientific.*

What if all of these events over those twenty-four hours represent an expression of an unfolding complex "plot," with "subplots" that involved interconnections of at least seven people's lives, as well as some animals and nature (i.e., rocks and clouds)?

After returning home, I remember on the one hand reasoning that something very sophisticated was going on, and on the other hand thinking that maybe I was becoming a synchronicity junky!

Truth be told, I resonated with the introductory quote to this chapter: *My life has a superb cast but I can't figure out the plot.* How could I figure out the "plot"—if there were one—when I couldn't keep track of all of the events and their interrelationships?

When we are faced with incredible complexity, what is our response? Do we say, "It's too complex, therefore it's probably random" and forget it? Or do we say, "It's too complex to be random," and keep trying to figure it out?

In my case, despite my skepticism, the decision was somewhat easy. The synchronicities did not go away. In fact, they kept on escalating, in ever more amazing—and humorous—ways.

Are you ready for ducks?

Chapter 9
Humorous Synchronicities with Ducks
Lesson: If It Walks and Talks Like the One Mind, It Probably Is

I do not believe in God because I do not believe in Mother Goose.
Clarence Darrow

Does the Universe have a sense of humor?

And if the One Mind does, how would we know?

Thus far in my synchronicity self-science journey, most of what I had experienced and recorded was strange, bizarre, improbable, and seemingly incomprehensible.

Yes, the unfolding synchronicities were sometimes exciting and even fun, but they were more often challenging and downright stressful at times.

When I would feel stressed by the emerging synchronicities, I would take solace in remembering the history of quantum physics, as well as other areas of mathematics and science that revealed ideas that seemed beyond understanding. Comforting examples in mathematics and science included the incomprehensible quantity of infinity times infinity (there is a field of mathematics that focuses on infinity), and the unknowable existence of physical matter that can only be inferred indirectly (called "Dark Matter").

Then, seemingly out of the blue, I observed that the pattern of synchronicities was shifting from the merely ridiculous to the ludicrous, and then on to the preposterous.

I suddenly realized that there was a complex cosmic comedy unfolding that was beyond anything I could have guessed or imagined. Not only was the emerging Grand Plot super-complex, but it was becoming super-silly as well.

Speaking of super-silly, what you are about to read may sound utterly off the wall.

We are about to explore a sequence of 19 duck synchronicities that occurred within a six-day period.

The number "19" is not a typo, and neither is the word "ducks."

These 19 duck synchronicities involved numerous people, including tenured professors, successful businessmen, the CEO of Canyon Ranch, a physician, an executive at Microsoft, a psychotherapist, a graduate student in health psychology at the University of Arizona, and some undergraduate students at the University of Arizona. They can all verify their respective participation. However, the hub of the wheel of these super-silly synchronicities was me.

I sympathize with Dr. Darrow, the famous lawyer who did not believe in Mother Goose, and by extension, in God. I too have seen no evidence for Mother Goose. Lacking evidence for her existence, the conservative approach is to disbelieve.

However, as you are about to read, I have witnessed a slew of super-improbable duck events that rivals the most extreme of any comedy routine I have ever seen.

And lest you wonder whether this initial Type III Duck Supersynchronicity was a fluke—a one-time sequence of events—I should mention that at least three more volleys of duck synchronicities have occurred over the past three years involving a total of more than 60 additional duck events.

Though I do not believe in Mother Goose, I have too much evidence not to believe in Type III Duck Synchronicities. And unlike

Dr. Darrow, I have compelling evidence from so many supersynchronicities that lead me to believe in a genuine Super Mind process.

If Dr. Darrow were to carefully consider the totality of this evidence, and attempted to understand and explain it, he would discover that the only potentially plausible explanation for the evidence is not only the existence of some sort of super-intelligent synchronizing process (which some would call God), but that this One Mind has a super sense of humor.

To help you see the big picture of the Type III Duck Supersynchronicity, I have prepared a summary list of the 19 synchronicities with their respective dates, followed by a descriptive account of what happened and how I responded to each.

Since some of the people involved prefer to remain anonymous, I have used initials or false names for them.

DATE	DUCK EVENT
1. Sunday morning, Feb 17	*I received an email about a four-legged duck from the Evolutionary Psychology program at the* University of Arizona
2. Sunday evening, Feb 17	*I learned of Mr. J's "Duck with arrow in heart" family crest*
3. Monday morning, Feb 18	*I read in my novel the sentence "First, you want to get all your ducks in a row?*
4. Monday evening, Feb 18	*Mr. J showed me two family crests, the second with three ducks in a row*
5. Tuesday afternoon, Feb 19	*I reached the scheduled point in my lecture where I describe the HBO Special "Life Afterlife" and "Lucky Duck" Productions, who produced the show.*

6. Tuesday afternoon, Feb 19	*A student handed me a plastic yellow duck she had in her pocket.*
7. Tuesday afternoon, Feb 19	*A student told me his four-year-old daughter had arranged 3 ducks in a row that morning.*
8. Tuesday afternoon, Feb 19	*A student told me about her son's nickname being "Duck" and about rediscovering her duck tea pot.*
9. Tuesday evening, Feb 19	*In a channeling, an intuitive brought up the phrase "If it walks like a duck…."*
10. Tuesday evening, Feb 19	*Martha shared her dream about Groucho Marx, and Betty told us she was reading "Duck Soup."*
11. Tuesday evening, Feb 19	*The intuitive told us about her pet duck Daisy, and that night I read about a character named Daisy in my novel.*
12. Tuesday evening, Feb 19	*Rhonda shared her transformative story of her and her mother healing a baby duck.*
13. Wednesday lunch, Feb 20	*Dr. K told me that Dr. D lives on* "Three Ducks Lane" *(named in Spanish).*
14. Wednesday night, Feb 20	*Just before my lecture, I bumped into Dr. D and he confirmed his street was named* "Three Ducks Lane."
15. Wednesday night, Feb 20	*Charles and Laurie Finklestein called and told Rhonda about "Honk!" (a musical based on the story of the Ugly Duckling).*

16. Thursday evening, Feb 21	*Dr. K saw* Tucson *"Adopt a Duck" month on TV.*
17. Friday morning, Feb 22	*I was on Mary Occhino's Sirius Radio show, where she mentioned a "water off a duck's back" story.*
18. Friday morning, Feb 22	*The caller on the phone, PG, mentioned her grandfather's pet duck*
19. Friday morning, Feb 22	*Mr. J came over, received an "Adopt a Duck" printout, and shared his town's name "Susy duck."*

We are ready to present the events in more detail. Groucho Marx, here we come.

1. Sunday morning, Feb 17 — *I received an email about a four-legged duck from the Evolutionary Psychology program at the Universityof* Arizona

On Sunday morning, February 17, 2006, I received an email from a professor in the Evolutionary Psychology PhD program at the University of Arizona (at the time, I was a visiting faculty member in their program), and read this seemingly crazy story about a four-legged duck. The duck's photo was also shown on TV. I thought nothing about the duck email at the time, except that the duck looked cute and that it was a curious genetic anomaly.

I had no idea it would serve as a synchronicity primer for what would transpire that evening with Mr. J.

2. Sunday evening, Feb 17 — *I learned of Mr. J.'s "Duck with arrow in heart" family crest*

Rhonda and I took Mr. J and his wife to dinner at North's Restaurant. After our meal, we somehow started talking about the meaning of names. Mr. J asked me what Schwartz meant, and I explained that it meant "black," and carried deep significance to me.

For example, during the day we can't see the stars—even though they are there—because we are blinded by the nearest star, our sun. The lesson is that sometimes we must enter the dark in order to see the light (i.e., the black of night reveals the stars hidden in the daylight).

I then asked Mr. J what his name meant. He explained that he did not know what it meant, but mentioned that he knew his family crest. He said it was a "duck with an arrow in its heart."

What a weird crest, I thought. As soon as Mr. J said that, I was reminded of the four-legged duck. I wondered, *Another weird duck?* My synchronicity detector began to process the possibility.

Was this a potential new synchronicity? Of course, I had no idea at that moment; I was simply open to the possibility. I could never have anticipated what was about to unfold.

3. Monday morning, Feb 18 — *I read in my novel the sentence First, you want to get all your ducks in a row?"*

As mentioned previously, I often read mysteries as well as non-fiction books—usually a few at a time—whenever I can. I try to read a few pages every day. I had just purchased Robert B. Parker's latest novel *High Profile* featuring Jesse Stone, Chief of Police in Paradise, Massachusetts. (This was the same Parker who writes the Spenser series.)

On page 136 in *High Profile,* the following conversation takes place:

"We maybe should ask him about that?" Suit said.

"Sooner or later," Jesse said.

"First, you want to get all your ducks in a row?"

"I'd settle for getting them herded into the same area," Jesse said.

Get all your ducks in a row?

Mr. J, whose family crest was a duck with an arrow its heart, was planning to get a group of very successful "gentlemen" into "the same area" and he was elegantly setting a carefully planned agenda that would get all his ducks in a row.

Yes, the phrase "get all your ducks in a row" is well known. However, I have read over 40 Parker novels, and many hundreds of mysteries by other writers, and I did not recall ever reading a sentence about ducks in a row in any of them.

Of course, my memory could be faulty (for example, as I reveal below concerning my early history with ducks). However, I knew we could later determine how many times mystery writers had used the phrase "ducks in a row" and calculate a fairly precise frequency of its usage. In fact, just prior to the final editing of this book, I discovered that Parker had used the phrase "ducks in a row" in one of his Spenser novels.

Much more important was the timing of my reading "ducks in a row." First a four-legged duck, then a family duck crest, and now ducks in a row. This was three seemingly unusual duck references in less than twenty-four hours.

I had no idea that the duck synchronicity sequence was just warming up.

4. Monday evening, Feb 18	*Mr. J. showed me two family crests, the second has three ducks in a row.*

I was scheduled to meet with Mr. J around 6:00 pm at the Arizona Inn to review the agenda for the "herd of gentlemen" we were scheduled to meet. When I arrived at the Inn, Mr. J had his computer set up with a detailed agenda. However, Mr. J also had a surprise for me: he had two samples of his family crest that he wished to show me.

To my eye, the first one looked like Donald Duck with an arrow in its heart at the top of the crest. The crest had other features that I could not easily discern at the time. I thought the duck was quite cute.

However, the second crest gave me the chills. It was simple, comprised only of ducks. It had three ducks in a row!

Three ducks in a row? This was a crest confirmation of the previous three duck synchronicities! What was going on?

5. Tuesday afternoon, Feb 19	*I reached the scheduled point in my lecture where I describe the HBO Special "Life Afterlife" and "Lucky Duck" Productions, who produced the show.*

I did not have time to ponder the meaning of ducks on Tuesday morning. I had multiple meetings at the University, plus I had to give two scheduled lectures. I follow a syllabus that is created at the beginning of the semester. The timing of what you are about to read—the lecture and its key phrase—was set into motion weeks before I learned that I would be meeting someone named Mr. J.

At 2:00 pm, I was beginning my lecture to my Psychology of Religion and Spirituality Class. The students were reading *The Afterlife Experiments,* and we were just about to discuss the beginning of an experiment with mediums conducted in my laboratory, which was featured as part of the HBO documentary titled *Life Afterlife* aired in 1999.

Once a year I give this lecture. I explained to students that the HBO experiment was made possible by Lisa Jackson, an award-winning director who worked for Linda Ellerbee (a famous producer of documentaries).

I then shared a bit of humor. I explained that it was bad enough to have to explain to colleagues and students that (1) I was conducting a controversial experiment with mediums on the topic of life after death, and then (2) explain that the research was funded by a television network (HBO) rather than a credible research agency like NSF or NIH, but (3) it was even worse to have to confess that the documentary was being produced by a company with the (some would say) silly name "Lucky Duck" productions.

As I heard myself saying the words "Lucky Duck" out loud, the previous day's ducks immediately entered my mind.

I literally stopped speaking.

I told the class I was seeing a connection with a possible emerging synchronicity, and since they would be learning about synchronicities in the next phase of the course (when they would be reading *The G.O.D. Experiments),* that I should probably share this particular synchronicity.

So I told the class we would take a bit of a digression, and I would tell them about a set of recent synchronicities involving ducks. Little did I realize that this would unleash a set of subsequent synchronicities that would ultimately lead me to learn the probable meaning of "why ducks" and "why ducks now?"

6. Tuesday afternoon, Feb 19 *A student handed me a yellow duck she had in her pocket.*

After the lecture, I was swarmed with students—more than any previous lecture.

One woman, whom I will call Joan, was beside herself. She told me she was sitting in class, hearing the duck synchronicities, and found herself putting her hand in the pocket of her sweater.

What Joan discovered shook her to her core. She said she had to show me, and ask me what it meant.

Joan then put her hand in her pocket and pulled out a little plastic yellow duck!

The swarm of students was shocked, as was I.

I asked her "How often do you carry a duck in your pocket to class?"

She said never.

I asked her how is it that she happened to have a duck in her pocket today, of all days.

She explained that she works with kids and drives them various places in her car, and that the previous week in her car she had found a little plastic duck on the floor and put it in the pocket of her sweater. She left the sweater in the car, then, thinking it might get cold that day, she decided to take the sweater (which had remained in the car up to that point) to class.

I asked Joan, "Why didn't you raise your hand in class and tell me?"

She said she had been too shocked, confused, and embarrassed. I understood.

I told her that in Appendix C of *The G.O.D. Experiments,* she would find a chapter titled "Synchronicity in New York City." It dealt with the number 11 and how I first discovered, empirically, evidence for synchronicity in my life. I agreed to meet with her after she had read the Appendix, and she gifted me with the little yellow plastic duck.

She was not alone.

7. Tuesday afternoon, Feb 19 — *A student told me his four-year-old daughter arranged 3 ducks in a row that morning*

Another student was bursting at the seams to speak; I will call him Jim.

Jim confessed to the group of students that that morning, his wife had been showering and could not find her shaver, so she asked her husband to try to find it.

He discovered that his four-year old daughter had taken the shaver and placed it in her room alongside three plastic ducks which she had carefully arranged in a row!

Jim said he had never seen (or at least noticed) before that his daughter had arranged three toy ducks in a row. When he heard me mention the duck synchronicities, he almost jumped out of his skin.

I asked him about whether the missing shaver / three ducks in a row constellation was a novel event in his household. He claimed that yes, it was. What made it meaningful for him, and for the rest of us, was the potential connection between his duck experience and other duck synchronicities that were taking place.

As you will soon discover, the web of emerging duck synchronicities extended far beyond this particular class, and was about to heat up and explode like a geyser at the Yellowstone National Park.

8. Tuesday afternoon, Feb 19	*A student told me about her son s nickname being "duck" and about her rediscovering her duck tea pot.*

I had no time to ponder what had just transpired. I had to get back to my office and put on my master's thesis advisor hat.

I was meeting with a student whom I will call Susan. We were reviewing details concerning her master's proposal investigating the effects of energy healing on cells that had been heat stressed.

Toward the end of our meeting, I experienced the intuition to ask her about ducks.

No, I had never asked any of my graduate student about ducks before—at least as far as I could remember.

I said to Susan, "I know this may sound a little strange, but my intuition is telling me that I should ask you if you and your family have any connection, in the past or recently, to ducks?"

Susan almost fell out of her chair.

First, she explained that when her youngest son was seven years old, they had lived near a pond in New Hampshire. One night the pond froze, and her son discovered that a duck was frozen in the pond. He tried to rescue the duck, broke the ice, and fell into the water. He screamed for his mother, who came to rescue both. Apparently, the duck survived and her son earned the nickname "Duck."

Years later, they moved to Arizona and the boy left his nickname in New Hampshire. Susan explained that her son eventually became a star quarterback on his high school football team. (I thought to myself that it was odd that Mr. J had been a star football player in high school, too.)

His coach decided to give him a nickname: he explained that since people often ducked when he threw the ball, that he would call the young man "Duck."

Susan's son became a lawyer, and now lives in San Diego with his wife and children, and sometimes still uses his old football nickname "Duck."

What was important to Susan was that just the day before, she had been thinking about this duck history because she had spontaneously decided to clean the top of the cabinets in her kitchen, and had noticed a teapot that had been placed up there. She had not thought about this teapot in years, she said.

The teapot was in the shape of a duck.

Meanwhile, I was thinking to myself, *I felt moved to ask a student I happened to have had an appointment with about whether she and her family has any association to ducks, and she shared with me two reasonably meaningful duck stories that were perfectly timed with the rest of the duck sequences that were unfolding at this unique moment in my life.*

How was I going to make sense of all this? Well, it just so happened that my next appointment provided the perfect opportunity to see whether the larger spiritual reality could provide a meaningful hint.

9. Tuesday evening, Feb 19 *In a channeling, an intuitive brought up the phrase "If it walks like a duck."*

Around 5:00 pm on Tuesdays, I held a regular off-campus meeting with a small group of people engaged in an exploratory "channeling" research project. This project was coordinated purportedly by a spiritual "Council"—a group of supposedly enlightened energy beings that claimed to have existed since the beginning of time and served as messengers of the Source.

The "Council" was allegedly channeled by an intuitive I will call Christine, a former physics teacher who subsequently received a master's degree in counseling. Christine became an intuitive, a medium, an experienced astrology practitioner and teacher, and also a psychic channel. For a few years she had participated in controlled mediumship and medical intuition research in our laboratory, and she was quite gifted. She has also worked for a while as a clairvoyant in the Metaphysics Department at a resort in Tucson.

Sometimes our group had included members from California. Fortunately, this particular session was small. In attendance was

Christine, myself, a friend of Christine's I will call Betty, a former employee of mine I will call Martha, and Rhonda. I decided to tell the group about my emerging duck synchronicities, including the four that had happened just that day (from Lucky Duck Productions to "Duck" the quarterback and the duck teapot).

Martha suggested that we should ask the spiritual "Council" what this might mean. I was curious, to say the least. The channeling session began, and the session was audio recorded.

The voice that came through Christine (she claims it does not come from her, but "through" her) more or less harangued me for a good ten minutes, claiming that the duck symbol was selected partly because (1) I resonated with ducks, and (2) I had a history with them. For the record, I have never been harangued by group of hypothesized spirits before.

I kept shaking my head no (and saying so as well). I could not remember any connection with ducks. I did not collect ducks. I did not read about them. I did not have a pet duck. I did not have a favorite movie about a duck. Nor did I remember ever lecturing about ducks.

What came out of her mouth next led me to gasp for breath: she said that I had been "given so much information, yet I never seemed to receive enough.". In a deep sense, this was true. As a researcher I was always seeking more evidence, more replications.

Then she said, "They are saying to me: If it walks like a duck, and talks like a duck ... ".

I would not be surprised if at that moment I looked white as a ghost—I sure felt that way. I found it hard to breathe; it was as if I had been hit in the solar plexus with an insight that provided a key of keys to a seemingly unsolvable mystery.

The reason was that at end of my lecture series about the survival of consciousness hypothesis and laboratory research about life after death, I always explain to students about how it may be impossible to "prove" beyond a shadow of a doubt that survival of consciousness exists—short of dying oneself.

However, the totality of the evidence is extraordinarily consistent with the hypothesis.

And in my book and lectures, I carefully use the metaphor, "If it walks like a duck, and talks like a duck, at some point it is prudent that we accept the evidence and conclude ... it's probably a duck!"

I had forgotten that I used this quote in my book and lectures. I had forgotten that this was the very metaphor I used to come to the conclusion that life after death was probably real.

I asked Christine later if she ever used this saying; at that point I had known her for five years, and had never heard her use it. She indicated that she never had done so by making the sign of a zero over her eye.

I asked her if this phrase had ever come up over the last twenty years of her channelings with the Council. She said that to the best of her knowledge, it never had.

I then asked her why she thought it might have showed up right now. She said something like, "You were asking about ducks, you wanted to know what it meant, you had no idea, and the Council had the answer."

As a scientist, I have not conducted formal experiments to examine whether there really is a spiritual Council. But regardless of "where" the message actually came from, the message itself was most curious. After all that haranguing, to then hear something that completely fit was surely far beyond chance. I felt that I had to take seriously the seemingly silly duck synchronicities.

As I explored with the group their current and past associations with ducks, more curious synchronicities emerged.

10. Tuesday evening, Feb 19 — *Martha shared her dream about Groucho Marx, and Betty told us she was reading "Duck Soup."*

Martha shared a dream she had experienced a few days earlier which featured an appearance by Groucho Marx. I asked Martha if she had ever dreamt about Groucho Marx before; she said no, and she had no idea why she had dreamt of him now.

Then Betty shared how she happened to be re-reading a book called "Duck Soup" about the Marx brothers!

This jogged my memory. As a child I had loved the Groucho Marx show, especially the duck that would fall out of the sky. I would watch it with my father.

And why did the duck fall out of the sky? It had a message in its mouth! The duck was, so to speak, "channeling"!

I could barely suppress my laughter.

11. Tuesday evening, Feb 19 — *The intuitive told us about her pet duck Daisy, and that night I read about a character named Daisy in my novel.*

Christine shared that she had a pet duck named Daisy. I assumed that having a pet duck was not all that uncommon, so I took Christine's duck experience with a grain or two of salt and dismissed it.

However, later that night while reading the Parker novel *High Profile,* I was introduced to a new character named Daisy. I knew that Daisy was not a common name in mystery novels. The timing of learning of Christine's duck being named Daisy and the new character in my Parker novel being named Daisy increased the likelihood that I should include Daisy the Duck as a probable duck synchronicity.

12. Tuesday evening, Feb 19 — *Rhonda shared her transformative story when she and her mother healed a baby duck.*

Much less common than having a pet duck is when two people—a daughter and mother—have a memorable experience using spiritual healing to heal a duck. Rhonda shared a very moving story with me about the apparent healing of a duck, which had happened when she was in college. I suspect that if we randomly sampled a thousand people, only a small number would report such an experience. What was important for Rhonda, and the group, was the sense that perhaps her connection to ducks would prove to be important. As you will see, she discovered an amazing one the next night.

Side Bar: Remembering Ducks in My Life

When Rhonda and I arrived home that night, we discussed ducks. The more we talked, the more I realized that I had a connection to ducks that I had forgotten.

Part of the reason I record synchronicities as they occur is because it is very easy to forget them and/or distort them.

I remembered that I used to have a walking stick with a duck handle. This was important, because I recalled looking at many different walking sticks before choosing the one with the duck.

I remembered that I had a golden-colored duck statue that was on my desk when I was at Yale.

I remembered that I had collected carved ducks during the period of time that I was at Harvard and used to vacation in Maine. The ducks were maybe four or five inches long, finely carved and quite beautiful. I don't remember what happened to them.

Then I remembered feeding ducks as a child. Lots of people enjoy feeding ducks, but I vaguely remembered seeing a home movie of myself as a child feeding ducks as well.

I recalled that I had an old VHS tape of clips from my parents' home movies that my brother had put together. I had not watched it in maybe five years. I dug up the tape, and Rhonda and I watched it together. Sure enough, there were two segments showing me as a child feeding ducks.

I could no longer claim that I had no prior affection or appreciation for ducks. They were part of my personal past.

Was this significant? I did not know, save for the fact that Christine, who purportedly channeled divine beings, had harangued me claiming that God had picked this symbol because I resonated with it.

It appears that she/"They" were right.

13. Wednesday lunch, Feb 20	*Dr. K told me that Dr. D lives on "Three Duck Lane" (named in Spanish).*

On Wednesdays I serve as the corporate Director of Development of Energy Healing at Canyon Ranch. This was not a day to ponder ducks. In fact, I wanted a mini vacation from ducks. However, I felt the need to share with two colleagues some of my evolving duck experiences. One of them was a physician whom I will call Dr. K.

Would Canyon Ranch have a potential duck connection? I did not seek an answer, and was afraid to ask. However, Dr. K brought up that Dr. D, a distinguished senior member of Canyon Ranch who had recruited me and who carries the torch for Energy Healing and Spiritual Wellness at the Ranch, apparently lives on a street whose Spanish name "via Tres Patos" happens to mean "Three Ducks Lane."

I found this interesting because (1) Dr. K brought this up spontaneously, and (2) I had requested something very unlike me and asked the Council group the night before if they knew how to say "duck" in Spanish!

I knew I would have to contact Dr. D and verify whether this was factually correct. As it turned out, I did not have to request an appointment with Dr. D; he literally bumped into me.

14. Wednesday evening, Feb 20	*Just before my lecture, I bumped into Dr. D and he confirmed his street was named* "Three Ducks Lane."

On Wednesday evenings in those days I gave a regular lecture at Canyon Ranch based on my book *The Energy Healing Experiments.* I almost never saw Dr. D in the evenings. However, whom did I bump into that Wednesday night, but Dr. D. We gave each other a hug, and with some trepidation I asked him about his street address. To my surprise, he confirmed that it meant "Three Ducks Lane." I shared that earlier that afternoon I had received the nickname "Ducktor Schwartz" from Dr. K, and that I would someday share with Dr. D some emerging synchronicities about ducks.

How many people live on a street not only named after a duck, but three ducks to boot? It was one thing for Dr. K to have known this fact about Dr. D and to have brought it up; it was another for me to then bump into Dr. D and confirm it.

I was convinced there would be no more duck synchronicities that evening. I was wrong, again.

15. Wednesday evening, Feb 20	*Charles and Laurie Finklestein called and told Rhonda about "Honk!" (a musical based on the story of the Ugly Duckling).*

By the time I got home from the lecture, I was exhausted. Rhonda was on the phone, and she seemed very excited by something. She announced that I needed to speak with Charles and Laura and hear about a remarkable synchronicity with them involving ducks! And then she handed me the phone.

Ducks again?

Rhonda and I were married in their unique custom-built home—a castle-like structure whose design was based on sacred geometry. We had not spoken with them in about a month.

When Charles and Laurie happened to call that night, for some reason Rhonda felt moved to ask them about whether they were experiencing anything right then involving ducks.

Oh boy.

They explained that their children were currently rehearsing to perform in a musical called "Honk!" based upon the story of the Ugly Duckling, and that they had been singing duck songs in the car all week! They began to notice other duck synchronicities in their lives (some of which they shared with us, but which I did not write down).

How many families would you guess at that moment had kids who were performing in a musical about ducks, and who were singing duck songs in their parents' car all week?

16. Thursday evening, Feb 21	*Dr. K sees Tucson "Adopt a Duck" month on TV.*

As far as I know, ducks did not come up again with Mr. J or others during our conversations at dinner. However, when I arrived home after dinner and Rhonda and I began to review our respective days, Dr. K called up laughing hysterically. He had just turned on the TV and saw a commercial for the Tucson "Adopt a Duck Month"!

Apparently, the Tucson Lung Association was raising funds through "Adopt a Duck Month" in Tucson. The next day, Dr. K found their website which described their "Tucson Ducky Derby."

I am not sure whether Dr. K and I ever laughed so hard together in our lives.

17. Friday morning, Feb 22 *I was on Mary Occhino's Sirius Radio show, where she mentioned a "water off a duck's back" story.*

For a few years, on Friday mornings at 10:15 am EST, I regularly did a half-hour interview with Mary Occhino on her successful radio show on Sirius XM satellite radio, titled "Angels on Call."

I wondered, *would ducks show up on her show?* They seemed to be showing up everywhere else at that time.

Mary accepts callers, and that day a woman named PG called who was excited because she had very much wanted to hear my interview with Mary, but had a client scheduled at that time. However, at the last minute the client had cancelled. PG was able to turn on the satellite radio, listen to the start of the segment, make a call, and actually get through.

She explained that she was a psychic who was good at seeing predictions and synchronicities in other people's lives, but had difficulty knowing when a dream or intuition applied to her own life.

Mary explained that one way we can know if there is something meaningful happening is if a dream or intuition is accompanied by a coincidence in our life—which Mary interprets as a "miracle"—and if a third related event occurs, she then takes the information very seriously.

Hearing this conversation, I felt intuitively that I should ask on the air if either of them had recently had any duck synchronicities.

Mary became very animated, and explained that on various occasions the previous week she had spontaneously used duck metaphors! She even had her producer confirm this on the air.

She explained that it had begun with a caller who was experiencing stress, and for some reason Mary had felt intuitively compelled to use the metaphor "water running off the back of a duck" as a way of helping the caller. She claims she never used duck metaphors, and did not know why she was using it then.

18. Friday morning, Feb 22 *The caller on the phone, PG, mentioned her grandfather's pet duck.*

The woman Mary currently had on the air, PG, then explained that her grandfather had recently died, and that the day before she had been speaking with a relative who was explaining in some detail how her grandfather had a pond with a pet duck that used to follow him around. She thought it was odd that this would come up in their conversation.

The combination of the caller wanting to talk to me specifically, facilitated by the canceling of her client, the fact that she was able to get through, her being a psychic, her question to Mary about how one knows when a message applies to our own life, the reference to synchronicity, my then feeling compelled to bring up ducks, and then the revelation of both of them having duck stories at this precise moment in their lives.... well, the combination seemed "too coincidental to be accidental," as Susy Smith used to say. This becomes important below.

19. Friday morning, Feb 22 *Mr. J. came over, received an "Adopt a Duck" printout, and shared his town's name "Susy duck."*

Following the show with Mary, I went to my email and found Dr. K's message mentioning the "Adopt a Duck" website. I went to the site, and decided to print it out for Mr. J. Just as the printer finished printing, who arrived at our door, but Mr. J.

I welcomed him, handed him the printout, and explained what had transpired with Dr. K and then Mary Occhino.

Mr. J then shared the story of how the town with his postal box had something to do with a "Susy" duck.

I realized that this was super-profound, not simply because he lived in a "duck" named town and was at that time considering moving to Tucson, which was currently celebrating "Adopt a Duck Month," but that the duck town had the name Susy.

I explained who Susy Smith was, her close extended family relationship with me, and her profound statement "It's too coincidental to be accidental."

What Does This All Mean?

Let's assume for the moment that if it walks and talks like a duck, then it probably is a duck.

Let's assume that this degree of Type III duck synchronicity—19 in a six-day period—is so far beyond chance that we can infer that some sort of a higher intelligence is required to orchestrate such a sequence of synchronicities.

Let's further assume that the hypothesized One Mind orchestrating these events might be trying to get a message across, one that is both serious and playful.

Could the message be that it was time for us to symbolically "walk like a duck" concerning synchronicities and the reality of the One Mind?

If we can apply the "walks like a duck" metaphor to evidence concerning survival of consciousness, why can't we apply the "walks like a duck" metaphor to evidence concerning the existence of the One Mind itself?

If the evidence "walks like Higher Intelligence," and it "talks like Higher Intelligence," maybe it is Higher Intelligence.

Well, if it is, it sure has a quack-like sense of humor.

Chapter 10
Lessons from Bear Synchronicities
Lesson: Going Inside is Essential for Discovering Synchronicities

Everything in life I share, except, of course, my teddy bear!
Author Unknown

One would think that after experiencing multiple Type III duck supersynchronicities that I would be prepared for anything. The fact is, I had not yet learned the phrase "Do not underestimate the universe." The duck synchronicities were, so to speak, a necessary step on the ladder of my awakening to synchronicity that would take me to, of all creatures, bears, including teddy bears.

As an adult, I had some Southwest Native American sculptures of bears, and even a Pacific Northwest Coast carved wooden bear mask (with a loon on its head). I do not recall having had a teddy bear as a child. I do remember an adorable fuzzy monkey puppet, a great set of Lionel electric trains, a truck with a shovel I could sit on that actually picked up dirt, but no teddy bears. Though I have admired bears over the years—their strength and beauty—I was basically afraid of them, and frankly knew little about them.

However, all that changed when a Type III bear synchronicity began to unfold. With it came some profound lessons that led to my increased understanding of the presence of synchronicities and the process of discovering them.

Since most of the people involved in these synchronicities prefer anonymity, I will only use the names of those who are comfortable being mentioned in this context.

"You Are Such a Teddy Bear"

My awakening to bear synchronicities began with a seemingly offhand comment—which apparently was meant as a compliment—that was said to me in Los Angeles after I had given an invited address at a conference on energy healing. The mother of a distinguished healthcare professional and healer came up to me, thanked me for my presentation and my honoring of her son's work, and then proclaimed, "You are such a teddy bear."

She went on to explain how my friendly and playful demeanor, coupled with my somewhat overweight and non-threatening physique, reminded her of a cuddly teddy bear.

Over the years I have occasionally been described as a teddy bear, but her statement was the first in the past few years, and probably the most emphatic. Though I was not aware of it at the time, it became Event #1.

A few days later, I had lunch with a colleague and a husband and wife team of energy healers at the Arizona Inn. The husband had been a successful businessman who had retired and then became a healer. The wife felt moved to share with me a technique she had discovered to help do "distant healing"—healing people over tens, hundreds, or even thousands of miles—especially for "spiritual protection," as she called it. What she would do was imagine a team of "teddy bears" and send them to protect the person.

Of course, I had no idea whether her imagined team of teddy bears had any effect—placebo or otherwise—on her distant clients. What I did realize was that I had never heard of such a treatment strategy before, and it happened on the heels of being called "such a teddy bear." This became Event #2.

I asked her why she had picked the teddy bear, and she explained how most children loved teddy bears and felt safe in their presence. Then my colleague reminded me that when we were doing our "master healer" experiments, the healers were requested to send healing energy to a large teddy bear that was placed in a chair near them.

I had forgotten about this novel aspect of our experimental methodology, and when we returned from lunch, I asked my colleague to show the bear to the husband and wife team as well as myself. Sure enough, there was the three-foot high, tan colored, adorable teddy bear. This was Event #3.

I asked my colleague why she had chosen the teddy bear as the "standardized non-living control subject." She told me that her daughter had collected over a hundred teddy bears, and so it seemed natural to her to choose one for this purpose.

How many colleagues or friends do you know who have a child that has collected over one hundred teddy bears? Two, five, ten, maybe twenty—but over one hundred? I realized this was Event #4.

At this point, my synchronicity antenna was up. I had entered into synchronicity alert mode.

A few days later, I had my weekly radio interview with Mary Occhino. I would usually receive a call ten to fifteen minutes before the actual interview with Mary so that I could hear her conversations with callers. On this day, what did I hear? Mary was taking about giving a teddy bear gift on the show!

I had been on Mary's show probably a hundred times by then, and I could not recall ever having heard Mary bring up teddy bears before. Event #5.

After the show, I was scheduled to bring my Land Rover Discovery in for an oil change. After checking in at the garage, I looked through the cases of Land Rover-related items for sale.

What caught my eye was a single Land Rover teddy bear!

The bear was maybe a foot high, and was dressed in a cute hiking outfit, from boots to hat, and including a tiny Land Rover shirt.

The timing of this observation was most curious. Aware that this could be an example of the VW bug effect, I asked the salesperson who handled these items how many Land Rover teddy bears they had in stock, and how often they carried them.

She explained that this was the only Land Rover bear she had, and that they had only stocked a handful over the past few years.

I could not resist: I bought the bear! I had no idea what I would do with it, or where I would place it, but I sensed I should keep it as a memento. This teddy bear became Event #6. (I have since returned to this dealership probably a dozen times since that day, and they have never had any more Land Rover teddy bears.)

After paying for the bear and service to my car, I placed the bear on the passenger seat next to me, and we drove to my University of Arizona laboratory. On the way, we passed the Harley Davidson store (which has since changed locations), and for some reason I decided to stop in. I was not consciously seeking to purchase anything; the idea seemingly just popped into my head.

I knew the manager at the time, and we greeted each other with a hug. He told me that it was curious timing for me to drop in, because a few nights earlier, he had been having a conversation with his sister-in-law who was visiting from out of town, and she explained that she had become a Reiki healer. The manager shared with her how he knew a professor at the University of Arizona who conducted research on energy healing.

Struck by the timing, and remembering the little guy sitting in my car, I decided to walk through the Harley Davidson kids section—something I rarely did—and remembered they had a large teddy bear display.

I reasoned:

- since I had not planned to visit the dealership that day,
- since the manager was having a synchronous experience with me related to energy healing, and
- since my first three teddy bear synchronicities all were related to energy healing, then

- I decided that I should get the little Land Rover guy a friend.

I selected a cute one-foot tall bear decked out in Harley Davidson attire, from boots to cap, with a little Harley Davidson shirt. I returned to my car, and placed the Harley Davidson bear next to the little Land Rover one. This experience at the Harley Davidson store became Event #7.

What was I going to do with two teddy bears? I had no time to think about it, because mid-afternoon I had to return home, pack, and drive to the airport for my planned trip to Lenox, Massachusetts. I was scheduled to give two invited lectures at the Canyon Ranch Resort in Lenox for "Celebrating Spirituality" week.

Little did I know that the bear synchronicities would escalate even beyond the duck synchronicities.

My Propitious Time with Dr. Ellerby

When I got to the Tucson airport, I bumped into Dr. Jonathan Ellerby, previously the Spiritual Program Director at Canyon Ranch, and author of *Return to the Sacred*. Dr. Ellerby had conceived and orchestrated "Celebrating Spirituality" week, and he was the featured speaker.

Though we were not seated together on the flight, we relished the fact that we would have time to commune in the Tucson Airport, the Denver Airport, and the ride from the Hartford Airport to Lenox.

Dr. Ellerby was aware that I was immersed in pondering the meaning of synchronicities, and how it could be possible for novelists and movie script writers to create specific images and phrases that could be precisely timed with certain people's lives.

Were these seeming synchronicities nothing more than meaningless connections made possible by very large numbers? In other words, could my moments of connection between a specific author's book and events in my life, or Dr. Ellerby's moments of connection between a specific script writer's movie and events in his own life, be explained entirely as chance occurrences?

Or was more involved?

Dr. Ellerby shared with me his belief that because creative writers tend to go inward to seek inspiration, and also because they are spontaneous, that they are more likely to "pick up" sacred transmissions and spiritual guidance that play a key role in the orchestration of complex synchronicities.

Dr. Ellerby speaks from a wealth of education and experience. He is a scholar of comparative religions as well as consciousness studies, and he has trained with distinguished Native religious leaders, medicine men, shamans, and healers. However, his views must also be put to the test.

We were in the Denver Airport at the time, and I vividly recall the moment when a deep insight—and a testable hypothesis—came to me. I realized that if there were a One Mind, a Higher Intelligence, and if it were "broadcasting" certain universal messages, then it would probably function as a clever "spiritual opportunist" and use any and every receptive being to receive Its messages.

This "God as Opportunist" hypothesis implied that It would seek out and find any source that could hear It, including creative authors of books and movies as well as open-minded, inwardly-aware healthcare practitioners, spiritual counselors, and even scientists. It could even conceivably include animals (and I was not planning to refer here to stuffed ones, but we may have to open ourselves to such a possibility).

I had not yet shared with Dr. Ellerby my seemingly silly teddy bear synchronicities—I mean, how could teddy bears have anything to do with intuition, inner awareness, and God as Opportunist?

However, I felt I should tell him, but before I could, it was time for us to get on our flight from Denver to Hartford, and Dr. Ellerby suggested we stop at a coffee shop on our way to our gate to pick up something to drink. I had not noticed the coffee shop, being completely "lost in thought." However, I was happy to comply, and I insisted on treating.

I went up to the counter, and my knees buckled. Sitting on the counter were two teddy bears.

Since before that morning I had not paid attention to teddy bears in stores, I had no idea how common teddy bears were at this particular coffee chain (I would soon discover they were fairly common).

However, what was odd, and noteworthy, was that I had been lost in thought, struggling with whether I should tell Dr. Ellerby about my emerging teddy bear synchronicities, and it was Dr. Ellerby who noticed the coffee shop and suggested we stop. The truth is, I would have gone right past the shop, as it was tucked in the corner to our left as we were walking by.

No, I did not purchase a third teddy bear. However, I did ask Dr. Ellerby if he would use my camera and take some pictures of me with the teddy bears, with the promise that I would explain later. This was Event #8.

I could never have guessed that the teddy bears would be a sign for my next core lesson in understanding the symbolic nature of at least one subset of synchronicities.

Dr. Ellerby's Bear Connections and the Shamanic Symbolism of Bears

I will never forget what I felt when I finally confessed, somewhat sheepishly, the emerging teddy bear synchronicities to Dr. Ellerby. I witnessed his complex reaction, and then received his enlightening explanation.

As I told the story of these synchronicities, Dr. Ellerby's facial expression shifted from shock to delight, from wonder to sadness, from playfulness to reverence. The reason for the complexity of his reaction was not only because Dr. Ellerby had a deep historic and spiritual connection with bears—which I did not know at the time—but that his understanding of the shamanic meaning of bears provided a key to the mystery that was plaguing me.

It is not my place to reveal Dr. Ellerby's bear history. However, I can share the Native American meaning of bears, as expressed in two classic books on the symbolic meaning of animals, *Medicine Cards* by Jamie Sams and David Carson, and *Animal Speak* by Ted Andrews. These two books have informed Dr. Ellerby's opinions on the subject.

For the record, prior to my experience with Dr. Ellerby, I had read such books as if they were novels. Prior to my synchronicity awakening, they were like Mother Goose to me—myths and fables, not potential symbolic expressions of meaningful qualities or aspects of reality.

According to Sams and Carson, the bear is a symbol of "Introspection." The poem that introduces the bear is as follows (formatted as it appeared in their book):

Bear
Invite me
Into the Cave
Where silence surrounds
The answers you gave.

To Andrews, what he terms the "Keynote" of the bear is:

Awakening the Power of the Unconscious.

Sams and Carson end their discussion of the bear with the following sentences:

> In choosing Bear, the power of knowing has invited you to enter the silence and become acquainted with the Dream Lodge, so that your goals may become concrete realities. This is the strength of Bear.

In his book, Andrews states that:

> It is a reminder for those with this totem to go within to awaken the power, but only by bringing it out into the open and applying it will the honey of life be tasted.

You can see the interrelated themes of introspection, awakening the power of the unconscious, the power of knowing, entering the silence, going within, inviting the questions, and being provided answers.

These themes all speak to the intuitive side of discovering and interpreting synchronicities. As mentioned previously, I have come to envision synchronicity seeking like typing. Just as our ability to type is enhanced when we integrate the use of both hands, our ability to discover and interpret synchronicities is enhanced when we integrate both reasoning and intuition.

So let me get this straight:

Did the "Opportunistic universe" know that it could awaken me to the fundamental Message of Bear—the essential role of introspection and quiet reflection in the detection and understanding of synchronicities—by being extremely clever and resourceful, using a complex set of "teddy bears" to ultimately get me to the Bear?

I saw the brilliance of the tactic, and marveled at how this might actually be true.

However, I would take more convincing (much more), before I could seriously entertain such a hypothesis. Once again, I said in my mind, *universe, if this is real, please reveal it in a way that can be documented.*

And once again, I was reminded of the phrase, "Be careful what you ask for".

The Continuity of Encouragement Regarding Bears

As you might have guessed, the bear synchronicities continued unabated. I will share the next four that happened in the series; to continue beyond that point might result in bear synchronicity overload.

Event #9 was very strange. I gave my lecture about *The G.O.D. Experiments* book and confessed the first series of raven synchronicities that I had encountered. To my surprise and delight, the audience was for the most part intrigued, if not enthralled.

When I returned to my room, I noticed that on the floor, opposite my room's door, were a dozen long-stemmed red roses and, if you can believe it, a teddy bear.

I actually sat down on the floor and photographed it. I have probably stayed in at least five hundred hotel rooms in my life, and I could not recall ever having seen a teddy bear in a hallway opposite my door (or any door).

As it so happened, the woman occupying the room opposite mine arrived as I was getting up from the floor. I asked her if the bear and the flowers belonged to her, and she said yes. She explained that it was her birthday, and that they had been delivered for her as a gift. However, she was unhappy that they had been left unattended outside her door. (I subsequently learned that Canyon Ranch's policy is to place such gifts inside a guest's room.)

Why was the mistake made in this instance? Was it for me to see the teddy bear, with roses to boot? Was the universe being opportunistic, clever, and resourceful? Was it attempting to provide evidence that could be documented?

Event #10 was even stranger. One of the physicians at Canyon Ranch in Lenox invited me to visit her home; I will call her Dr. T. I have only been invited by one other Canyon Ranch physician to visit their home.

I was honored to accept the invitation. Dr. T's home had two front entrances, the main one leading to her living room, which was quite fancy and filled with art, and a second one leading to her family room; we took the latter entrance. When I walked into her front room, my knees buckled again.

Sitting on a chair in the family room was a gigantic, four-foot tall teddy bear. Another fairly large one was sitting on the sofa, and there were other teddy bears sprinkled around the room.

Out of all the homes I have visited, I could not recall ever having visited one where the owner was so attracted to teddy bears that she featured them so prominently in a room like this. (For the record, there were no young children living in the house.)

It turns out that she had a special affinity to bears, which extended beyond the family room to other rooms in her home.

Was this another sign from the universe?

Event #11.

Later on in the week, a particular guest was quite taken with my talk on *The G.O.D. Experiments,* and we spoke privately. He was reading a novel that happened to take place in the Pacific Northwest Coast and which mentioned ravens, and he asked me if I would like to read it. I was thrilled with the gift.

I forgot to include the book's title in the notes I took at the time these events occurred (the same notes I am referencing while writing his chapter). However, my notes clearly indicate that a bear was featured prominently in the plotline of the book.

How many times has a stranger given me the novel they were reading? I cannot remember another instance. Was this another "opportunistic moment" for a resourceful One Mind to act?

Finally, Event #12. I was being driven back to the Hartford Airport, and the driver and I engaged in conversation. He asked me about my current writing, and I told him I was beginning to work on a book on synchronicities. I then shared with him some of the emerging teddy bear / bear synchronicities. He became super-excited because, only a few days prior to speaking with me, he had been driving on a country road less than a few miles from Canyon Ranch, where he had seen a bear crossing the road. He had pulled over so that he and his passenger could watch the bear amble across to the other side.

I asked him, "How often do you come upon bears crossing the road while driving?" Since he is a professional driver, he spends significant time on the road. He said he could not remember the precise frequency, but prior to this, he had not seen a bear crossing the road in at least the previous two to three years.

Was this yet another sign, this time with a real bear?

Getting the Message

I have come to recognize, and finally accept, that it is not only my openness to synchronicities that leads me to see them more frequently. Nor am I (at least consciously) "making" these synchronicities appear.

I am an avid and apparently accomplished "watcher" of synchronicities, and it appears that I have been quite adept in surfing them as well. Moreover, it appears that I may be "attracting" them, partly because I now speak openly about them, and also because I "ask for signs" as well. However, it also appears that I have been getting ever more proficient at "tuning in" to them, not only as a "surfer" but also as a "participator," in the sense that I seem to "go with the flow" of synchronicities relatively effortlessly.

If there is a guiding process—a "wave-like" process (e.g., like waves on an ocean), as hypothesized in quantum physics—then my ability to detect and follow the grand wave may be playing an increasing role in my discovery of synchronicities, as well as my understanding of their possible meaning.

First ducks, and now teddy bears. Would you believe me if I told you it is now time for the Emerald City, and Oz?

Chapter 11
The Green Emerald and the Magic of Oz
Lesson: Supersynchronicities Can Reveal True Magic

The power of Thought,
the magic of the Mind!
Lord Byron

We have explored a number of seemingly impossible—some might say "magical"—super-improbable sequences of synchronistic events, from 11s, dragonflies, and ravens to roses, ducks, and bears. These fact-based accounts sometimes sound like a complex mixture of *Alice in Wonderland, Harry Potter,* the *Da Vinci Code,* and *The Twelve,* all rolled into one. And they are only a small fraction of the total number of Type III Synchronicities I have observed since beginning the practice of synchronicity self-science.

However, of all the seemingly miraculous aspects of this true-life journey of discovery, the one that fills me with the most humility, wonder, and awe is the fact that the human mind—our minds—can discover such incredible patterns in the first place, and that we can then collectively think about these patterns and potentially make sense of them. We can develop our personal super minds to discover these complex relationships.

Some people may find it difficult to fathom how it could be possible for 19 duck synchronicities to have been conceived and coordinated within a six-day period. And as Dr. Feynman reminds us, most physicists cannot fathom how light can be a wave extending out infinitely into space, and also be a "massless particle" precisely localized in space (the photon being a particle with apparent zero rest mass). However, our minds can readily record the ducks, measure the photons, and discover their seemingly impossible—if not "magical"—qualities, even if we cannot understand their essence or meaning, at least at present.

As I began to entertain the possibility that I was being "taught" about the nature and purpose of synchronicity, one synchronicity at a time, the appearance of "green emerald" synchronicities heralded another great awakening. I began to wonder: *could the synchronicity process be leading me to acknowledge, and subsequently celebrate, the power and magic of our own minds to discover the power and magic of synchronicity?*

Here's what happened.

It Began With a Strange Analogy

It was February 23rd, 2008, and I had just received a copy in the mail of a book titled *Irreligion: A Mathematician Explains Why Arguments for God Just Don't Add Up* by Dr. John Allen Paulos.

The details of this witty and critical (as well as sometimes curiously illogical) book, though interesting, are not pertinent here. What is important is that early on in the book, the author drew a strange analogy by saying, and I paraphrase slightly, "All emeralds are green. What would it mean if you found a red one?"

I was reminded of Professor William James' famous example: "If you wish to upset the law that all crows are black, you need only find one white crow". I wrote a note about this in my copy of *Irreligion,* and didn't think anything more about it. However, I would soon realize that writing notes about this analogy was to become Event #1.

Later that afternoon, after completing my writing for the day, I turned on the television and discovered that *The Wiz* was playing. The movie, released in 1978, was based on the acclaimed 1975 Broadway musical that garnered seven Tony awards, including the award for Best Musical. The story is based on the Wizard of Oz, and much of the story takes place in Emerald City.

I had not seen the Broadway show or the movie before. However, I did purchase a soundtrack of the show shortly after I started my tenure at Yale in 1976, and quickly learned all the songs by heart. The lyrics were bright and clever, and the music was upbeat and bouncy. I would often sing along with a cassette tape of the soundtrack in my car on my commute from Guilford to New Haven.

As I watched the movie, the connection between Dr. Paulos' green emerald analogy and *The Wiz's* portrayal of Emerald City caught my attention. This became Event #2.

There was an improbable timing of a combination of several events:

- the book *Irreligion* arriving that February morning,
- me noticing the green emerald / red emerald analogy in the book (I had never come across such an analogy before),
- *The Wiz* being on television that afternoon (it is not often broadcast), and
- me turning on the television on a Saturday afternoon and finding the movie playing (I rarely watch television on Saturday afternoons).

Nevertheless, these Type I Synchronicities could have been mere chance or coincidence, and at the time I treated them as such.

However, later that night, I was startled to notice in the mystery novel *The Closet of Curiosities* (the Preston and Child novel I was reading at the time) that the authors described a huge green emerald in the office of the Director of a New York City museum. I could not remember the last time I had read about a large green emerald featured in a mystery or science fiction book. This became Event #3.

The following morning, I returned to the novel and read how the wife of the museum Director was wearing a large green emerald. This became Event #4.

At this point I knew next to nothing about emeralds: their colors, chemical makeup, history, or symbolism. My own jewelry was limited to silver or gold, turquoise stones (due to my devotion to Native American art), and a single diamond (the dramatic synchronicity involving this diamond was reported in some detail in a chapter in *The G.O.D. Experiments).*

Consequently, I decided to ask Rhonda if she knew anything about emeralds. What she told me was revealing and timely.

First, I learned that Rhonda's birthstone was the emerald. To confess my ignorance, I know virtually nothing about birthstones, and would not have guessed that it was Rhonda's stone. Though the chance was one in twelve that Rhonda's birthstone could have been an emerald, it qualified as Event #5, given its timing with the previous instances involving emeralds.

Second, Rhonda had spent the previous twelve years of her life in Seattle, where we were also married, and Seattle is sometimes referred to as the Emerald City. The Seattle / Emerald City connection really took me by surprise, and it became Event #6.

Third, Rhonda shared with me that she had a book on the "Emerald Tablets" referring to "Thoth" (also known as Enoch). The reason this was curious was because the place in the house where I typically read novels at that time featured a painting by a local artist that had been gifted to me, which portrayed an Egyptian character that turned out to be Thoth. In other words, I was reading about emerald analogies (Event #1), a huge green emerald in the Director's office (Event #3), and the wife of the Director wearing a large green emerald (Event #4) in the presence of a painting portraying a character described in the "Emerald Tablets." This became Event #7.

At this point, it seemed prudent to educate myself on green emeralds. As fate would have it, that night I was scheduled to introduce Professor Rustum Roy, a distinguished materials scientist and member of the National Academy of Sciences, at his lecture on new research on the structure of water at the University of Arizona School of Medicine.

Dr. Roy had published many hundreds of scientific papers related to materials and gems, and I thought he might be a good source of expert information.

We were scheduled to have dinner with a group of colleagues, including Dr. Iris Bell. Dr. Bell has both an MD and PhD, and we have been colleagues and friends for almost forty years. (I mention her expressly because of what was about to transpire in our upcoming research meeting. But this is getting a bit ahead of the story.)

The first hint that green emerald synchronicities were ramping up came when Rhonda and I arrived at the restaurant, and ended up being seated next to Dr. Bell and two of her friends who were visiting from out of town. Rhonda pointed out to me that all three of them were wearing green outfits!

I could not remember the last time I was surrounded by women all wearing green attire. I asked Dr. Bell about this, and she too was surprised. She claimed that each of them had dressed for the evening independently, and yet had all ended up wearing the same color. Because of its oddity, I considered this to be Event #8 (especially in light of what I learned in our subsequent research meeting, to be revealed below).

While I did not have time to tell Dr. Roy anything about my emerging interest in emeralds, or what had transpired over the previous two days, we did have a brief conversation after dinner. It turned out that one of his PhD students was not only an authority on emeralds, but held a patent for growing man-made emeralds. Given the timing of my emerging emerald awareness and my dinner with Dr. Roy, I interpreted this as Event #9.

We traveled in separate cars from the restaurant to the university auditorium where Dr. Roy was speaking. I gave my brief introduction and then Dr. Roy gave his formal lecture, which was approximately an hour long.

Somewhere in the middle of the lecture, Dr. Roy said something utterly unique. Apparently spontaneously, he decided to use the "black crow" quote from Professor William James. However, what he said was: "In order to disprove the law that all crows are black, you need only find one *green* crow."

He later claimed that he was not aware of why the William James crow quote had popped into his head at that moment. He also was not aware that he had misrepresented the color analogy of the quote by replacing the "white crow" with a "green crow."

The birthing of the green emerald synchronicities began with me reading a bizarre analogy about green versus red emeralds, and the parallel to Professor James' "black crow—white crow" comparison did not escape me. Only two days after reading this analogy, a distinguished professor spontaneously uses the Professor James quote and unknowingly replaced the word "white" with "green." This became Event #10.

It was clear that something at least as bizarre as the duck and bear synchronicities was going on. It was also clear that the synchronicities involved connections between many people, including multiple MD's and PhD's.

The Green Emerald Synchronicities Escalate

The next week contained a slew of creative and amusing emerald synchronicities. I will highlight a few to give you the flavor of their persistence.

For example, when I met with Dr. Bell for our research meeting and asked her whether she had any connection to emeralds, she shared three facts, each of which qualified as a synchronicity.

First, she explained that she had recently purchased an expensive piece of jewelry featuring a green emerald. This was timely because, according to Dr. Bell, it was the only fine piece of jewelry she had purchased in years. Event #11.

Second, she told me that she had a favorite emerald green toy laser sword (a lightsaber), apparently a favored color of the Jedi Warriors in Star Wars. Though I knew Dr. Bell had an appreciation for Star Wars, I did not know it involved an emerald green lightsaber. Event #13.

Third, and most amazing, was that Dr. Bell was in the process of finishing a new book on alternative medicine, and the metaphor she employed throughout the book was of the Wizard of Oz, including mentions of Emerald City!

I had never met a professional who used the Wizard of Oz as a theme in their written work. The timing of this was sufficiently propitious to justify calling it Event #14.

Dr. Bell suggested (only partly tongue in cheek) that "maybe God was saying if you like this one, here is another one!"

Finally, I have to mention two green emerald synchronicities that connected Rhonda, Mary Occhino, and me. I had shared with Rhonda that night my earlier conversation with Dr. Bell. I then turned on the television, and the movie *Romancing the Stone* was playing. Rhonda immediately told me I needed to watch this film. I had probably seen the movie a couple of times over the years, but had little memory of the plot. It turned out that the reason why Rhonda wanted to watch the movie was that the stone they were seeking happened to be a large green emerald. Event #15.

In light of these synchronicities, I decided during my morning radio interview with Mary Occhino to ask her if she had had any connections to green emeralds—did they mean anything to her?

Mary got quite excited and shared that just the previous day, her "guides" had instructed her to go into a secondhand store where she had discovered, and almost purchased, a large costume ring that was crafted to look like a green emerald. Mary claimed that she did not own any green emeralds, and had never seriously thought of purchasing one, real or fake. Event #16.

Green Emeralds and the Wizard of Oz

As I pondered this confusing synchronicity mystery, the first thing that came to mind was that I had been terrified as a child by the original 1939 Wizard of Oz movie.

I was born in 1944, and recall seeing the Judy Garland movie when I was maybe four or five years old. I recall not only hiding behind the seats for much of it, but covering my eyes with my hands, every now and again peeking through the tiny slits between my fingers.

As I reflected on these childhood fears, I remembered the deep and frightening voice of the towering Wizard of Oz, the powerful and destructive tornado, and the hideous Wicked Witch of the West—especially her being dissolved toward the end of the story, screaming to her death as she melted into the floor. I had identified with the cowardly lion, in spades.

Meanwhile, people often tell me that I must have great courage not only to conduct research that integrates body, mind, and spirit, but also to share these discoveries with the general public in popular books addressing life after death, energy healing, and a greater spiritual reality.

However, I do not experience this as courage; I typically sense it as being a great opportunity for adventure and discovery, combined with a scientific and ethical responsibility to discern and share. Though I try to keep my child's heart alive, and appreciate the importance of maintaining a "beginner's mind," the fact is that I am a senior scientist who has been around the block many times.

What the green emeralds and the Wizard of Oz reminded me of, however, was the implicit, if not explicit, fear that is evoked by the bizarre, mostly unpredictable, and seemingly unimaginable nature of Type III Synchronicities.

This type of unusual evidence can evoke fear of the unknown as well as fear of the unknowable. In the face of an apparent all powerful and infinite intelligence orchestrating the universe, one can feel pretty insignificant, if not utterly powerless.

Then, of course, there is the fear of being duped, foolish, and stupid, if not insane, to believe that all this (and more) just might be true. Though the history of science is replete with examples of how experiments have revealed that some of our most cherished assumptions, beliefs, hypotheses, and theories were incomplete if not wholly incorrect, most of us do not relish making major mistakes, especially in pubic.

In my case, I often feel like I am between a rock and a hard place, and I have forebodings about either outcome.

On the one hand, if supersynchronicities are real, then extreme skeptics, as well as many senior mainstream scientists, will likely attack me as well as the work. This has been part of the history of science; I have experienced it many times before, and it continues to the present day.

On the other hand, if supersynchronicities are merely coincidences or can be adequately explained by other conventional causal mechanisms (recall the VW bug hypothesis), then a potential tidal wave of extreme (and supposed) spiritual people will likely attack me as well as the work. I have experienced firsthand the wrath of a handful of psychics and other supposedly spiritual people when their beliefs or values have been challenged.

So, there is potential for strong criticism whether I am right or wrong. Nonetheless, I know that there are a growing number of people who are becoming more open to these sorts of experiences, and they will want to understand them. This book is especially for those people.

However, an important reminder for all of us is that the Wizard of Oz was a professional illusionist who deceived his followers into believing he had great powers.

Who is living the illusion: evidence-based intuitive people witnessing (apparent) synchronicities, or materialist scientists dismissing them?

Which would be more frightening to you—to learn that a significant and growing number of highly educated, seemingly successful, and supposedly sane individuals were being duped by the complexity of life and expressing some sort of Logic Deficit Disorder, or that the universe was in some fundamental and deep way more "magical" than even our wildest fiction writers could conceive?

Among other uses, the emerald is apparently considered by many people to help calm a troubled mind. If that is true, then we have here an extraordinary juxtaposition of ideas. On the one hand, we see the multilevel terror explicitly and implicitly presented in the Wizard of Oz, combined with the multilevel solace and enlightenment explicitly and implicitly found in the symbolism of the green emerald. However, the predominance of these synchronicities was not about the Wizard of Oz story, but rather the green emerald stone itself, and secondarily the emerald green color.

It may also be helpful to briefly share with you two more emerald related synchronicities that occurred around the time of Dr. Paulo's green emerald analogy and Dr. Roy's "green crow" talk.

I happened to be driving along First Avenue in Tucson when I noticed what turned out to be an emerald green Chevy "muscle car." Unlike VW bugs, which are fairly common, how often do we come upon glaringly emerald green painted cars—be they old Chevy's (or VW's, for that matter)?

I then met Rhonda for lunch and told her about my close encounter with the emerald green car. We marveled at how relatively rare such an experience is, within the context of all the other related synchronicities.

After lunch, I spontaneously decided to have my (more conventionally-hued) black, sporty car washed. While the vehicle was going through the washing process and I was preparing to pay, Rhonda discovered that among the car wash's collection of model cars for sale was a glaringly emerald green muscle car! They had only one. As you can probably guess, I purchased it as a memento. To the best of my knowledge, that was the first (and only) emerald green anything I had ever purchased.

For the record, since that special day, Rhonda and I have had our respective cars washed at this establishment at least two dozen times, and we have never come upon another emerald green model car for sale.

If the universe, the Super Mind, the Great Spirit, the Ground of Being, the Infinite Intelligence, the One Mind—or whatever term you prefer—was somehow involved in orchestrating the slew of green emerald and emerald-associated events that were seemingly circling all around me during this period, the cleverness of Its selection deserves our deepest respect and awe.

However, what also deserves our deepest respect and awe is the power of our own minds to discover such amazing patterns in life and uncover their potential meanings. I could not agree more with Lord Byron when he said: "The power of Thought, the magic of the Mind!"

Yes, the reality of synchronicities has its challenges and associated fears, as implied via the parable of the Wizard of Oz. But it also reveals the power and magic not only implicit in the Synchronizing Process, but also in our minds that can discover it.

The green emerald is a symbol of:

- love,
- hope,
- prophecy,
- comfort,
- reason,
- wisdom, and
- spring

Not a bad combination of symbols!

If this involves the One Mind teaching us about Its synchronous nature, I humbly say, "thank you."

Chapter 12
Coincidence Science and My Supersynchronicity Tipping Point
Lesson: Self-Science is Key to Discovering Supersynchronicity

Synchronicity is an ever present reality
for those who have eyes to see.
Carl Jung

Sometimes it feels like I can no longer avoid synchronicities. It appears as if some sort of synchronicity floodgate has been opened which refuses to be closed. Though I still try from time to time to deny the existence of synchronicities, my attempts at avoidance have been regularly crushed by ever-increasing waves of seemingly impossible—yet surprisingly delightful—Type III Synchronicities.

One of my all-time favorite Type III Synchronicities—which might be described as my synchronicity tipping point—occurred in the context of attending my first university-based research seminar on the topic of synchronicity, which happened to be held when I first began the process of writing this book in 2008.

The seminar presentation was being given by Dr. Bernard Beitman, a former distinguished professor and chairman of the

Department of Psychiatry from the University of Missouri. The presentation took place at the Division of Perceptual Studies in the Department of Psychiatry and Neurobehavioral Sciences of the University of Virginia Health System.

It turned out that my learning about this particular synchronicity seminar was, in itself, a synchronicity.

Moreover, the numerous synchronicities associated with this scientific presentation on synchronicity continued to happen before, during, and immediately following the seminar.

As you are about to see, if there ever were a time for me to conclude that synchronicities were real—and that it was time for us to figure out how they operated and what they meant—that time was heralded by the events surrounding Dr. Beitman's synchronicity seminar.

Learning About the University of Virginia Synchronicity Seminar

In January of 2008, early in the process of writing this book, I was about to give an invited presentation in San Francisco at a conference sponsored by the Forever Family Foundation on the possibility of life after death.

The conference consisted of a "who's who" of scientists working in this controversial area. The speakers included Dr. Bruce Greyson, then the Carlson Professor of Psychiatry and Neurobehavioral Sciences and Director of the Division of Perceptual Studies at the University of Virginia Health Sciences.

I had known and admired Dr. Greyson for close to a decade, and I was looking forward to hearing him speak. On the first day of the conference, before either of us had given our respective presentations, we had the opportunity to have lunch and catch up.

While walking to the restaurant, Dr. Greyson shared a curious event that had happened to him recently. He told me that the previous week he had received two unsolicited manuscripts on the topic of synchronicity, one written by a psychiatrist, the other by a psychologist.

At this point, I had not told Dr. Greyson that I was writing a book about synchronicity. This became Event #1.

I said something to the effect of, "How interesting. Can you tell me about the manuscripts?"

Because Dr. Greyson had not yet read the manuscripts (and also did not have permission from the authors to share their information with others), he was not in a position to tell me about them.

However, he did mention that one of the authors, a respected academic psychiatrist, was scheduled to visit his family near the University of Virginia in March of that year, and Dr. Greyson had arranged for him to give a seminar on synchronicity at that time.

"Really?" I replied, "It turns out that I am going to be in Virginia in March, giving a keynote address at The Monroe Institute. Is The Monroe Institute near you?"

Dr. Greyson explained that the Institute was only a forty-five-minute car ride away. This became Event #2.

When we compared the date of the seminar and the date of my address, it turned out that the events were just two days apart! This became Event #3.

For the record, I had not been to Virginia for almost a decade. I asked Dr. Greyson if I could attend the seminar, and he said yes.

I was thrilled. Was it possible that somehow, seemingly independent events had been arranged so that I would have the opportunity to meet a respected senior scientist who was doing serious work in the area of synchronicity?

I further wondered whether it was a synchronicity that I was going to have the chance to attend a research seminar on synchronicity at this propitious time in my professional and personal life.

A Synchronicity Greets Me upon Arrival in Virginia

Rhonda accompanied me on the trip to Virginia. Our plane left Tucson on March 22nd at around 1 pm Mountain Standard Time, and we arrived at The Monroe Institute at around 10 pm Eastern Daylight Time. The Monroe Institute staff had graciously saved dinner for us, and we enjoyed our meals with two senior staff members.

I innocently asked them if anyone who had participated in activities at the Institute had been inspired to create their own offshoots or centers based upon Monroe's teachings.

We were told that a former Monroe Institute participant had in fact created his own center just outside the grounds of The Monroe Institute. If you can believe this, the institution was called The Synchronicity Center! This became Event #4.

When I heard this, I almost choked on my dinner. In addition to the synchronous timing of the Monroe Institute event and the synchronicity seminar that was taking place at the University of Virginia, I had now learned about the Synchronicity Center, just down the street from where we were having our meal.

Little did I know at the time that subsequent synchronicities—some involving the word "synchronicity" itself—would continue to unfold in ever more improbable ways.

A Synchronicity Article at the Division of Perceptual studies

The most striking synchronicity involving the word "synchronicity" itself occurred shortly after our arrival at the Division of Perceptual Studies. Dr. Greyson and his distinguished team of scientists had just moved into new headquarters there, and were in the process of setting up their computers, having their electrically-shielded subject research chamber assembled (it had arrived from the manufacturer that morning), and unpacking books for their new library.

On the floor were duplicate copies of various journals and magazines, and we were told that we were welcome to take some if we wished.

I noticed that amidst the piles of journals were some issues of a journal called *The Journal of Religion and Psychical Research* (JRPR), which now has a more contemporary title, *Journal of Spirituality and Consciousness Studies* (JSCS). This particular journal caught my eye because I had published two articles in the JRPR about research mediums contacting the late Susy Smith shortly after her passing, and Susy was the originator of the phrase "It's too coincidental to be accidental". This became Event #5.

I picked up a journal from the pile and skimmed the table of contents. To my utter amazement, the third article was titled *The Space Between: A Study in Synchronicity*. I could not believe my eyes. Event #6.

There I was, preparing to meet Dr. Beitman and hear him speak about his new research on synchronicity and what he calls coincidence science, and I was holding in my hands a journal containing an article with the word "synchronicity" in the title.

Moreover—and this is particularly significant—a research medium who had received a number of evidential and verified communications from Susy Smith since her passing had told me twice, both times within the previous two months, that she was being "guided" to impart to me the following key to solving how spirit communication and energy healing works:

"to look at the 'space between' the numbers in the mathematical series sometimes called the Golden Mean".

Hence, the title of the article was meaningful to me at multiple levels. This was Event #7.

The article was written by Michael Cocks (someone I had never heard of) who, at the time of the article's publication, was listed as the Vicar of Hororata, Canterbury, New Zealand, and former Chairman of the Christ Church Council of the Christ Church Diocesan World Development Committee.

I had no idea whether he or his article had any scientific credibility or significance. However, the title certainly caught my attention given the twice-offered advice that I pay attention to "the space between."

It turned out that there were multiple extra copies of this particular journal issue, which happened to be twenty-five years old at the time (published in October of 1982, Volume 5, Number 4). I decided to take one for Dr. Beitman, and give it to him after his presentation.

I would soon find out that while this synchronicity was going on inside the laboratory, an amusing parallel sequence of synchronicities was simultaneously occurring outside of the lab (which I would learn about only after the seminar had ended, and which are beyond the scope of this chapter).

I wanted to examine the statistical probability of this particular issue of the journal being available, and ponder the possible meaning of this sequence of synchronicities about synchronicity, but I had to wait until my return to Tucson to have sufficient time to consider this information.

The Statistical Improbability of the Synchronicity Article

In my over thirty years of work as a scientist, visiting investigators in laboratories in the US, Europe, and the Far East, at no time had the investigators made available duplicate copies of old journals for their visitors. If Dr. Beitman had not happened to be visiting the Division of Perceptual Studies at precisely the time its investigators were moving into their new headquarters and setting up their library, and if I had not happened to be in Virginia at the very same time, this event would not have been noticed (at least by me). In other words, the fact that journals were being given away was a rare event in itself.

When I first picked up the journal, I noticed that of the ten articles (including book reviews) contained in that volume, only one article had the word "synchronicity" in the title.

However, the question arose in my mind: *did this particular journal publish many articles on synchronicity?*

Upon returning home, I discovered that inserted within the journal was a detached piece of paper containing an index of the complete set of articles found in the four issues of the volume. The list included titles of twenty-six additional articles that had been published in Numbers 1–3, resulting in a total of thirty-six articles published in Volume 5.

I discovered that there was only one article out of the thirty-six that had the word "synchronicity" in the title.

I had subsequently discovered that, conveniently contained in the back of Volume 5, Number 4, was an Index of topics that had been discussed in the entire volume. I calculated that there were 169 different topics listed, some with multiple citations. For example, the topic of Jung's archetypes was discussed in 11 articles; the topic of Buddhism was discussed in seven articles.

However, I found that the topic of synchronicity was discussed in only one article. This suggested that the topic of synchronicity was not a common one in this journal, at least in Volume 5. (1 divided by 169 is 0.6% or p<.006).

I then felt inspired to look up *The Journal of Religion and Psychical Research* online and discovered a list of titles of all the articles published in the Journal from 1979—2003. It turned out that out of the 1660 articles listed, only seven (or 0.4%) had the word "synchronicity" in the title. It is curious that this was the first and only journal out of the many available that I happened to pick up and examine.

It's the Combined Pattern that Matters

By itself, the appearance of this article on synchronicity at that particular historic moment (Dr. Beitman's excellent presentation on the science of synchronicity) was intriguing, but not necessarily exceptional.

However, when combined with the other synchronous events that occurred in the context of Dr. Beitman's presentation, the resulting sequence or pattern of synchronicities becomes statistically and conceptually extraordinary.

To summarize the sequence of events:

- Dr. Greyson received not one, but two unsolicited manuscripts on synchronicity the week before he saw me in San Francisco (he had never received unsolicited manuscripts on synchronicity before).
- I happened to have begun writing a book on synchronicity at around that time (something I had never done before).
- I happened to be scheduled to speak at the Monroe Institute around the same time that Dr. Beitman happened to be visiting with family in Virginia. Because of the

timing, Dr. Beitman was able to give a presentation on his new research on synchronicity (he had never spoken to Dr. Greyson's team before). Our respective timings were synchronous with each other and multiply determined (i.e., multiple factors or causes).

- Soon after arriving at the Monroe Institute, I discovered that there happened to be a Synchronicity Center right next door to The Monroe Institute property.
- When visiting the Division of Perceptual Studies, I discovered that they were giving away duplicate copies of old journals, and the one journal I happened to pick up had an article on synchronicity (I had never visited a laboratory where old journals were being given away before).
- I inferred, and later verified, that this journal had a history of rarely publishing articles either with "synchronicity" in the title or in the body of the articles.
- The title of the synchronicity article began with the words "The Space Between"—a phrase a psychic had used not once, but twice when speaking with me in two previous months. She had claimed that "understanding the space between" contained a key to understanding how synchronicity works (I had never heard the phrase "the space between" applied to consciousness studies before receiving this advice from the psychic.)
- The journal I happened to pick up that contained the article on synchronicity, was the same journal that had published two of my articles on evidence involving research mediums, information purportedly received from the late Susy Smith. Hence my prior history with the journal happened to be related, via Susy, to the topic of the article on synchronicity.

Though this specific sequence of eight synchronous events about synchronicity per se is itself super-improbable, the sequence takes on much greater significance when you recall from Table I in the Overview that it is only one of more than a hundred categories or themes of sequences of Type III Synchronicities I have experienced and charted (and supersynchronicities continue to this day).

Can you imagine what kind of probability value we would obtain if we were to calculate the conditional probability combining more than one hundred Type III Synchronicities? Here the phrase "astronomically improbable" becomes an understatement. Only the most resistant and avoidant of minds could dismiss or try to "explain away" such a number as being down to "random chance."

People vary in their experience of synchronicity. Some people live in a sea of synchronicities where the waves are so tiny as to be almost imperceptible—the sea seems almost perfectly still—and therefore they presume there are no synchronicities.

Others are immersed in choppier waters, leading them to notice the waves from time to time.

Some people (perhaps relatively few) live in areas where the waves are often quite large. These people regularly notice synchronicities and usually enjoy them. Extending the metaphor, we can say that some people seek the waves and become professional surfers, while a few tackle the largest swells, sometimes called "monster waves," because they can be dangerous.

In writing this book, I have become, so to speak, a professional synchronicity surfer. It seems high time that we acknowledge the existence of synchronicity waves and come to understand how they occur and what they mean.

And the only way we will do this is if people start investigating supersynchronicities (what Dr. Beitman calls "serial coincidences") seriously. He considers me to be an authority on supersynchronicities (he has called me the emerging "master of serial coincidences").

One of the wonderful attributes of the science of supersynchronicity is that we can, as individuals, conduct the research at virtually no financial cost. All we need to do is to decide to become synchronicity self-scientists and begin the process of personal—and transpersonal—discovery.

As Chico Marx once said (when dressed as Groucho Marx) "Who you gonna believe, me or your own eyes?"

Are you ready to become a synchronicity self-scientist and discover if you can see synchronicities with your own eyes? Or, if you are already an experienced synchronicity surfer, are you ready to understand your experiences at a deeper level, opening the way to even greater supersynchronicity adventures?

Marcel Proust said it well: "The real voyage of discovery consists, not in seeking new landscapes, but in having new eyes". Are you ready to see with "new eyes"?

The truth is, our physical eyes are severely limited. For example, we can only see a sliver of the total spectrum of photon frequencies that exist in the Universe. With our physical eyes, we are mostly blind to infrared and ultraviolet light, and we are also unable to see radio waves on one side of the spectrum, nor cosmic rays on the other.

It was through the power of our minds, and our capacity to imagine beyond our senses, that we were able to create the technology to "see the invisible," with the development of new sensors coupled with computerized information-processing systems.

Are you ready to awaken even further to your own supersynchronicities?

CHAPTER 13
SUMMING UP THE 11 *LESSONS: FOSTERING YOUR AWAKENING TO EVIDENCE-BASED SPIRITUALITY AND DIVINE TIMING*

I am open to the guidance of synchronicity, and do not let expectations hinder my path.
The Dalai Lama

We are now ready to take stock of what we have learned thus far about the mystery and majesty of synchronicities—especially supersynchronicities—which will further help you apply this knowledge in your daily life. Remember that remaining open to new discoveries and awakenings is vital to achieving success in the self-science of synchronicities and divine timing.

Let's review the 11 key lessons, each accompanied by some hypothesis-like statements that more accurately reflect the scientific and qualified nature of the conclusions.

The reason I have listed them here first as "lessons," followed by more conservative statements concerning their possible truth, is partly because I wish to encourage you to explore them, and partly because my emerging conclusions are based on substantially more evidence than was feasible or reasonable to present in this book.

And as Sherlock Holmes reminds us, "There is nothing like first-hand evidence".

Lesson 1: Follow the Evidence that is Way Beyond Chance.

Pay close attention to events that are highly improbable, because the more improbable they are—especially Type III Synchronicities—the more they may reflect genuine non-random processes.

Lesson 2: The Evidence is Always Friendly

Even if the evidence does not support what we have been taught to believe—or want to believe—we should remember that the data are always "friendly": they are not out to get us, but to potentially awaken us. They are helping to lead us to truth.

Lesson 3: Spirit Can Play a Role in Synchronicity

The invisible realm of spirit (including people who have passed on) may have the potential to direct and guide us, and therefore be part of the synchronicity process.

Lesson 4: Symbols Can Play a Role in Synchronicity The meaning(s) of synchronicities may be complex, and not only reflect a "plot" or "purpose," but also involve symbolic expressions as well.

Lesson 5: Synchronicities are Associated with Our Intentions

It is possible that our intentions, questions, and requests may play a role in the manifestation of specific synchronicities.

Lesson 6: The Universe Can Reveal that It is the Higher Source of Synchronicity

Whatever the Higher Source of synchronicity is called, this Source may have the capacity to teach us about Itself and help us to discover what It (the One Mind) is doing, if we are open to learning this.

Lesson 7: Never Underestimate the Genius of the One Mind

Try to be open to the occurrence of phenomena, regardless of how strange, unpredicted, or unfathomable they may appear to you; just because they may seem to be impossible does not necessarily mean they are not real and that they should be rejected.

Lesson 8: If It Walks and Talks Like the One Mind, It Probably Is

If evidence from various combinations of synchronicities points in a particular direction, it is prudent for us to consider coming to the conclusion suggested by the evidence. This includes considering the hypothesis that some sort of Higher Intelligence or One Mind may be involved in supersynchronicity.

Lesson 9: Going Inside is Key for Discovering Synchronicities

It may not be sufficient to look for external explanations and predictions to discover synchronicities; synchronicity-seeking seems to require us to be equally good at intuiting as we are at reasoning.

Lesson 10: Supersynchronicities can Reveal True Magic

Some synchronicities have the potential to lead us to the conclusion that the essence of magic is a fundamental quality of the Universe. ("Magic" here is not equated with deception, but rather with that which is beyond verbal description.) And the greatest magic of all may be the extraordinary power of the mind to discover and comprehend this truth.

Lesson 11: Self-Science is Key to Discovering Supersynchronicity

The discovery of synchronicity, both individually and collectively, may require the active participation of each of us. Self-science may be a required process for discovering the breadth and depth of synchronicity.

We would do well to heed the advice given to Dr. Eleanor Arroway as a child by her father in the movie *Contact,* the same words she later heard repeated as an adult, purportedly emanating from somewhere on a distant planet: "Small steps, Ellie; small steps".

Though we have taken a number of significant steps in this book, they are still but "small steps" on the ladder of possible explanations and mechanisms that appear to be involved in synchronicity. However, I would like to offer you what I have termed Quantum Synchronicity Theory as a possible means of moving forward into greater understanding of synchronicities, which I introduce in Chapter 15.

Paying Special Attention to Details

It has been said that "the devil is in the details." The same can be said of the Divine and its role in synchronicity: "The Divine is in the details, too." It is in the complex patterns of the details discerned that the true genius of Divinity is revealed.

Here is how Sherlock Holmes put it: "You know my method. It is founded upon the observation of trifles". To the untrained eye, the little details are seen as "trifles," unimportant, and justifiably ignored. However, to the trained eye, these little details are observed to sometimes hold the keys for solving mysteries.

If you are not willing or able to examine and understand these essential details, you will not be able to see the brilliance of the possible One Mind in all this, let alone discover the apparent complexity of the multiple levels of the simultaneously-expressed plots with which it is entangled.

This is a core part of the process of developing our synchronicity intelligence. When asked about his ability to solve crimes, Holmes replied:

"They say that genius is an infinite capacity for taking pains," he remarked with a smile. "It's a very bad definition, but it does apply to detective work".

Following Holmes, my opinion is that it applies to supersynchronicity detective work as well.

Not Being Hindered by Expectations

As I have stated in various ways throughout this book, if there is one thing I have learned from science in general, and synchronicity self-science in particular, it is to be prepared for surprises.

We must not let our expectations hinder our paths, as the Dalai Lama reminds us. We must be continually open to new discoveries, while at the same time holding firm to the goal of discerning true gold from fool's gold.

Of course, in one sense we should allow ourselves to be guided and helped by our expectations—be they hunches, hypotheses, or theories. Expectations can help focus our attention and direct us to new discoveries. The key is to be helped, not hindered, by our expectations.

Again, quoting Holmes, "I have already explained to you that what is out of the common is usually a guide rather than a hindrance".

The Tools of Self-Science Are Affordable

This book is based almost entirely on the notes I took either immediately or shortly after the specific events in question occurred. Eventually, I started carrying a pocket-sized digital camera in addition to my notebook, as well as an even smaller digital tape recorder (of course, all of these tools are now combined in a smartphone). Whatever tools you choose to use—whether it's a simple notebook, the back of napkin, or the latest technology—it is helpful to record events as they occur. Otherwise, you will increase the probability not only of forgetting important events and their timing, but also misremembering them later on.

I envision the creation of user-friendly software that will not only enable us to keep better track of complex sequences of synchronicities, but will also help us to detect patterns and standardize the calculation of their conditional probabilities. Moreover, I envision the expansion and implementation of this software, enabling people from around the world not only to discover interpersonal and transpersonal synchronicities, but also to contribute to the creation of a global synchronicity self-science database.

Understanding and Honoring the Heart of Science

Recall Dr. Sagan's comment about "the heart of science" requiring that we be ready and able to give up cherished beliefs if they turn out to be false. Unfortunately, my experience has been that most of us—including mainstream scientists—find it extraordinarily difficult to practice this in our personal lives, let alone our professional lives.

Yet we need to strive to understand and honor "the heart of science," which holds the greatest hope for us to rise above our current destructive biases and beliefs and preserve our ability to see with new eyes.

Parables like *The Celestine Prophecy* and *The Twelve* also hold a special promise of not only opening our minds and hearts, but also inspiring us to go beyond our limited senses and conceptions.

Inspirational science fiction movies like *Contact,* as well as spiritual comedies like *Evan Almighty,* can serve as parables concerning the capacity of the human mind and heart to reach beyond their current understanding and limitations.

What connects these fictional works is the phenomenon of synchronicity.

If we are going to do science, we might as well do it with heart. If any field of science requires that we use our minds and hearts for discovery and awakening, it is the science of synchronicity.

As Dr. Sagan writes in the novel *Contact:* "Do you want to take a ride?"

And then the hawk crashed into my window….

Chapter 14
The Surprising Hawk Moment and the Wright Brothers Message
Lesson: Synchronicities Can Be Timely Reminders

The Wright Brothers created the single greatest cultural force since the invention of writing. The airplane became the first World Wide Web, bringing people, languages, ideas, and values together.
Bill Gates

You might think that after having experienced, documented, and analyzed so many astronomically improbable synchronicities, that I would stop being surprised. You might even wonder if I had become bored with them. The answer is quite the contrary, and I can blame this state of affairs partly on the creativity and intensity of the One Mind.

This chapter is a case in point. What you are about to read occurred after I had thought I had completed a full draft of this book, from the Foreword, Introduction, and Chapter 1, to the Questions and Answers, Appendices, and Suggested Readings.

At that time, in 2010, I had intentionally stopped this book at 11 lessons. I decided to save the remainder of the synchronicity chapters with their associated lessons for a sequel to this book. The reasoning for stopping at 11 lessons per se was not a synchronicity; it was a conscious choice that celebrated the first Lesson involving the number 11.

I was just finishing what I thought was the very last chapter (Chapter 13, which you just read), and suddenly a hawk flew straight at me and crashed into my window!

That's correct—a large hawk flew directly into my window. Talk about catching my attention.

This startling event inspired my writing an unplanned Epilogue for this book, and that's how in 2010 this book actually ended.

However, in the final editing stage in late 2015, we decided to take three of the substantial theory and science appendices which had been placed there because they were more challenging to read, and elevated them to become chapters in a new Section Three. Though my Epilogue with its important final take home message could no longer serve as an ending for the book, I felt I needed to honor what the hawk moment had taught me, and by extension, could teach you. Hence, I am transforming the Epilogue into Chapter 14, and we are now ready to celebrate it.

The View from My Study

My study looks out on our backyard, which at the time I wrote this chapter included two finch feeders that typically have ten to thirty yellow and brown finches pecking away at the seeds, plus a seven perched hummingbird feeder whose perches are sometimes all occupied. On the ground are often anywhere from five to twenty quail and doves. In 2015, as I was transforming this Epilogue into Chapter 14, I noticed that I could now see a total of ten bird feeders in our yard.

Maybe once a day, a large brown hawk swoops into the yard with the goal of feeding as well. As it makes its descent, the menagerie of birds flees. Sometimes a bird will crash into a window, get stunned or injured, and the hawk will have earned a meal.

As I happened to be finishing what was then the very last chapter of this book, I noticed out of the corner of my eye a hawk swoop in.

The birds fled, as they always do. None hit the window. The hawk perched on the first tier of our four-tiered natural stone water fountain. I thought nothing of this other than that I was enjoying the hawk's presence.

As I watched the hawk, the strangest thing happened. It suddenly took off toward the window and, seemingly while making eye contact with me, flew directly into the window!

In the eight years I had lived in my home prior to that moment, I had easily spent over a thousand days (a conservative estimate) writing in my office, during which time no hawk has ever crashed into my window. I have spent another thousand plus days since then writing in my office and I have not witnessed another hawk slam into the window.

I got out of my chair, concerned for the hawk, and looked down. There he (or she) was, somewhat dazed, looking up at me.

I called for Rhonda to witness what had happened, and the hawk flew into a tree to the right of the fountain.

We watched as it perched there for a while before going after some courageous finches who had ventured back to the feeders.

The hawk then alighted on the ground maybe ten feet from the window, and looked up at me again, clearly staring.

Rhonda and I watched some more, and then the hawk finally took flight and flew off toward the mountains.

The Message of the Hawk

As listed in Table I in Chapter 1, I had at least one Type III Synchronicity involving hawks, but I had never experienced something quite like this. I wondered what the hawk had been doing there. Was this merely a coincidence, or something more? Was there a possible message here?

I decided to retrieve my copies of *Medicine Cards* and *Animal Speak,* as I was fairly certain I had previously looked up the mythology of the hawk at the time of my Type III hawk synchronicities, but since I rarely attempt to put such knowledge into long-term memory, I could not recall the stories about the possible meaning of hawks.

The information I read—or rather, reread—could not have been more perfect. This included the fact that this hawk incident served as a reminder of how I had originally planned to end this book, which I had forgotten all about!

In *Medicine Cards,* the word for hawk is "messenger." The accompanying poem reads (and is formatted as it was typed in the book):

Hawk
  Messenger of the Sky
    Circle my dreams and teach me
      The message as we fly.

The first paragraph reads:

"Hawk is akin to Mercury, the messenger of the gods. Hawk medicine teaches you to be observant, to look at your surroundings. Observe the obvious in everything that you do. Life is sending you signals".

You will recall from the previous chapter the discussion about self-science, the making of observations, and the seeking of evidence of meaningful synchronicities—which are "life's signals."

The authors went on to write:

"You are only as powerful as your capacity to perceive, to receive, and use your abilities".

As I read this particular sentence, I began to wonder: *was the surprising and propitious appearance of the hawk simply there for me, or more importantly, was it there for you, the reader, too? Was the hawk message actually directed toward you, the reader, as a reminder of "your capacity to perceive, to receive, and use your abilities" to unleash your inner powers?*

What do you think?

In *Animal Speak,* the keynote words for the hawk are "Visionary power and guardianship". The author writes: "Hawks are one of the most intriguing and mystical of the birds of prey. They are the messengers, the protectors, and the visionaries of the air".

Four pages are devoted to the hawk, ending with the following passage:

The sky is the realm of the hawk. Through its flight it communicates with humans and with the great creator spirit. It awakens our vision and inspires us to a creative life purpose.

The hawk "awakens our vision." Was this a symbolic home run, or what?

You may not believe it—and I had a hard time believing it, too—but it's true. The sudden appearance and behavior of this hawk turned out to fit perfectly with my original plan to end this book. The hawk's actions had caught my attention, triggering me to (re-)read about hawks, which rekindled my memory.

And once again I was reminded that the real is sometimes surreal.

A Wright Brothers Moment?

To preserve the profound timeliness of the hawk and the original ending of this book, I have not rewritten what follows next. Except for minor editing, it reads as it was originally written in 2010 when it was going to form the Epilogue.

As my weekly lecture at Canyon Ranch on *The Energy Healing Experiments* from the years 2006 to 2009 can verify, I regularly ended my presentation with the Wright Brothers Lesson. Of course, there had been no mention of a surprising hawk synchronicity in these lectures, since the hawk event had just happened a few minutes prior to writing this very Epilogue.

It is now time to bring this book to a close as I had originally planned. If my original ending was to be the cake, this surprising synchronicity becomes its icing. The connection between the Wright Brothers and the bizarre appearance of the hawk is both self-evident and profound.

As you probably know, prior to the Wright Brothers, it was not known whether human beings could ever fly with a powered, heavier-than-air craft. Many inventors had tried and failed. However, on December 17, 1903, Orville and Wilbur Wright succeeded in flying the first powered, controlled heavier-than-air plane.

However, what I mean by the Wright Brothers Lesson has nothing to do with airplanes, technology, the evolution of flight, or any of the ensuing controversy. It also does not matter that the first flight lasted only twelve seconds, or that many people didn't even believe it had really happened, or didn't seem to care (which soon changed!) It has to do with the change in consciousness that took place when we truly realized that flight was indeed possible. Though it would be years before flight became commercial and ultimately taken for granted, the fact remained that after December 17, 1903, we knew that flight was possible, and that knowledge permanently changed human consciousness.

After having read this book, you may now want to consider two key questions:

1. If you were agnostic or skeptical before, did the totality of the evidence lead you to become convinced that supersynchronicities are possible?
2. Or, if you already were convinced of the reality of supersynchronicities (even though you likely wouldn't have used the nomenclature), are you now convinced that these extraordinary phenomena can be validly studied scientifically?

Was this, metaphorically, a Wright Brothers Moment for you? If not, how many more synchronicity flights, so to speak, would you want to see before you could conclude that supersynchronicities were possible?

As you can probably infer, I asked myself this question many times. I ultimately decided that I had witnessed and recorded more than enough evidence of repeated supersynchronicities to conclude that they were not only possible, but that they were actual. For me, the synchronicity plane had taken off.

But it may not have taken off yet for you.

As I sat down to finish what I thought was to be the final chapter of this book, I realized I had forgotten that this was how I had originally intended to end it.

And then the hawk crashed into my window—it flew, so to speak, into my face. Not only did the symbolism of the hawk fit squarely with my invitation to you to become a synchronicity self-scientist so that you could potentially confirm this for yourself, but the hawk literally embodied flight!

And where did the famous Wright Brothers Moment, that historic first flight, occur? Nowhere other than Kitty Hawk, North Carolina!

Has this book ended on a seemingly absurd note, even more so than how it began? Is it like the timely appearances of ravens and ducks and green emeralds, which you will recall included a "green crow"? Is all this for the birds, or is it time that we learn to fly?

What do you think?

Are you going to develop your own capacity for self-science and experiencing supersynchronicities?

And, if you are interested in exploring our emerging scientific theories and understanding of synchronicity, Section Three awaits you.

Chapter 15
Understanding Pseudo-Skepticism and Another Hawk Moment
Lesson: Synchronicity Favors the Prepared Mind

Chance favors the prepared mind.
Dr. Louis Pasteur

In a lecture at the University of Lille on December 7, 1854, Dr. Louis Pasteur said, "In the fields of observation, chance favors only the prepared mind".

Jung stated it this way: "Synchronicity is an ever present reality for those who have eyes to see".

I was reminded of these famous quotes in the process of writing this additional unplanned chapter. What you are about to read illustrates how the synchronicity journey continues for those of us who are prepared to see. It also illustrates the continued development of my personal synchronicity intelligence, and by extension, yours as well.

Here is what happened.

Literally during the process of my writing this post-book completed, extra chapter on pseudo-skepticism, a super-timely Type III

Synchronicity occurred. The set of events actually interrupted and interfered with my writing the first draft of this chapter.

It was only after I had the opportunity to take a break from what was unfolding that I came to see the potential take-home synchronicity lesson of this chapter.

To help you experience the actual discovery and reflection process *as it unfolded,* what I have done is only minimally edited the next few pages. I did change the formatting in certain places so that it would be easier for you to distinguish between the unexpected events that were occurring – **indicated in bold text –** and the text that I was writing for the chapter. I also added the Event #'s during the editing process.

Here we go.

Why I Decided to Write This Special Section

I have written this extra chapter not only to responsibly defend this book from unjustified and unfair pseudo-skepticism, but to help all readers—true skeptics and believers alike—to discern rational and responsible critiques of this book from irrational and irresponsible ones.

In *The Sacred Promise,* I was inspired to write a lengthy chapter titled "Healthy and Unhealthy Skepticism about Spirit," which was labelled as Appendix D and placed at the end of the book. In this Appendix I explicated the difference between genuine and pseudo-skepticism.

I helped the reader understand the nature of pseudo-skepticism by constructing seven critical statements made by seven different fictional pseudo-skeptics (I simply labeled them #'s 1—7) and corresponding rational responses to each critique made by a second fictional character defending the veracity of the work.

Curiously, the evening before Param Media and I were completing the edits of what we thought was the final organization of *Super Synchronicity,* I received an email from a gentleman I did not know who has worked as a high school teacher for more than two decades.

In his email he mentioned the following:

I have just finished reading The Sacred Promise

No surprise; I loved it and I especially enjoyed Appendix D referring to Pseudo-skeptics.

Thank-you for defending yourself and us against the bullies in our school yard.

An interesting and insightful phrase, "bullies in our school yard." It is not uncommon for pseudo-skeptics to sometimes behave in bombastic and bullying ways.

And curiously, a week or so earlier, I had received an email from a successful television producer who read *The Sacred Promise* twice and sent me four pages of notes and questions concerning the book.

He too was especially appreciative of Appendix D. He said that I was quite "courageous" in taking on pseudo-skepticism, and he wrote that "the best defense is a good offense."

Wow—I have to stop typing right now. I can't believe this. A hawk just flew into my office window, scattering the birds. Event #1 (Hawk in what became Chapter 14, see below).

It is 11 am. Event #2 (recall how my synchronicity journey began with the number 11; see further replication below).

Now the hawk has flown on top of one of our bird feeders, and is intensely staring at me.

After a minute, he (or she) just flew into the tree closest to my window. I have called Rhonda, and told her what is happening. She has gone outside and sure enough she can see the hawk still sitting on a branch in this tree, apparently dazed a bit.

What is truly extraordinary about this utterly unexpected hawk window moment is that only yesterday afternoon did the idea come to me to convert what had once been the Epilogue—which featured a hawk flying in my window—into an additional synchronicity lesson. I had just titled Chapter 14 *"A Surprising Hawk Moment and The Wright Brothers Message."*

I had then mailed the new Chapter 14 and revised Table of Contents to Param Media in the late afternoon.

More importantly, it was only just an hour ago that I worked on the latest edits of the new Chapter 14, which I had received back from Param Media earlier this morning. Event #3 (timing with this hawk moment).

And now a hawk has flown into my study window.

You will recall in the previous chapter that I had only experienced one instance in my life where a hawk had flown into my window, and this unique event occurred just as I thought I was ending the first completed draft of this book in 2010.

Now, here I am in 2015, spontaneously writing a possible new section to what we thought was the final organization of this book, having just completed my responses to the editing of Chapters 9–

15 and the Questions and Answers Chapter, and then suddenly a second hawk moment has occurred.

If you are skeptically inclined, you might wonder, "Is Schwartz making this up? Is he trying to pull the wool over my eyes? Is he imagining or hallucinating the hawk?"

For the record, if I had been reading this instead of just writing it, I might also entertain such thoughts. I am a well-trained questioner. I often say that my middle name is "Question" (which includes the question "If).

However, I would balance these "knee-jerk questioning" reactions with more reasoned and responsible considerations such as, "Is Schwartz really stupid enough to do this?" I would ask, "Is Schwartz unethical enough to do this?" I would raise the question, "Has Schwartz possibly lost his mind but is extraordinarily good at hiding it from his colleagues and friends?"

Having raised these questions, I would carefully evaluate the evidence from this book (and his previous books and scientific publications) and determine whether the totality of the evidence supported the skeptical responses that Schwartz must be stupid, unethical, and/or insane.

If one examines the evidence thoroughly and fairly, a rational and responsible conclusion presents itself. Despite what some

super-critics have falsely claimed, the facts are that Schwartz shows no obvious evidence of excessive stupidity, lack of ethics, or psychopathology. If Schwartz were all (or some) of these things, he is a master at disguising them.

What is important for me at this moment is that we not dishonor (1) the highly improbable event of the hawk flying into my window, nor (2) the precise time it happened to occur (11 am).

So with deep gratitude what I am doing is formally thanking the universe (including the hawk) for this surprising gift, and honoring it by completing this unanticipated extra chapter on pseudo-skepticism.

Returning to writing the chapter, I have just re-read what I was writing before the hawk-window moment occurred. I had been mentioning two recent emails commenting on my appendix on healthy and unhealthy skepticism at the end of *The Sacred Promise,* and was I sharing how part of this appendix addressed seven core pseudo-skeptical criticisms of the work.

To keep the present section brief, what I will do is list eight of the top standard skeptical criticisms of these kinds of phenomena in general, and the evidence reported in this book in particular, with brief commentary about each.

If you have read this book from cover to cover, and you ...

I have to stop writing again. I just heard a bang, and noticed that the hawk had returned. It just flew into the very tall window to the left of the fireplace in our living room which I can see to the left of the computer monitor in my study. Event #4.

I looked at the time and it was 11:44 am. I said to myself, *If this had happened a minute later at 11:45, that would have added up to 11 and would have been a second 11 synchronicity.*

And in the process, *bang!* the hawk flew into the living room window a second time! Event #5.

I looked at the time and it was now 11:45 am. This added up to 11. Event #6.

Needless to say, this combination of events has never happened before.

Rhonda just came in, and I told her what happened. I said I think the hawk flew back to the tree in view of my study window. Rhonda has gone outside and said sure enough, the hawk is there. At which point the hawk took off, again.

What has just transpired reminds me of a quote from a famous scientist whose name I cannot recall. I slightly paraphrase it below:

"I didn't say this was possible. I said it happens."

I think I will take a break and hopefully complete this section in a bit....

No sooner had I typed the five asterisks above then Rhonda spontaneously walked into my study. Since I was ready to take a break, I asked Rhonda if it was okay with her if I read her the birthing of this extra chapter.

After hearing just the first few paragraphs, Rhonda noticed a hawk fly into the tree outside the window, and I stopped reading the text to look at the hawk.

Then, a second hawk flew into the tree, and Rhonda began hearing them screeching back and forth, apparently communicating with each other!

Rarely have we ever seen two hawks in our backyard at the same time (maybe 3 or 4 times over a span of 9 years). However, neither one of us has ever seen two hawks in the same tree talking to each other. This is a first. Event #7.

Rhonda has just gone outside and is trying to shoo them away so that the smaller birds can return and safely eat from our feeders. She came back in, and then heard one of the hawks screeching again. Despite her efforts, the two hawks have returned to the tree. Event #8.

Rhonda is going out to shoo them away again.

This is very unusual, and maybe meaningful.

I decided to take an hour break to clear my head and ponder what just had transpired.

So let's return to my list of eight top pseudo-skeptical claims against the phenomenon of synchronicity and the self-science process of observing and analyzing them in real-life.

1. Anecdotal
2. Mistakes of perception and memory
3. Cherry picking
4. Pseudo-science
5. Easily explained by chance
6. Seeing patterns where none occur
7. Theoretically impossible
8. Unethical observer

Rather than referring to all of the evidence in the book, I will honor the new Chapter 13 and the new Chapter 14 Type III Synchronicity featuring:

- the appearance of the hawk-window moment at what was to be the end of the book in 2010,
- the timing of the transformation of the then hawk-window Epilogue into Chapter 13 and Synchronicity Lesson 12, and then editing the new Chapter 13 in 2015 this morning,
- the appearance of not one, not two, but three hawk-window moments during the writing of this extra chapter at the end of the book, and
- the mid-writing transformation of this hawk window chapter to become Synchronicity Lesson #13

I list each pseudo-skeptical criticism with a brief commentary. Note that I provide further detailed criticisms against pseudo-skepticism in Chapter 15.

Is It All Anecdotal?

Yes, all this is "anecdotal" in that it all comes from real-life. Concerning the present events, the hawks were real, the windows were real, the clocks were real, the documents were real, etc. What pseudo-skepticism would have us do is label real-life events as anecdotal, treat them all as hearsay or uncontrolled, and then dismiss them. To dismiss evidence from real-life as being invalid and useless is sadly irrational as well as irresponsible.

Mistakes of Perception and Memory?

Yes, sometimes people make perceptual errors, and human memory is far from perfect. Responsible self-science requires that the experimenters (e.g., me and the hundred-plus people I have experienced synchronicities with) be super-mindful of our capacity for error. However, the fact is that the vast majority of what has been reported in this book, including in this chapter, was actually recorded at the time the events were witnessed, or shortly thereafter. The hawks and times reported in this chapter were recorded literally as they occurred. Many events reported in this book were witnessed by two or more people, and many were photographed or recorded. Only someone practicing pseudo-skepticism would assertively claim that these synchronicities could be explained as being errors of perception and memory.

Cherry Picking?

Yes, if we look for things, we are more likely to find them. However, does that mean that all the evidence reported in this book can be explained by selectively picking good examples and ignoring bad examples or evidence that does not fit? Was I cherry picking the hawks today, or the precise times that they occurred? The answer should be obvious—absolutely no.

Pseudo-Science?

A common strategy in pseudo-skepticism is to assert that something is pseudo-science and thereby summarily dismiss the data and the investigators. Of course there is bad science. But there is good science, too. Some of the very best controlled scientific methodologies are actually employed in controversial areas like parapsychology precisely because these areas are so controversial, and are therefore highly scrutinized. There is nothing inherently unscientific or pseudo-scientific about carefully applying the basic methods of science to the laboratories of our personal lives. Quite the contrary: applying self-science to daily life and fostering the living of "evidence-based lives" is to be applauded. To dismiss responsible self-science as being pseudo-science is both dishonest and anti-intellectual.

Easily Explained by Chance?

Some readers may already have a grasp of conditional properties and will understand how highly improbable outcomes can translate into the probability of observing a given set of synchronicities appearing in a finite period of time. You will recall how we calculated some astronomically improbable numbers in the context of exemplary Type III Synchronicities. Let's briefly consider the hawks hitting my window. Prior to 11 am today, I had only witnessed a hawk fly into my window once (Chapter 14), and it happened precisely at the time I was completing the first draft of this book. I explained that this was one occurrence out of a total of at least 1000 occasions I had sat at this window before I finishing the book, and that another 1000 occasions (conservatively calculated) had transpired since ending the book. That's one out of 2000. However, each occasion involves a few hours, ranging from maybe 1 to 6 hours at a time. If we pick 3 hours as the average, that comes out to 6000 hours total.

But this is only part of the story. The hawk had to hit the window exactly as I was finishing the first draft of this book. How often do I end a book in this manner? The answer up to that time was once (in 2010). And most importantly, the meaning of the hawk happened to directly relate to my error in forgetting to end the book with the core take-home message about flight and the Wright Brothers. The probability of this occurring is obviously miniscule.

Now, let's add the second hawk moments, a total of three occurrences, as I was trying to write this chapter, after we had just completed the ending of the book a second time (late 2015). The truth is that only someone engaged in pseudo-skeptical thinking could assert with a straight face that the timing of all these events can be easily explained by chance alone.

Seeing Patterns Where None Occur?

Humans not only see patterns, but they create them too. Sometimes people believe they see patterns where none exist. Moreover, humans see motion in flashing images, for example, and we experience the color yellow on a digital monitor when in fact there are only red, green, and blue pixels on the screen. Does this mean that all or the majority of the patterns and potential meanings I have reported in this book are "projected illusions" of my mind? Of course not. Highly trained psychologists are taught to be cautious and careful in seeing patterns and inferring meaning, and I was blessed to receive such advanced training. If a person dismisses all such Type III Synchronicities as due to faulty or fantasy pattern recognition, they are sadly ignoring the evidence and are engaged in pseudo-skepticism.

Theoretically Impossible?

Mainstream scientists—especially devoted materialist scientists—have faith that their philosophical understanding of the nature of reality is correct. I say "faith" because they hold on to their materialist beliefs despite areas of strong evidence to the contrary. Moreover, they argue that it's only a matter of time before materialist science will discover a materialist explanation for the present challenging evidence that seriously questions their meta-theory. If any area of evidence threatens the foundation of mainstream materialist thought—and I was trained as a materialist—it is Type III Synchronicities. If we (1) accept that the evidence reported in this book is real (i.e., it's not fake or erroneously observed and reported), and we (2) accept that the combination of the improbabilities of the observed events and their patterns rationally and responsibly imply that some sort of invisible intelligence, script writer, orchestrator, and/or conductor, is required to manifest such patterns, then (3) this supports emerging postmaterialist theories which propose that mind or consciousness is at least as primary in the universe as information, energy, and matter. Contemporary theories in physics and psychology now indicate that all of this, and more, is possible. To assert that this is theoretically impossible, especially in the face of careful logic and evidence, is to engage in erroneous and unhealthy pseudo-skepticism.

The Hypocrite?

Probably the lowest, most irresponsible, and completely anti-scientific technique employed by certain pseudo-skeptics is to try to damage the reputation of controversial pioneering scientists by making false accusations and attacking their character. Science and reason, by their very nature, cannot devolve into personal attacks, but amazingly, such obvious logical inconsistency and hypocrisy seems lost on these people. They appear to champion science, but are actually acting against and suppressing the ideals of scientific inquiry.

Some of my colleagues and I have been attacked by these pseudo-skeptics, and it is not hard to find awful and untrue things said about us online. In my view, it seems that many of these pseudo-skeptics are afraid. They are terrified of facing reality, of having to confront their own internal weaknesses and false beliefs, which would necessitate a transformation of consciousness within themselves. They are afraid of ascending to higher levels of mind, and so they try to pull others down.

I understand their fears. But I suggest that they stop hypocritically attacking others, and instead have the bravery to look at the confusion and fear in their own minds and hearts. It is easy to accuse others, but so difficult to admit one's own faults. Like everyone else, I too have faults, but being unscientific is not one of them.

These pseudo-skeptics are the most irrational and unscientific of all the pseudo-skeptics, but they are also often the most vociferous. We should not feed these "trolls" (as they are called on the Internet).

Celebrating Healthy Questioning and Skeptical Thinking

One of the greatest gifts of having a human mind is our ability to conceive and raise questions. Einstein said that "The important thing is not to stop questioning". The more we learn about science, and the more we learn how to think, the better we become at asking questions, especially if we allow intuition to feed our reasoning.

The better prepared we are to imagine and accept possible synchronicities, the better we are at seeing, studying, and benefiting from them.

I end this chapter with the hope-filled lesson that "Synchronicities favor the prepared mind."

This makes our journey of learning all the more valuable as we explore and advance the laboratories of our personal and collective lives, and increase our Synchronicity Intelligence.

Section Three
Theory—Emerging Scientific Understanding

It is a capital mistake to theorize before one has data.
Insensibly one begins to twist facts to suit theories,
instead of theories to suit facts.
Sherlock Holmes

Chapter 16
Staircase of Explanations: From Skepticism to Spirit

The history of science shows that theories are perishable. With every new truth that is revealed we get a better understanding of Nature and our conceptions and views are modified.
Nicola Tesla

It is possible to organize the primary alternative theories of synchronicity in terms of a ladder or staircase of explanations, beginning with the simplest and most conventional explanations, and moving upward toward the more complex and controversial explanations. The lowest steps or rungs encompass the skeptical explanations; the highest steps or rungs reflect the One Mind explanations.

My intent here is not to present this comprehensive analysis in great detail. Nor is my intent to provide additional compelling evidence from multiple Type III Synchronicities to justify our careful consideration of the highest steps on the synchronicity staircase, which would require another book to do it justice. However, it is feasible to offer a brief introduction to the levels of possible explanation here so that you can begin to envision the bigger picture.

Table II lists twelve types or categories of theories. I will briefly explain each of them in the context of the evidence presented in this book.

Though we can apply this analysis to any type of synchronicity, I have chosen to focus mainly (though not exclusively) on the

Type III Synchronicities discussed in Chapter 12 that illustrate the evidence for my "Supersynchronicity Tipping Point," partly because it is likely that you read this material fairly recently, and partly because it addresses many of the steps in Table II.

As you will see, my examination of the totality of the evidence has led me to the conclusion that some combination of the explanations represented by the uppermost five steps on the staircase are not only important, but essential, if we are to understand and harness our emerging experiential understanding of the reality of synchronicity.

Table II
Steps on a Staircase of Possible Explanations for Synchronicity

Step 12 The One Mind—Collective
Step 11 The One Mind—Personal
Step 10 Higher Spiritual Beings
Step 9 Human Spirits
Step 8 Human Intention and Energy
Step 7 Biophysical and Social Self-Organization
Step 6 Geophysical and Astrophysical Forces
Step 5 Psychological and Social Causes
Step 4 Beyond Probable Chance
Step 3 Chance Coincidences
Step 2 Selective Attention
Step 1 Deception—Self or Other

We will start at the bottom, and consider each step in turn as we ascend the staircase.

Step 1 Deception–Self or Other

People sometimes misperceive information about themselves or others, and therefore either lie to themselves or to others about purported patterns and sequences of events. For example, cognitive psychology research on human memory and eye witness testimony shows that memories are often inaccurate and distorted, and like the classic "fisherman's" account of the size of their catch, changes over time.

Can the totality of the evidence reported in this book be explained—or explained away—as primarily a function of misinformation and/or disinformation?

The factual and verifiable nature of the events described in Chapter 12 involving multiple scientists and several others clearly rules out Step 1 as a plausible explanation. Moreover, each of the Type III Synchronicities reported in this book involved multiple credible witnesses who participated in the reported events and verify that they actually happened. Therefore, Step 1 is not a rationally acceptable explanation.

Step 2 Selective Attention

This hypothesis makes the claim that when people pay special attention to specific categories of information, they will be more likely to observe them. We discussed in Chapter 1 how if you have an interest in VW bugs, for example, you will more likely seek them and, therefore, more likely see them.

The issue here is not whether selective attention was involved in the detection of patterns and sequences of events—after all, if you are not paying attention, then you are not likely to notice synchronicities. What matters here is whether or not the events were sufficiently probable to allow us to claim that our perceptional priming (our preparation for selective attention) was sufficient to explain their appearance.

In the case of Chapter 12, not only was each event highly improbable by itself, *but the timing and sequencing of the collection of events was significantly more so,* and similarly for each of the Type III Synchronicities reported in this book. Therefore, even though as bona fide self-scientists we need to be paying careful attention, Step 2 is nevertheless ruled out as a rationally acceptable explanation for the total patterns and sequences of events reported in this book.

Step 3 Chance Coincidences

As we have discussed numerous times in this book, an apparent relationship observed between two or more events can occur simply because of chance alone. This is not meant to imply that the events themselves were not caused, but that the seeming *relationship between them* was not mediated causally.

You will recall my discussion of the software program I designed that makes it possible to document the chance occurrence of sequences of events in huge data sets, involving hundreds of thousands or millions of events/"flips" per "trial."

Using random-event generators—created by electrons or photons, or by computer algorithms—I can collect a million random "flips" of an electron, for example, in a fraction of a second, and call this a "trial." I can then repeat this process hundreds, thousands, or even millions of times, and calculate the actual sequences of events that happen via chance alone. Dr. David Hand's book *The Improbability Principle* addresses the probability of obtaining individually highly improbable events (or sets of events) given large enough samples extended over long enough periods of time.

To determine whether chance per se is a likely explanation, it is essential to calculate conditional probabilities, which was discussed earlier in this book. Each of the Type III Synchronicities reported in this book involve conditional probabilities, which are easily estimated to be in the millions, billions, trillions, octillions, or beyond.

In Chapter 12, for example:

- Dr. Greyson had never received two research manuscripts in a single week on synchronicity (or even one, for that matter, and he had been an editor of a major scientific journal for more than a decade).
- He had never invited a scientist to speak about research on synchronicity at his research division before.
- I had never attempted to write a book on synchronicity before.

- I had never been invited to give a presentation at the Monroe Institute before (though I had once visited the Monroe Institute approximately fifteen years earlier).
- I had never visited an Institution that was located a stone's throw from a Synchronicity Center.

Each of these events by themselves was super-unique. *None of them had ever happened before.* Moreover, the confluence of their timing was even more extraordinary. All this was just the beginning of the Type III Synchronicity reported in Chapter 12.

Therefore, Step 3 is not a rationally acceptable explanation for the evidence reported in this book.

Step 4 Beyond Probable Chance

This hypothesis acknowledges that a given set or sequence of events may be improbable, or even highly improbable, but the results could still be due to chance.

Just because the probability of a given set of events might be one in ten million, billion, trillion, or even octillion, this does not mean that it could not have occurred by chance alone.

The truth is, as discussed before, even extraordinarily improbable events can happen every now and again, especially given enough time and events.

Hence, the sequence of Type III events reported in Chapter 12, as extraordinarily improbable as their combined occurrence and timing was, could have occurred by chance.

In other words, the sequence could have been a "fluke."

However, I did not report only one Type III Synchronicity; I reported a dozen of them—beginning with the Type III Synchronicity of the naming of the term "supersynchronicity" reported in Chapter 1.

My next book will reveal even more extraordinary and improbable sequences. At some point, it becomes unreasonable to conclude that these replicated observations of patterns, or sequences, of highly improbable events could have occurred by chance alone.

Step 4 is not a rationally acceptable explanation of the totality of the evidence reported in this book.

Step 5 Psychological and Social Causes

If the patterns and sequences of events justify our concluding that they are probably non-random in origin, the search then begins for possible causes that might explain them.

The simplest, most straightforward, and scientifically responsible place to begin is to look for conventional (everyday) causes. This is where I looked first.

There are a host of psychological or social causes that could be responsible for two or more events occurring at the same time.

For example, my meeting Dr. Greyson in San Francisco may not have been a synchronicity. We had each been invited to speak at this conference, and we had co-spoken at conferences before. Step 5 would therefore seem to be able to explain our being present at that meeting at the same time.

However, Dr. Greyson receiving two synchronicity manuscripts a week prior to our meeting could not be explained simply in terms of Step 5. He had not requested that the authors send him their respective papers; in fact, prior to spontaneously receiving them, he did not even know that the authors were writing them.

Similarly, Dr. Greyson telling me about receiving these two manuscripts shortly after our seeing each other could not be explained simply in terms of Step 5. Only a handful of people knew I had begun writing a book on synchronicity, and he was not among them.

Further, my being scheduled to speak at the Monroe Institute two days prior to one of the authors who was giving a research seminar on his synchronicity manuscript at Dr. Greyson's Division at the University of Virginia could not be explained simply in terms of Step 5. Dr. Greyson did not know that I was scheduled to speak at the Monroe Institute at that time.

If Dr. Greyson had previously known that I was writing a book about synchronicity—or if I had told him so when we first met in

San Francisco—I would not have attributed his telling me about the receipt of the two manuscripts on synchronicity as being a possible synchronicity itself. Rather, I would have explained it in terms of Step 5.

Or if he had previously known that I was scheduled to come to Virginia, and he had consciously arranged the seminar so that I could be in attendance, we would not have classified it as a synchronicity. I would have again explained it in terms of Step 5.

You might be wondering: was it possible that Dr. Greyson had read my mind telepathically, even unconsciously, and this is what caused him to tell me about the manuscripts? Even more unconventional (and controversial), was it possible that Dr. Greyson somehow knew "intuitively" that I was coming to Virginia, and he unconsciously arranged the seminar to fit with my schedule? Such potential "paranormal" mechanisms need to be included in the list of possible explanations, as you will soon see when we reach Step 8.

My preference is that we not skip any steps.

The skeptical mind might also wonder: maybe Dr. Greyson had known that I was writing a book, but he had forgotten about it? Or maybe Dr. Greyson had known that I was coming to Virginia, and had forgotten about that? Also, maybe I had misremembered whether Dr. Greyson knew I had a growing interest in synchronicity (maybe he had read Appendix C in *The G.O.D. Experiments*), or I had mentioned my trip to him in a forgotten email correspondence.

Though highly improbable, they are, in principle, possible.

However, this would not explain the uncanny timing of the two unsolicited manuscripts that Dr. Greyson had received just prior to coming to San Francisco. Nor would it explain the fact that the actual scheduling of Dr. Beitman's seminar was related to his vacation plans to visit with relatives who happened to live near the University of Virginia.

The beauty of Type III Synchronicities—especially those containing ten or more sequences of events—is that even if a couple of the events prove to be non-synchronistic, they do not significantly reduce the super improbability of their occurrence.

When carefully examined, we discover that Step 5 is not a rationally acceptable explanation for the combined sequence of events found in Chapter 12, nor, for that matter, for any of the Type III Synchronicities reported in this book.

While there is an abstract logical possibility that individual pairs of events might have Step 5 explanations, the combined events for any of the Type III Synchronicities require that we consider additional steps on the staircase.

Step 6 Geophysical and Astrophysical Forces

This explanation proposes that the possible cause (or causes) of the observed patterns and sequences of events might be due to geophysical and astrophysical forces, such as barometric pressure changes, fluctuations in the earth's magnetic field, solar flares, or changes in gravitational fields produced by the movements of the planets. I include this possible hypothesis partly to be thorough, and partly to recognize that research has been conducted documenting that various physical, chemical, biological, and psychological processes can be influenced by such invisible mechanisms (as perceived by our conventional five senses). Even the decay of certain radioactive substances has been documented to be modulated by cycles of solar flares occurring over the timescale of many years.

However, even if one or more of these hypothesized forces played a role in either creating the sequences or fostering our awareness of them, we would still be left with having to explain how the patterns of the sequences were non-random in the first place. In other words, we would still be left with the question, "who or what was orchestrating the forces that were causing the sequences?"

In other words, if an event (whether synchronistic or not) can be explained by appealing to geophysical and astrophysical forces (the laws of physics), then it is still the case that these forces would require their own prior explanations. In any case, it certainly appears that Step 6 is an insufficient explanation for the totality of the evidence reported in this book.

Step 7 Biophysical and Social Self-Organization

This hypothesis is derived from general systems theory as expressed in contemporary chaos and complexity theory. The basic idea is that nature is replete with examples of complex systems that seem to "self-organize," meaning that they appear to have come together and function as a complex orchestration of components without seemingly requiring the presence of some sort of "designer" or "orchestrating agent."

I have come to question whether "self-organization" theory is sufficient to explain the emergence and evolution of complex systems, especially super-complex systems, at all levels of nature.

Though systems "appear" to self-organize—for example, the growth and development of biological organisms containing millions, billions, or trillions of cells, all derived from a single cell—*it is well known that biological self-organization requires the functioning of DNA, a sophisticated blueprint that somehow directs the organization and growth process, as well as the presence of complementary causal mechanisms in the external environment, in order for a healthy and optimal system to emerge.*

The longstanding and heated debate about whether it is sufficient to explain biological evolution in terms of random mutation guided by "natural selection," or whether some sort of a Higher Intelligence is required to help orchestrate the process, is possibly getting hotter than ever.

In my book *The G.O.D. Experiments,* I explain how I came to the conclusion that a non-guided or "blind" theory of self-organization was by itself insufficient to explain complex non-random events connecting and forming humans and animals; if you are interested in this question, I invite you to read the book.

Consider the combined sequence and timing of the previously discussed events involving:

- Dr. Greyson,
- Dr. Schwartz,
- the Monroe Institute,

- Dr. Beitman speaking on synchronicity,
- the new space of the Division of Perceptual Studies being completed,
- the giving away of old journals, in particular an issue of a journal containing an article on synchronicity (with multiple copies of that issue available),
- my curious historic connection to this journal, and
- the content of the article related to what an intuitive who "channels" had said not once, but twice

Is it possible that somehow all of this could be explained simply in terms of some sort of non-intelligent "self-organization" process extending not only over space (Arizona, Missouri, and Virginia), but over time (at least a few months) as well?

Can you envision such a self-organizing process extending over thousands of miles and continuing over an extended length (or even any length) of time?

Of course, from a purely abstract point of view, the answer to this hypothetical question could be "yes."

However, this is also like asking whether fourteen extraordinarily improbable sequences of events—fourteen Type III Synchronicities—not just one or two, could have occurred simply by chance alone.

Again, from a purely logical point of view, the answer could also be "yes."

The deep question becomes whether "yes" is a reasonable and probable answer.

For example, it is logically possible that your spouse of twenty years is actually a tree and not a human, and you have simply been programmed by aliens to perceive the tree as if it were your spouse. This may sound crazy (and I believe it is crazy), but it is abstractly logically possible. However, as crazy as this sounds it is actually more likely to be true than saying that biophysical and social self-organization principles are sufficient to explain Type III Synchronicities. In other words, it is more likely that your spouse is actually a tree than the speculation that simple self-organization somehow creates sophisticated Type III Synchronicities.

The precise *timing and order* in which the events occurred, plus their *apparent symbolic meanings,* suggest that something beyond simple self-organization is going on. The evidence suggests that additional mechanisms are involved, and that the patterns even look like "plots" (as in writing and scripting) rather than the random and spontaneous self-organization of letters on a page.

My analysis at this point is that Step 7 is not a rationally acceptable explanation for the totality of the data reported in this book, and that it is our intellectual and ethical responsibility to actively explore additional possible explanations on the higher steps of the staircase.

Step 8 Human Intention and Energy

We are about to enter the realm of consciousness, energy, quantum physics, and parapsychology. Some of you may be familiar with this research and theory, and you may accept, if not believe, it. Others may not be familiar with this work, or may question or dismiss it altogether.

This is not the place to make the case for the plausibility of Step 8 explanations. I encourage you to read books written for the general public such as Dr. Dean Radin's *Entangled Minds,* Dr. Diane Powell's *The Psi Enigma,* Lynne McTaggart's *The Intention Experiment,* and my book, *The Energy Healing Experiments,* to understand why Step 8 explanations are viable and essential.

Here is the basic hypothesis: It is possible that the emergence of patterns and sequences of complex events is determined to some degree by the conscious as well as unconsciousness beliefs, intentions, wishes, and desires of the people involved in the synchronicities, whether they are aware of this fact or not.

We have seen examples of this possibility in numerous Type III Synchronicities reported in this book. You may recall a simple yet dramatic example of this in Chapter 8 involving my consciously "asking" whether ravens might appear, and then they did.

Of course, my replicated observation of the ravens in that Type III Synchronicity could have been a coincidence. The timing of my asking the questions, and the ravens' appearance, might have been due to chance.

However, in light of research reported in the representative sample of books cited above, it is possible that the timing of my making these requests could have reflected some sort of "precognitive" or "presentiment process" on my part. It is conceivable that somehow my consciousness could have affected the minds of the ravens, triggering their precisely timed flight. It is also possible that my requests were heard by higher spirits, and that they somehow influenced the ravens, but this would take us to Step 9 and above.

Partly because Step 8 explanations are so controversial—and partly because there is much to ponder in the Type III Synchronicities I have already revealed—I have decided to postpone sharing additional multiple Type III Synchronicities, which speak directly to the plausibility of Steps 8 and above, for a sequel to this book.

My purpose here is not to convince you that Step 8 is both probable and consistent with important scientific evidence, but rather to make you aware of its logical and evidence-based possibility in light of contemporary physics, neuroscience, and psychology.

In sum, it is entirely possible that one or more events within a complex Type III Synchronicity might involve Step 8 processes.

However, by itself Step 8 cannot rationally and responsibly account for the totality of Type III Synchronicities reported in this book.

Step 9 Human Spirits

Is it possible that some synchronicities are mediated by spirits? That the living consciousnesses of people who have passed on can play a role in connecting and coordinating our lives?

Of course, if you are not open to the possibility of survival of consciousness after death, then Step 9 is immediately ruled out.

Moreover, some of you may resonate with a statement purportedly attributed to Einstein, as reported in Stacy Horn's non-fiction book *Unbelievable,* about the history of parapsychological research in Professor JB Rhine's parapsychology laboratory at Duke University:

"According to Helen Dukas, Einstein's secretary, Einstein once said, '*Even if I saw a ghost I wouldn't believe it*'" (33).

Or, as a skeptic once said to Dr. Margaret Mead, the distinguished anthropologist, "These are the kind of data I wouldn't believe, even if they were true!"

However, I have responsible reasons for proposing that we seriously entertain the possibility of Step 9.

The first is that I have conducted extensive research on the possibility of life after death, reported in three books—*The Afterlife Experiments, The Truth About Medium,* and *The Sacred Promise*—and the totality of the evidence is consistent with the idea that consciousness continues after physical death. Moreover, at least four laboratories have independently replicated and extended our observations using double-blinded and triple-blinded procedures.

Also, laypersons have written reports documenting evidence of after death communication that are compelling, if not convincing, as illustrated by Rhonda Eklund Schwartz's non-fiction book *Love Eternal* (New Edition published by Param Media).

The second reason is that early on in my synchronicity self-science journey, I was exposed to the possibility that spirit might be involved with synchronicity.

You will recall in Chapter 3 how I received a message purportedly from the late Susy Smith via a medium in the Midwest. In the email I was told about the movie *Dragonfly,* and that I would be meeting someone important to the research.

Presuming that fraud was not involved here, the question arises: was the medium somehow reading my mind, plus the mind of the composer of the score to the movie *Dragonfly* (a Step 8 hypothesis), or was she reading Susy's mind from the other side (a Step 9 hypothesis)?

If she was doing the latter, Susy was clearly playing a role in making me aware of upcoming dragonfly synchronicities.

There are many ways that spirit might play a role in our lives and contribute to the synchronicity process. What matters at this moment is that we realize that there is a reason to entertain the possibility of the reality of the Step 9 explanation.

Step 10 Higher Spiritual Beings

Step 10 proposes that higher spiritual beings or "higher frequency energies" can sometimes play a role in the appearance of synchronicities in our individual and collectives lives. These higher spiritual beings are sometimes called "guides" or "angels."

If you already had difficulty imagining the possibility that Step 9 might be valid, you will find Step 10 almost impossible to entertain. However, it is important to keep in mind that the idea of higher spiritual beings is not at all illogical or irrational. On the contrary, as noted by Dr. John H Spencer in *The Eternal Law,* even the great twentieth century logician, Kurt Gödel, a close companion of Albert Einstein, believed that we are connected to higher beings. As Gödel puts it: "There are other worlds and rational beings of a different and higher kind".

The Type III Synchronicity reported in Chapter 12 is especially curious, because it includes the fact that an intuitive supposedly channeled information not once, but twice. Moreover, this information was featured in the article on synchronicity that I happened upon at the seminar on synchronicity research at the University of Virginia. The details of the precise timing and content involved with that article, and the journal in which it was published, combined with the fact that I discovered it at a research seminar on synchronicity, played a pivotal role in it becoming my synchronicity tipping point.

The intuitive was Christine, the woman you met in Chapter 10 whom I witnessed purportedly channel the phrase, "If it walks like a duck." Christine had participated in a variety of experiments in my laboratory spanning mediumship, medical intuition, healing, and channeling research. She was never 100% accurate—no intuitive is—but she was typically more often correct than incorrect, and like a superstar baseball player, not only did she hit homeruns from time to time, but every now and again she hit one out of the park.

In the process of writing this section, I happened to notice a curious pattern of events that might possibly represent an emerging synchronicity:

- The initial stimulus for me to finish this book came from my reading of William Gladstone's novel *The Twelve.*
- When I made the list of possible explanations for synchronicities, the total count came out to 12. (I must admit, I would have preferred 11.)
- The group of guides that Christine supposedly channels are 12 in number, and They claim that this number is spiritually significant.

If more than chance coincidence, how would you explain this if not at least by considering Step 10?

Step 11 The One Mind—Personal

Step 11 takes us to the penultimate level of possible explanations of the source of synchronicities: the Higher Intelligence or the One Mind hypothesis. There are at least two fundamental levels on which the One Mind might operate. The first is personal, where the One Mind would have the capacity to connect with each of us as individuals and play a role in our relatively local lives and synchronicities.

The chapter that most directly addresses this possibility is Chapter 7, which reviews the rose-God Type III Synchronicity. However, we can infer the existence of some sort of Higher Intelligence or the One Mind in most of the chapters of this book, including Chapter 12.

It would take many pages to show how it is possible to analyze the configuration of synchronicities that extended across space (from the Southwest to the Southeast) and time (at least several months), and reveal an unfolding organization implying the existence of some sort of super high level of creative, practical, and playful intelligence in the process.

What is important here is to recognize the possibility that careful and thorough analysis of Type III Synchronicities can lead to the strong inference of the existence of the One Mind in the appearance of synchronicities. The key term here is "inference."

The process of logical deduction that encourages physicists to infer invisible matter ("dark matter") or invisible "fields" of energy is the same type of process of logical deduction that encourages us to infer the existence of invisible intelligence ("dark mind") in Type III Synchronicities. Therefore, Step 11 is a highly plausible explanatory hypothesis on both rational and empirical grounds.

Step 12 The One Mind—Collective

Step 12 presents the greatest challenge to our intelligence and imagination. It is for me, personally, the most daunting, humbling, and awe-inspiring hypothesis that has ever challenged my human mind.

This is the hypothesis that proposes that, in order for us to ultimately envision the source and mechanisms of Type III Synchronicities, it is essential for us to posit the existence of some sort of Higher Intelligence or One Mind operating at a collective (and even universal) organizing level.

Step 12 addresses the deepest implications of the take home message of novels like *The Twelve.*

If a Universal Synchronizing Process operates via the One Mind, we can think of it as being required to play the combined role of composer, arranger, and conductor. I find it helpful to use the metaphor of a jazz symphonic orchestra to express this profound idea.

Jazz is an individual as well as group or collective process. I know the process firsthand, because I played professional jazz in high school and college. The larger the group is (I have played in trios and quintets, as well as big bands of thirty or more musicians), the more complex the process is. And a symphonic jazz orchestra may involve the coordinated music making of more than a hundred musicians.

The composer envisions the melodies, harmonies, and rhythms, and creates a structure, organization, and flow.

Then the arranger takes this core organization of information provided by the composer and expresses it across multiple instruments. The simplest of melodies, such as 'Twinkle Twinkle Little Star,' can be arranged in myriad ways.

It has been my experience that only by attempting to orchestrate a melody yourself can you fully appreciate the degree of intelligence, creativity, and aesthetics required to produce a beautiful and lasting arrangement of music. In my opinion, the arranging process is as difficult (if not more difficult) than the composing process.

Finally there is the conductor, who serves the critical role of helping the musicians to coordinate their individual parts so as to produce an organized and effective collective performance.

What jazz adds to this already complex process is that at various points, individual musicians are given the opportunity to improvise within the underlying structure of the chord progressions and rhythms. In smaller ensembles, each musician may have their turn to play a solo while the others offer background support.

People can serve as composers, arrangers, or conductors, and sometimes they do all three.

We have a difficult enough time envisioning the whole of a complex symphonic score when we focus on our own particular melodies and harmonies. Having played in classical orchestras, I know how hard it is just to perform one's one part well, and to do so in the context of the orchestra as a whole.

It is unfortunate that when we are focusing on performing our individual parts, we often seem unable to experience the fullness of the music as a whole. The same limitations of awareness and understanding apply to living our personal lives in the context of our greater collective lives.

Can you imagine what it would take to compose, arrange, and conduct a super-orchestra, especially a jazz super-orchestra, containing millions of people? And what if you were attempting to compose a "meta-score" that could creatively unite billions of people worldwide playing simultaneously and yet allowing—and fostering—their individual improvisations? This image helps us appreciate that the One Mind is truly a Super Mind.

The greatest spiritual visions reported throughout history infer the existence of some sort of infinite intelligence and beneficence—some sort of a Super Composer, Arranger, and Conductor—whose grand mission is to foster both our individual and collective lives.

If we were to look for evidence of such a Super Mind, one place we could look for it would be in patterns and sequences of events that not only connect disparate people, but also reveal a unifying purpose or plot, what some call the "Divine Plot."

Patterns of Type III Synchronicities across individuals may provide such scientific evidence.

Meanwhile, when we are busy playing our individual instruments—focusing on our individual lives and challenges—we may not have the time, energy, skills, or inspiration to discover whether there exists an emerging super-complex yet unifying score that is ultimately available to us all.

I am reminded of the lyrics in one of James Taylor's songs where he sings, "Look up from your life". What synchronicity self-science does is nurture our intentions and abilities to look up from our own lives and discover a bigger picture.

Is there a pattern, for example, to the unfolding of the Type III Synchronicities reported in this book?

Was the sequential order of these Type III Synchronicities "random"? Or, is there a "higher order" to these Type III Synchronicities waiting to be discovered?

As I came to discover, the answer to this challenging question clearly seems to be "higher order," and it is supported by additional Type III Synchronicities. More importantly, these "patterns of patterns" and "sequences of sequences" reveal the emergence of a higher order that transcends us as individuals.

What matters here is not whether the Step 12 hypothesis is ultimately true. What is important is that we make sure to include it in our list of possible explanations, and that we remain open to the possibility of discovering it in our individual and collective lives.

With this overview in mind, we can now turn our attention to Quantum Synchronicity Theory in the next chapter, and explore how the combination of accepted fundamental observations and theories in quantum physics and systems science provide a new integrative framework for conceiving and applying synchronicity to our personal and collective lives.

Chapter 17
Introduction to Quantum Synchronicity Theory: Looking Ahead

In fact, it is often stated that of all the theories proposed in this century, the silliest is quantum theory. Some say that the only thing that quantum theory has going for it, in fact, is that it is unquestionably correct.
Machio Kaku, PhD

It is generally acknowledged that the most successful—and weirdest—theory in the history of science is quantum physics. As I have come to discover in my synchronicity self-science journey, there are curious and revealing parallels between quantum physics and the nature of Type III Synchronicities.

Some of these parallels are extraordinarily challenging, as well as enlightening. Not only do they offer the hope of providing a new understanding about synchronicity, but they potentially point to the next great step in our understanding of nature and the universe as a whole.

Honoring Thoughtful Skepticism

I am going to do something unusual here and feature the writings of a well-known super-skeptic and atheist to help make the case for Quantum Synchronicity Theory (QST).

I wish to thank Dr. Victor Stenger, author of the book *Quantum Gods: Creation, Chaos, and the Search for Cosmic Consciousness* for two pages he wrote that initially turned my mind upside down, and subsequently gave me one of the fundamental keys to QST.

Based on his long history of skeptical writing, I would predict that Dr. Stenger's position is that synchronicities can best be explained by the five lowest steps (from misperceptions and coincidence to simple psychological causes), and that the five highest steps are probably poppycock.

For example, he writes:

"Goswami [a professor of physics] has no basis for inferring superpowers of the mind from quantum mechanics or claiming that they are empirically verified. In fact, the data now show that beyond any reasonable doubt that these powers do not exist" (179).

Statements like "beyond any reasonable doubt" and "these powers do not exist" pretty much slam the door on any possibility of Steps 8—12.

I doubt that Dr. Stenger will disagree with my specific description of quantum physics, since I am using his precise words. I also would hope that he would not disagree too much with my showing its apparent parallel to the emerging evidence of Type III Synchronicities, since the logic is straightforward and obvious.

However, I anticipate that he might take serious issue with one of my conclusions, as you will soon see.

"Waves Are Not Real"—Or Are They?

Our focus will be on one aspect of quantum physics, which is typically referred to as "wave-particle duality." Briefly, it is now well established in replicated experiments that in the presence of a single slit, photons (which, according to Dr. Stenger, are massless particles or quanta of light) create a pattern of dots—a single column—which are particle-like in their distributions.

However, in the presence of two slits, instead of creating two similar columns of dots which are particle-like in their distributions, what is observed are multiple columns of dots which are wave-like in their distributions—meaning they can be described using mathematics originally crafted to measure the interference patterns of waves (for example, as observed in water).

Many physicists, as well as individuals Dr. Stenger calls "quantum spiritualists," have interpreted this to mean that not only is light both a wave and a particle, but that how it appears to us depends upon how we measure it—in other words, using one slit or two.

What Dr. Stenger wrote that initially turned my mind upside down was his claim that actually "there are no waves, just particles". Moreover, to justify his conclusion, he quoted a high school lecture attributed to Dr. Richard Feynman, who said:

"I want to emphasize that light comes in this form—particles. It is very important to know that light behaves like particles, especially for those of you who have gone to school where you were probably told something about light behaving like waves. I'm telling you that it does behave—like particles" (184).

This sounds pretty definitive to me.

And in one sense, they are absolutely correct.

When the experiments are conducted, what are detected on arrays of photomultipliers are distributions of little dots—what look like individual, localized events.

We do not see "waves" per se; what we see are collections of dots.

What physicists mean by the "wave-like" nature of light is that the patterns or sequences of the dots are arranged in such a way that they resemble interference patterns of waves seen in ripples of water—especially if we were to "connect the dots."

When we connect the dots, the resulting lines are wavy in appearance. And the wavy-appearing lines can be described precisely by equations originally designed to quantify distributions of numbers that make up wavy lines.

Dr. Stenger goes on to explain how these mathematical "wave functions" can more accurately be described as "state vectors" (which is beyond the scope of the current discussion). What is important here is that he concludes that the wave function is "fictional," meaning it is merely an "abstract invention."

I completely agree with Dr. Stenger's simple point: that photons look like particles. However, I could not disagree more with his conclusion that waves are therefore "fictional."

Understanding our disagreement is key not only to understanding my fundamental issue with his argument; it is also key to understanding how it helps us make sense of the quantum nature of synchronicity. Moreover, it helps us to understand the underlying debate between super-skeptical people and spiritual people.

Waves Are "Organizations" of Particles: Though Appearing "Nonmaterial," They Are Conceptually as "Real as Steel"

It is an experimental fact that in the double-slit condition, the light is detected as individual dots. The light has not lost its "quantum" or "particle" essence.

In this obvious sense, there is no "wave": light is still a "particle."

However, it is also an experimental fact that in the single-slit condition, the distribution of these "particles" can be described as if the particles are "organized" or "arranged" like particles, whereas in the double-slit condition, the distribution of these "particles" can be described as if the particles are "organized" or "arranged" as waves.

What Dr. Stenger prefers to do, quite emphatically, is label the "organization" and "arrangement" of the dots as "fictional," and in some deep sense "not real."

For him, only the dots are real, not their arrangements.

The question is, are only the dots, and not their arrangements, real?

If this is how you think, and we apply this identical logic to patterns and sequences of real-life events, then yes—ravens, ducks, and green emeralds can be real, but not their arrangements (e.g., the pattern and sequence of their appearance).

Ravens, ducks, and green emeralds are "quanta" in the sense that they are discrete units or dots of information. Since their arrangement would be by Dr. Stenger's definition abstract, a "fiction" of the "inventor" who was trying to describe it, then the arrangement could be dismissed as immaterial (pun intended) and ignored.

Returning to quantum physics, it is precisely the unpredicted observation of the "wave-like" arrangement of the distributions of the individual photons in the double-slit condition that raises the profound experimental and theoretical questions regarding light as a particle and a wave.

We cannot use the mathematics developed for particles to predict and describe the distribution of dots in the double-slit experiment. Whereas the distribution of dots is predicted by particle mathematics in the single-slit experiment, the distribution of dots is predicted by wave mathematics in the double-slit experiment.

Yes, in the simplest sense, there are no waves on the ocean. The water molecules do not travel across the surface of the water; what they do is mostly move up and down. It is the organization of this pattern over space and time that "travels."

Let's be practical for a moment and think about the surfer. What the surfer rides on across the surface of the water is not the movement of the individual water molecules—which are mostly moving up and down, and can be described as particles—but the organization of their patterns over space and time.

Concluding that the "wave" the surfer rides is "fictional" misses both the adventure and essence of what she or he is doing on the water. If Dr. Stenger really does not believe in the reality of waves, then he should try telling that to surfers and sailors.

Also in the simplest sense, there are no waves of sound in the air. The individual air molecules do not travel from the musician's instrument to the listener's ear. What they do is mostly move up and down. It is the organization of their patterns over space and time that "travel" to the listener and comprise the beauty and complexity of music.

Concluding that the sound "wave" is fictional misses the essence of both the art and science of music. Being both a performer and listener, I perceive the wave-like information aspects of the air molecules as both meaningful and "real."

A final example is when people "do the wave" in a football or basketball stadium. Properly coordinated and timed, it looks a gigantic wave is traveling around the stadium. Clearly the spectators are not moving around the stadium; they are merely standing up and down and waving their arms. However, the pattern of information that defines the movement is witnessed as travelling around the stadium.

Waves function as information. They carry form, pattern, and ultimately meaning. It is true that they are not "physical things." What they "are" is the arrangement of things; it is the arrangement of things that make them what they are.

However, in a deep sense, "waves as organizations" are as "real as steel," since it is the arrangement or organization of particles of steel that define theoretically what we mean by steel. As particle physics reminds us, it is the number and organization—the arrangement—of electrons, protons, and neutrons that create the metal we observe as steel.

In other words, if we used Dr. Stenger's logic, it would seem that we would have to conclude that "steel" itself was actually "fictional," since to particle physicists only electrons, protons, and neutrons are real (unless we were further tempted to consider subatomic particles as real, and carry this logic of reductionism one step lower).

Taking Stock: The Math is Not the Territory; the Math Is the Map

To summarize, at the quantum level, light (as well as electrons and possibly all fundamental particles) appears to exist as "particles" localized in time and space. This quantum particle-like) property applies to things that have mass—our normal sense of material—as well as things that presumably have zero rest mass, such as photons of light (though some physicists might argue that light has a miniscule amount of mass).

However, laboratory research reveals that the distribution of the quanta behaves quite differently depending upon the experimental conditions—in the single-slit condition, the dots are arranged as predicted by the mathematics used to describe particles, whereas in the double-slit condition, the dots are arranged as predicted by the mathematics used to describe what we observe to function as waves.

The kind of logic that dismisses wave-like distributions as unreal misses something fundamental, not only about quantum physics but about the whole of nature and the entire universe. If we are inclined to envision wave-like patterns over time—sequences of events in time and space—as fictional and unreal, we will be less likely to discover these patterns, and should we happen to discover them, we will be more prone to confer little importance or meaning upon them.

Furthermore, if Dr. Stenger were correct, then all that would be real would be the fundamental particles, since all material objects are only what they are more or less due to the arrangement of their particles. And so, if Dr. Stenger is correct, then it would seem that he does not even exist, since he, too, would be just an arrangement of particles; since the arrangement according to him is a fiction, and since it is just this arrangement that gives him individual corporality, then if the arrangement is unreal, then he, too, is unreal. Therefore, if Dr. Stenger is correct, he does not exist—and never did.

I once asked Dr. Paul Davies, the author of numerous books on physics and God and winner of the one million dollar Templeton Prize in 1995, what his understanding was of the nature and essence of a field. We were two of approximately ten senior scientists who had been invited to attend a small private working conference in Seattle.

Most of us were first introduced to fields in grade school science. We were given a bar magnet, a piece of paper, and iron filings. We were instructed to place the paper over the magnet and gently sprinkle the iron filings on the paper. Instead of forming a seemingly random pile, we witnessed the filings lining up in concentric curves. The little particles of iron seemed as if by magic to arrange themselves in an orderly fashion. The explanation for what placed them in this precise order was the organizing power of invisible magnetic fields.

When I asked Dr. Davies about the nature and essence of fields, he responded by saying something to the effect of, "You have taken multiple physics courses. You know what a field is. A field is something we measure with our equations". Then he walked away. I was initially a bit disappointed by his seemingly dismissive response. However, I later realized that he was not being flippant; he was simply being honest.

The truth is that most physicists have no idea what a field is, except insofar as it works in their equations. To many working physicists, the existence of a simple magnetic field—like the existence of a wave—is often assumed to be "fictional" and an "invention of mathematics" which is useful to the extent that it works in practice.

As mentioned previously, Dr. Feynman announced in his Nobel Prize lecture that he did not understand quantum physics, and he was convinced no one else did either.

As someone who appreciates engineering and technology, I deeply appreciate the practical. My attitude is—if the math works, let's use it.

However, extending the metaphor that "the map is not the territory," it is essential that we not lose sight of the fact that "the math is not the territory."

We must remember this.

The math does not arrange the iron filings around the magnet.

The math does not create the wave-like distributions of the photons in the double-slit experiment.

The math does not compose, arrange, and conduct a jazz symphony.

And the math does not compose, arrange, and conduct patterns and sequences of what we might call "quantum synchronicities," be they of ravens, ducks, or green emeralds.

Like maps, math is a tool. I am not only interested in the tools (although truth be told, I actually love tools). I am more interested in how we can use the tools to understand both the properties and essence of the territory.

What QST does is encourage us to discover the many parallels between quantum physics and synchronicity—we have reviewed a possible parallel to wave-particular duality here—and then take the integration one step further.

QST inspires us to expand our conception of quantum physics and psychology by opening our minds to the possibility that replicable and meaningful patterns of sequences of events can occur, not only in a double-slit experiment, but in the laboratory of our daily lives.

QST proposes that the task of becoming a sophisticated synchronicity self-scientist is not merely to collect data systematically and accurately. Our goal is to be discerningly open to analyzing the patterns and sequences of the events in a manner that can reveal not only the explicit ordering of the events, but their implicit potential symbolic meanings as well.

Words and Ideas Are More than Dots

If you are reading this in a printed book (or an eBook), what you are seeing are dots distributed on a page. In a deep reductionistic sense there are no letters, words, phrases, concepts, insights, or opportunities on this page; there are only dots organized in apparently non-random ways. And the distribution of black dots in the context of the surrounding white paper (or screen) result in reflection of an extraordinarily high number of patterns of photons to your eyes which are initially registered as dots.

However, if you see more than this—if you are reading my words and hopefully understanding them—then you are going beyond the simple exposition of quantum physics as conceived of by physicists such as Dr. Stenger. You are going beyond the dots to their patterns and sequences. You are seeing the "waves" and "fields" in terms of their organization and arrangement.

QST encourages us to see both the dots and their patterns. It encourages us to connect dots, and even to be open to discovering that the connected dots may have deep meaning and purpose.

Can we develop better tools for analyzing patterns and sequences of events—be they photons and electrons, or ravens and roses—and discover their possible organizations and meanings?

I am convinced through my own self-science synchronicity journey that we can. In fact, all of us can.

The hope and promise of synchronicity self-science awaits us.

Chapter 18
"A is and is not equal to A": A Synchronicity Equation

The worst form of inequality is to try to make unequal things equal.
Aristotle

I could not end this book without briefly sharing a joyful mathematical (and personal) synchronicity between William Gladstone's *The Twelve,* my writing of this book, and its applications to understanding the essence of synchronicity. We can think of this as my awakening to the synchronicity equation.

I should prepare you for the fact that this chapter will get a bit abstract, and may at times even seem like nonsense. Feel free to sample a little taste of this chapter or savor the whole serving. We include it not only because we are convinced it is nutritious for the mind, but like many acquired tastes, is a genuine delicacy.

As I was reading *The Twelve,* I began to notice its emerging focus on synchronicities. Then I came to Chapter 4, titled "Understanding Understanding." I had not read the phrase "Understanding Understanding" in at least a decade.

I was reminded of a graduate student I knew when we were doing our doctoral work in what was then called the Department of Social Relations at Harvard. This became Event #1. Years later he returned to Harvard as a tenured professor and was writing a book titled "Understanding Understanding." This was Event #2.

And I was reminded that Bill had also been a doctoral student in the Department of Social Relations, though he decided to leave graduate school and pursue a career in publishing instead. This was Event #3.

I then noticed that Chapter 4 began by mentioning how the main character, Max, had attended Phillips Andover Academy, which is situated twenty miles from Boston.

I had spent a semester doing clinical training at the Phillips Andover Academy as a graduate student in clinical psychology at Harvard. I had not thought about the Academy in decades. This was Event #4.

I continued reading and learned that Max was now attending Yale. I knew that Bill had been an undergraduate at Yale, and I smiled at some of the similarities between Bill and his fictional character Max. I had been a professor at Yale. This was Event #5.

A bit further into the book, I discovered that Max was fascinated by Alfred North Whitehead, who was at one time considered the world's leading systems thinker. Whitehead had also been a distinguished Professor at Harvard

As it so happened, Dr. Whitehead had been a hero of mine, but I did not know that Bill had as deep a fondness for him as I did. This was Event #6.

Bill went on to write about how "All knowledge was contained within the limits and possibilities of the systems in which human beings interacted". I was aware that this understanding is central to systems thinking. In fact, I had worked closely for a year with a Yale undergraduate on a project where we defined systems as a "set of limits." This was Event #7.

Then Bill wrote a sentence that really caught my attention: "Max saw in a flash that the ultimate limitation was being human". And then on the next page, Max shared one of the deepest and most important philosophical and mathematical insights that I had ever read about—in a textbook, journal article, or non-fiction book.

After referring to "Lux et Veritas" (Light and Truth, Yale's motto), Bill wrote a sentence that was elegantly simple and absolutely brilliant at the same time.

He wrote the formulation that "A is and is not equal to A" as the ultimate equation in explaining how to penetrate the impenetrable intellectual domain of "understanding understanding." The formulation took my breath away.

Could it be that Max had discovered "the ultimate equation" and that it was expressed by the simple phrase, "A is and is not equal to A"?

At first glance, the equation "A is and is not equal to A" may sound like nonsense. But nothing could be further from the truth.

As my mind quickly shifted from *what?* to *wow!,* I realized that Max (a.k.a. Bill) had provided an essential insight for understanding both quantum physics and synchronicity.

Here is how Bill described Max's awakening:

The realization of "A is and is not equal to A" changed the parameters for all logic, and the conclusions that purely logical theory could provide. The realization changed the axioms upon which general mathematics were based, and thus would have an impact on all hard scientific investigations.

Max's mind started spinning.

It could be the answer to our very existence... our life's purpose, he mused. *We're all connected and not just in superficial ways.*

It is beyond the scope of this chapter to discuss in detail how Bill reveals the essence of Max's bold insight, or the Yale professor's clinical response to Max's wild and seemingly grandiose idea. Indeed, the novel spends some time wrestling with the question: is Max brilliant or simply schizophrenic? If "A is and is not equal to A" is true, then maybe Max was both!

I understood being in such a quagmire. I experienced a similar challenge when the systemic memory hypothesis first came to me as a professor at Yale. (This hypothesis claims that all systems comprised of recurrent feedback loops, from the micro to the macro, extending from subatomic particles to super-clusters of galaxies and all levels of systems in between, have some form of dynamic memory.) For over a decade I did not know whether this insight was brilliant, crazy, or a combination of the two.

When I wrote the first draft of what became *The Living Energy Universe,* the manuscript was given to Bill to read for possible publication. I included just one equation in the book to encapsulate the thesis. I was pretty sure the reader would not notice it or give it much thought. However, Bill read the draft and said, "What convinced me that your theory was correct is the one formula you included in the book".

Returning to Max's formula, I was awestruck as I realized the deep truth in what Bill wrote: " 'A is and is not equal to A' resolved fundamental philosophical knots. It explained away paradoxes and enabled a higher level of abstraction for ever more complex mathematical systems".

This will get a bit abstract here. However, once you appreciate the basic logic, I will be able to show you how it helps us understand the weird and mysterious nature of both quantum physics and synchronicity.

Systems, Subsystems, and Supra-Systems: How "A Is and Is Not Equal to A"

Simply stated, we typically assume that 1 = 1, that 2 =2, and so forth. This is so obvious as to be taken literally to be true, and we hardly give it a second thought.

However, we know that 1 can be expressed as ½ plus ½, and 2 can be expressed as 1 plus 1.

In a deeper sense, "1" the "whole" is also "1" the "combination" of two parts (½ plus ½). And "2" the "whole" is also "2" the "combination" of two parts (1 plus 1).

Simply stated, something can be a "whole" in one sense and also be a "combination of parts" in another sense.

Notice that the "whole" can itself simultaneously be a part of something that is greater than itself. In systems thinking, it is said that the whole (system) is composed of parts (subsystems), and at the same time the whole (system) is also a part (subsystem) of a larger whole supra-system).

Hence, "1" the system (whole) can also be thought of as being composed of parts (subsystems: "½'s") and simultaneously be a part (subsystem) of a larger whole supra-system: "2").

What can we do with this abstract systemic logic?

For one thing, we can make sense of the unfortunate conclusion about the reality of particles versus waves proposed by Dr. Stenger, as discussed in the previous chapter, as well as celebrate its applicability to increasing our understanding of synchronicity.

Dots Are, and Are Not, Equal to Dots

You will recall that Dr. Stenger sees dots (called photons) in the double-slit experiment—as do all scientists who work with the raw data. The dots represent "A's" in Max's equation.

Since Dr. Stenger assumes that A equals A and only A, he concludes that only dots as individual dots exist.

If only dots exist, then the surprising wave-like distributions of the dots would be presumed to be fictional and unreal. However, if dots are not only "wholes" unto themselves, but also are "parts" of something greater—organized by force fields—then the dots can be viewed as being particles and also being expressions of invisible but real wave functions. In other words, dots are, and are not, equal to dots. And though the real may at times seem surreal, it is still real.

Of course, if your belief structure demands that only dots exist—especially if you emotionally prefer a dot-based universe—then you will be psychologically inclined to interpret the abstract and seemingly surreal formula that Max proposed as being a fiction or "invention" and summarily dismiss it, just as you would dismiss the abstract nature of waves. To do so, however, is neither scientific nor based in reason. (It would also logically and scientifically entail that you do not exist.)

From Dots and Letter A's to Quantum Synchronicity Waves

Synchronicities are like letter A's. In one sense, each event can be thought of as an individual, isolated event, and nothing more.

However, in another sense, each event can be thought of as being part of a larger string or sequence of events, which together reflect a greater and higher whole.

I suspect that in his heart of hearts, Dr. Stenger would honor the critical role that observations and evidence play in the responsible and ethical practice of science. He even wrote on page 206, "In any case, the final test as it always is in science is what the data say". I could not agree more.

I also suspect that Dr. Stenger agrees with Dr. Carl Sagan's vision that our ability to give up our most cherished beliefs in the face of new data is the "heart of science." It is also often very hard to do.

Max affords us a new logical tool for examining and understanding data. His analysis applies as effectively to quantum physics as it does to synchronicity. The equation provides us with a powerful tool for making it easier for us to discover and embrace new information and even change our minds.

If you started reading this book as a skeptic, has your mind been changed? Are you now open to the genuine possibility of supersynchronicity? If it has not changed, what does this tell you about the nature of your skeptical mind?

Commentary—Skeptical About Skepticism

John H Spencer, PhD
Author of the multiple award winning
The Eternal Law: Ancient Greek Philosophy, Modern Physics, and Ultimate Reality

Doubt everything or believe everything:
these are two equally convenient strategies.
With either we dispense with the need for reflection.
Henri Poincaré

Super Synchronicity dives deep into the synchronicity ocean, shedding the light of scientific understanding on many of its underlying mysteries, while facilitating our ability to co-create and ride the higher waves. Gary Schwartz has offered us a brilliant pioneering book that will encourage desperately needed foundational changes to the ossified assumptions of materialistic science.

How wonderful it would be if only the scientific community as a whole could abide by its own professed principles of objective and unbiased examination of evidence, without clinging to preconceived (and clearly false) assumptions about reality. The irony (and hypocrisy), of course, is that many scientific materialists vociferously critique religious believers for refusing to rationally examine evidence that may appear to threaten their beliefs, while they themselves do the same thing.

Richard Dawkins, for example, has no hesitation to vehemently attack the notion of faith, and yet he seems to ignore the fact that Max Planck, one of the greatest scientists in history and the chief originator of quantum physics, completely disagreed with him on this crucial point. This is illustrated in the following quote from Planck:

"Anybody who has been seriously engaged in scientific work of any kind realizes that over the entrance to the gates of the temple of science are written the words: *Ye must have faith.* It is the quality which the scientists cannot dispense with".

While it is true that Dawkins, a guru for atheists, has been a prolific voice in the realm of popular science, Planck's unique genius ushered in the development of quantum physics. Whose views carry more weight for you?

One of the main problems here, specifically in relation to the scientific study of synchronicity (and other related paranormal phenomena, such as precognition, telepathy, and so forth), is that most people – including many scientists – do not really understand the foundations of science itself. Similarly, far too many spiritual/religious people also lack the depth of understanding of science, and therefore tend to bring further confusion to all these issues. The first step, therefore, is to admit that we do not really know what we are talking about in any deep sense, which then offers us the hope to move forward and gain further clarity.

Let's consider one simple, but powerful, example of how further rational reflection on the skeptic's own assumptions leads to the implosion and transcendence of those very assumptions.

Is Synchronicity Self-Science Unscientific and Pseudo-Science?

One way the skeptic would like to attack the content and purpose of *Super Synchronicity* would be to say that what Gary is doing is not scientific because you cannot replicate or verify his synchronistic experiences in a controlled laboratory setting. The skeptic would continue by saying that since Gary's claims in this book are not scientific, we should therefore dismiss them as pseudo-science. However, the further hidden foundational assumption here is that only knowledge gained through controlled scientific experimentation is genuine and true knowledge. So, let's start with this foundational assumption:

The essence of the skeptic's argument (if they were to bother – or have the ability – to articulate it clearly) is:

1. Only knowledge gained through laboratory experimentation is genuine and true knowledge;
2. Laboratory experimentation requires being able to replicate the relevant conditions;
3. Gary's supposed synchronistic experiences cannot be replicated in a controlled laboratory setting;
4. Therefore, Gary is practicing pseudo-science with respect to the study of synchronicity.

Now we will consider each assumption in reverse order, starting with Assumption 3. It is true that Gary's specific experiences cannot be replicated in a laboratory setting—you can't move his house into the lab and sit around waiting for the next billion years hoping that, by chance, some hawks will fly into the window while he finishes writing *Super Synchronicity*. But, so what?

How much of what we experience in daily life can be replicated in the same way in a lab? Your close friend suddenly calls you after you have not seen each other for five years, and you are moved to tears from the joy of reconnecting; can that exact spontaneous emotional experience be replicated in a lab? But even when various paranormal phenomena have been subjected to laboratory conditions, the results are still, more often than not, rejected by the stubborn skeptic, so it seems that the criterion of replication is arbitrarily applied only when it is convenient for the skeptic to do so.

Next, let's consider Assumption 2. First, as Gary noted earlier in this book, we cannot put stars and galaxies in a lab here on earth; we have to observe their motions and discover the hidden patterns, similar to how he observed synchronistic events and tried to discover their underlying patterns.

Furthermore, despite the vital necessity of experimentation, science as a whole cannot be reduced to experiments. Indeed, Einstein, and many other scientific pioneers, did not do experiments. They were theorists. And without scientific theory, there is no viable way to make sense of experimental data, or even to know how to set up a useful experimental arrangement in the first place. Understanding data depends upon good theory, and developing theory depends upon good data. Both approaches are equally necessary to science, but that means that the whole of science cannot be reduced to pure theory; nor can it be reduced to pure experimental data. Therefore, Assumption 2 is deceptive, because it is leaving out the role of scientific theory, as well as insight, creativity, imagination, and even the mysterious. As Einstein famously put it:

> The most beautiful experience we can have is the mysterious. It is the fundamental emotion which stands at the cradle of true art and true science. Whoever does not know it and can no longer wonder, no longer marvel, is as good as dead.

Finally, let's consider Assumption 1. Interestingly, although it is the foundational assumption, it is the easiest to refute, and once refuted the entire skeptical argument fails. Assume first of all that it is true: that only knowledge gained through laboratory experimentation is genuine and true knowledge. The immediate – and devastating – self-destructive nature inherent in this assumption is that *there is no scientific experiment that could ever prove that we need a scientific experiment to achieve genuine and true knowledge.*

Assumption 1 is actually philosophical in nature (some would say metaphysical), and it is decidedly not scientific. Therefore,

Assumption 1, by its own standards, cannot be genuine and true knowledge. This means that either the skeptic holds onto this assumption through sheer stubbornness, in which case the argument is neither genuine nor true, or the skeptic rejects the assumption, in which case the whole argument against Gary loses its foundation and falls apart. In other words, the skeptic's argument fails either way.

But let's assume for a moment that my logical analysis is completely wrong, and let's also assume that all of Gary's rigorously detailed observations and highly plausible explanations are all unscientific. Again, I would have to say: so what? All of reality cannot be compressed and forced into the container of our current scientific knowledge. Reality is bigger than science; otherwise, we would not be able to make any new scientific discoveries.

In any case, even if we are all deluded about synchronicities, what matters here is that synchronistic events are *meaningful,* and no one has the right to take away the meaning, the personal significance, of a given event.

I wonder if a skeptic would tell their daughter that her wedding day was meaningless? After all, a wedding is nothing more than an arbitrarily defined social convention, and we are quite comfortable (skeptics included) in attributing great meaning to this day (and to many other such conventions). Why, then, the sudden hypocrisy in outlawing Gary's personally meaningful experiences, especially given that he is seeking objective patterns rather than mere social convention? What are the skeptics so afraid of?

The Hawk and the Rattlesnake

In my book *The Eternal Law,* I provide the following analogy, which, given Gary's unique hawk experiences, is even more relevant. Indeed, it is quite puzzling how materialist skeptics say we must adhere only to their narrow (and false) assumptions about science, while then refusing to listen to those many scientists who say that materialism is false.

It is as if the rattlesnake is asking the hawk to explain how they catch their prey, then restricting the hawk to speaking only within the rattlesnake's conceptual and experiential limitations.

Every time the hawk begins to describe stalking prey from the air, the rattlesnake protests that this way of speaking is illegitimate or irrational, since nothing can hunt from the air.

The hawk is then forced to use metaphors, analogies, and so forth to describe what it is like to fly, which the rattlesnake dismisses as not being logically rigorous and going far beyond what is possible to experience.

The hawk replies that all hawks experience hunting from the air every day, at which point the rattlesnake has had enough and slithers away.

The rattlesnake thinks that the hawk is absurd, but the hawk simply shrugs its wings, takes flight, and continues to catch prey in ways beyond the conceptual grasp of the rattlesnake.

I am not belittling snakes, by the way. On the contrary; imagine what an incredible hunting team the rattlesnake and the hawk would make if they were to work together! But in order to do so, the snake must first accept the reality of flight.

However, it seems rather pointless to fly without direction or purpose, and the greater our depth of understanding, the higher we can ascend – and also, the more safely we can land.

Quantum Synchronicity Theory and "A is and is not equal to A"

In addition to Gary's highly detailed observations, he has also turned our attention to the beginnings of what could potentially be more fully developed into Quantum Synchronicity Theory (QST), which can help us to increase our understanding of synchronicities. As Gary notes, William's insight that "A is and is not equal to A" is very significant. It helps us understand, for example, how in quantum physics the "dots are, and are not, equal to dots."

Interestingly, in 2007 I submitted my PhD thesis at the University of Liverpool, which included a discussion about how the statement "A = A" is both true and not true (a discussion I also included in *The Eternal Law,* which was published in 2012). William's *The Twelve* was published in 2009, and I did not read it until the summer of 2015. We were thinking in very similar ways on this topic without knowing each other or our respective writings. Was that all by chance?

I have had many extraordinary synchronistic and other profound spiritual/mystical experiences, all of which, to varying degrees of depth and intensity, have played a significant and transformative role in my life. If skeptics still want to deny the reality of synchronicities, then let them stay slithering on the ground while the rest of us enjoy the view from above.

Chapter 19
Techniques for Observing and Understanding Synchronicities

There is nothing so practical as a good theory.
Kurt Lewin, PhD

Inspired by the process of writing this book, in 2015 I created a workshop for guests at Canyon Ranch titled *Synchronicity and Spiritual Wellness.* Though my focus as a scientist is on helping guests discover and understand the reality of synchronicity, guests want to learn specific techniques and tips for observing and understanding synchronicities in their personal lives..

Being a conservative academic, I tend to be reluctant to share information that I have not established through scientific research. Though the evidence for the existence of supersynchronicity is extensive as reported in this book, there is no research that I am aware of that evaluates specific techniques for enhancing our ability to observe and understand synchronicities.

What follows is a short list of personal impressions concerning my learning about how to observe and understand synchronicities, especially supersynchronicities.

1. **Develop an open mind.** This includes not only being open to the reality of synchronicity, but being open to the potential novelty of the synchronicities as well. If our

minds are closed or dismissive, we will not have the "eyes to see."

2. **Keep a running record of your observations.** There is no substitute for chronicling potential synchronicities when they occur (or shortly thereafter). I use my smart phone for writing texts, recording audio messages, taking photographs, and even recording videos. In addition, I have a separate email account for sending myself emails documenting synchronicities. The process of recording synchronicities not only increases the accuracy and completeness of the information, but it fosters in creased awareness of potential synchronicities as well.
3. **Spend time reviewing your synchronicities.** Each time we review the synchronicities, not only may we see deeper connections, but we also increase our memory for the synchronicities as they are unfolding.
4. **Celebrate your synchronicities when they occur.** I do this for multiple reasons, including (a) increasing my awareness and memory for the events when they happen, (b) learning more about the possible connections between the synchronicities, especially when the synchronicities involve other people, (c) expressing instantaneous gratitude to the Universe for the presence of the synchronicities (i.e. letting the Universe know that I have noticed It's potential involvement with the synchronicities, and that I deeply appreciate them), and (d) having fun with the whole process. Also, if you discover a special piece of jewelry, art, or other memento of a given synchronicity, purchase it if speaks to you. Rhonda and I have purchased over a hundred pieces of jewelry, art, and other mementos which not only honor the synchronicities but remind us of their occurrence and specialness.
5. **Enjoy the process of becoming a synchronicity detective.** I am a great fan of gifted detectives in literature, especially Sherlock Holmes and Nero Wolfe. I treat the mystery of synchronicities as a playful and creative challenge, something

to savor. This includes being comfortable in not knowing whether a given chain of serial synchronicities has a meaning, or what the meaning (s) might be.

6. **Develop increased discernment in entertaining alternative interpretations.** Sometimes synchronicities are essentially random coincidences, and they should be treated as such. Other times synchronicities are "too coincidental to be coincidences" as Yogi Berra said, or are "too coincidental to be accidental" as Susy Smith said, and should be explored further. Sometimes synchronicities can have multiple layers of meanings – including (a) for you, (b) for one or more other people, and (c) for your web of interrelationships, and all of the meanings may be relevant in some situations. And sometimes synchronicities are not literal, they are symbolic, and we need to be open to exploring historical symbolic meanings and how they might apply in a given situation. The more sophisticated we become in developing our discernment, the more adept we become in observing and understanding synchronicities. This includes becoming our own "friendly devil's advocates" and being skeptical about whether a particular event deserves to be labelled a synchronicity and examined. We all have the potential to fool ourselves and engage in self-deception; being mindful of this helps us keep such tendencies to a minimum.
7. **Ask questions and request information of others, including the Universe.** My personal experience, including knowing many people who are avid supersynchronicity experiencers, is that allowing ourselves to ask questions of others, including the Universe, increases the number and significances of synchronicities observed. The increase is more than just selective attention; the fact is that super highly improbable sets of synchronicities can occur when we request their occurrence.
8. **Develop relationships with synchronicity buddies.** Synchronicities buddies not only provide us with increased

> opportunities to have synchronicities, they provide us with the inspiration to be mindful of potential synchronicities in the first place. Also, it makes the process of discovery and evolution all the more meaningful and enjoyable.

Each of these personal impressions can be investigated in future synchronicity research. So many opportunities for discovery and exploration...

Twelve Frequently Asked Questions and Answers: From Randomness to Openness

1. When did you become convinced that synchronicities were real?

Though I have now had hundreds of extraordinary evidential Type III Synchronicities, and even supersynchronicities across multiple Type III Synchronicities, there was no single event or combination of Type III Synchronicities that marked the time when I became convinced of the reality of synchronicities.

As I pondered this question, I came to realize that I had become convinced that synchronicities were real when I could no longer keep track of them all! I had experienced so many Type III Synchronicities that I could no longer recall the detailed accounts of a significant number of them. I found I had to go back to my notes, and then I would marvel all over again at what had happened. Indeed, it was the "astronomical improbability" (introduced in Chapter 1) of the accumulated Type III Synchronicities that logically and emotionally led me to accept their reality

2. Based upon your discoveries to date, what have you concluded about the nature of reality?

The overarching conclusion I have reached can be summarized in the sound bite, "never underestimate the universe." I have learned to be ever more humble in thinking that I know what reality is, or what is truly going on. The more synchronicities I uncover, as carefully and responsibly as possible, the more clearly I can show how remarkable reality really is.

I introduced the idea that "randomness does not occur by chance" in *The G.O.D. Experiments* partly through physical and statistical evidence, and partly through a careful integration of quantum physics and systems science. The totality of the evidence reported in that book, and extended in this book, strongly suggests that science's core assumptions about the existence and nature of chance and randomness need to be reexamined, probably deeply revised, and even potentially rejected. I am mindful of the fact that the reexamination of randomness addresses a fundamental assumption in science and extends from quantum physics, through evolutionary biology and psychology, to astrophysics.

My second book addressing synchronistic phenomena, currently in progress, focuses on reexamining the randomness hypothesis in light of contemporary evidence and theories spanning quantum physics, evolutionary biochemistry, complexity, and contemporary consciousness science.

We can no longer view reality exclusively, or even primarily, in simple material terms. Think about this: in quantum physics, light is presumed by most physicists to be a "massless" particle (zero rest mass)—which immediately makes it "material-less" (i.e., devoid of matter) when at rest. These "material-less" entities somehow gain some sort of "materiality" when in motion; but how can something material-less be in motion and gain materiality? These entities can then be organized by invisible fields (according to wave mechanics) that are non-material in nature (i.e., abstract entities in equations). Add to this the existence of consciousness and intelligence, and extend this beyond the individual to a Higher Consciousness or One Mind, and one's vision of reality is expanded accordingly.

In light of the increasing real-life evidence for synchronicity, coupled with its transformative implications for how we view the nature of reality, it is not surprising that I regularly experience my personal and professional life as surreal. A more accurate way of saying this is that the experience of surrealism is becoming a frequent reality-based experience in my life.

3. How do your observations speak to atheist claims that there is no evidence for Intelligence or Mind in the cosmos?

My heart goes out to people who have concluded "beyond a reasonable doubt"—a phrase used often by Dr. Stenger in his book *Quantum Gods*—that the concept of a Higher Intelligence, the One Mind, a Super Mind, or God is irrational, delusional, and completely inconsistent with the scientific evidence (or more appropriately, the lack of evidence).

Dr. Stenger states this position forcefully:

> We should see evidence for God in the cosmos, in life on Earth, and in human activities. However, using our own senses and the scientific instruments we have developed to aid those senses, we find no evidence for God or any form of supreme spirit.

However, contrary to Dr. Stenger's apparently definitive dismissal (and dismay), *Super Synchronicity* documents that we can responsibly and effectively use "our own senses"—coupled with relevant, reasoned analysis—to obtain compelling and replicable evidence of higher-order organization and structure to life events.

The logical approach to collecting evidence of synchronicity is not dissimilar, in principle, to the way in which quantum physicists obtain compelling and replicable evidence of higher order organization and wave-like structure revealed in the distribution of dots (photons) in the double-slit experiment. I discuss this in some detail in Chapter 17, which introduces Quantum Synchronicity Theory. And although Dr. Richard Feynman might be tempted, if he were here, to label this as "Quantum Flapdoodle," I would caution him to remember that sometimes what seems like "nonsense" turns out to be "essence"; the deciding factor in experimental science is ultimately data, which, of course needs to be correctly—or most reasonably—interpreted or understood.

What is important to recognize here is that evidence for Higher Intelligence and a Greater Mind can be found in the patterns and sequences of life events, presuming that you are open to collecting this information and analyzing the patterns that unfold. If you are convinced "beyond reasonable doubt" that such evidence does not and cannot exist—as Dr. Michael Shermer concludes in his Foreword to *Quantum Gods*—you will not volunteer to play the game of synchronicity baseball and will never get to first base.

Similarly, while the skeptics disbelieved that the Wright Brothers actually flew their plane, such skepticism did not stop the plane from flying. It simply meant that such skeptics would themselves never be able to create a flying machine. As Dr. John H. Spencer makes clear in *The Eternal Law,* if the greatest scientific pioneers had followed such a fundamentalist skeptical approach to science, then science would never have developed. If we cannot imagine anything beyond where we currently are, then there seems to be little hope of moving forward in any kind of systematic, scientific way.

Moreover, the sequences and patterns of life events are often not only replicable (they behave non-randomly), and potentially have symbolic meanings, but the complex unfolding of patterns implies a "secret" structure or storyline that can potentially be described in narrative terms. Dr. Dale Harrison, formerly at the Elon University School of Communications, calls this the "Holy Grail of Synchronicity Science."

Addressing this implicit narrative in synchronistic events is one of the greatest quests for future synchronicity science.

4. What is the most surprising aspect of synchronicities that you have witnessed?

Probably the most surprising aspect of Type III Synchronicities that I have witnessed involves the apparent playfulness, humor, and even silliness in some of these Type III Synchronicities. The string of nineteen duck synchronicities is a hilarious case in point.

If a Higher Intelligence, or the One Mind, is involved with Type III Synchronicities, this divine power sometimes displays a super-sense of humor.

5. What are the qualities of people who seem to have recurrent multiple synchronicities?

My personal observations suggest that people who experience genuine and frequent synchronicities tend to be

1. creative,
2. open-minded,
3. compassionate,
4. caring,
5. playful,
6. curious,
7. courageous,
8. genuine,
9. intelligent,
10. discerning,
11. mindful,
12. intuitive,
13. appreciative,
14. successful, and
15. sane.

They are distributed across gender, age, religions, professions, cultures, and financial demographics.

6. How do you feel about sharing your personal awakening to synchronicities, especially with super-skeptics?

The primary feeling I experience is one of nervousness.

I realize that some people are going to dismiss these experiences out of hand and label them (and me) using unwarranted derogatory terms like "sloppy thinking" and "pseudo-science."

I expect that some people are going to miss the forest for the trees. Some super-skeptics are going to discover minor errors I may have made concerning one or two branches or twigs on a given tree (maybe I made an innocent miscalculation or citation somewhere), and use this as an excuse to not only throw out the whole tree, but the entire forest as well.

However, believing in Yale's motto "Lux et Veritas"—Light and Truth—I prefer to shine light on the truth, even when the truth is seemingly bizarre—if not unbelievable—at times.

7. **In what sense can synchronicity be brought into the laboratory?**

Since synchronicities typically occur in real life, and we do not have control over them, we cannot manipulate them per se and study them parametrically. In this sense, synchronicity self-science is more like astrophysics than quantum physics, as we cannot put a galaxy in a test tube and study it under ideal laboratory conditions.

On the other hand, Dr. Beidman and colleagues have created a reliable personality test titled the "Weird Coincidences Scale" to measure people's reports of different kinds of synchronicities. It is also possible to conduct "intervention" experiments to determine to what extent people can be taught to improve their ability to detect and accurately interpret synchronicities. And it is possible to conduct "micro" experiments looking for evidence of synchronicities between people in quantum events such as observed in electronic noise circuits, or even double-slit experiments.

8. **What convinces you that quantum physics and parapsychology both are part of the tapestry of synchronicity?**

This is an important and complex question, and is the foundation of my next book on synchronicities. Chapters 16 and 17 provide introductory answers to this two-part question.

However, the quick answer is that synchronicities are like quanta, in that they have particle-like and wave-like properties—meaning that they are discrete events on the one hand, and show patterns of relationships, implying that they are organized by some sort of dynamic energy and field process, on the other. Moreover, the discovery of synchronicity is improved through becoming increasingly intuitive and following one's hunches and gut impressions—in other words, becoming more psychic. And yet, we must never lose our grounding in rationality and discernment.

9. Can synchronicities ever be dangerous?

Certain sequences of synchronicities can be stressful at times, and they can sometimes make you feel that you and/or the world are going crazy, but that is likely mostly due to the fact that our society as a whole has not openly embraced them as genuine aspects of reality. One can become "overloaded" with synchronicities and even potentially "overdose" on them. Also, one may be tempted to "jump to conclusions" about possible interpretations of a given sequence of synchronicities and end up making unwise choices in one's life.

In principle, I could imagine someone seeking negative or dangerous synchronous events, and unfortunately discovering them. And scientific integrity requires that I not rule out the possibility of the existence of negative spirit mediated synchronicities in certain situations. However, I have encountered less than a handful of instances of this possibility as of the time of writing this section.

10. How do we figure out what synchronicities mean?

This is one of the most challenging questions facing future synchronicity self-science. In the case of synchronicities involving animals or myths, seeking out well-recognized sources such as books like *Animal Speak* can sometimes be useful. However, it is advisable to be discerning and cautious, seasoning what you have tasted with a grain or more of salt. Skilled therapists, especially trained Jungian analysts, can also sometimes be helpful. Dr. Bernard Beitman addresses the meaning of synchronicities in his book *Connecting with Coincidence.* If any challenge requires the highest functioning and integration of reasoning and intuition, this is it. If any faculty requires the development of our synchronicity intelligence, this is it.

I should mention that apparently supersynchronicities can have multiple levels of meaning. For example, a specific supersynchronicity may contain specific meanings for the individuals involved in the serial synchronicity (e.g., in Chapter 2, the specific meaning of the number 11 for me) as well as a "meta" or universal meaning about supersynchronicity itself (e.g., the take-home lesson of Chapter 2, "Follow the evidence that is way beyond chance").

11. Can you foresee a time when awareness of synchronicity will be a part of mainstream belief and everyday life?

Absolutely. If synchronicities are real—and they certainly seem to be—then it is only a matter of time before this fact will become known, better understood, and increasingly part of contemporary culture. To the extent that synchronicities can serve as useful guides in our lives, they will come to be sought after and adopted. My goal and vision is for humanity to someday reach the point where every person has experienced at least one supersynchronicity in every workplace and every home.

12. How can people learn to become adept at discovering and in terpreting patterns of synchronicities?

The approach taken in this book is that synchronicity self-science involves the coordinated integration of reason and intuition.

Dr. Jonas Salk, the discoverer of a successful polio vaccine and the founder of the Salk Institute for Biological Studies, wrote an inspiring book in 1983 titled *The Anatomy of Reality: The Merging of Intuition and Reason.*

Besides being a brilliant exposition of systems thinking, the book illustrates how the merging of intuition and reason results in discovering and awakening what cannot be achieved by either on their own.

I believe that books like *Super Synchronicity* can provide pointers and examples. In the future, workshops can be developed for fostering both reasoning and intuitive synchronicity-seeking skills. People can develop synchronicity self-science groups in their local communities to mutually nurture each other's abilities.

My experience is that when small groups come together, they can serve as catalysts for each other, and synchronicities will increasingly emerge between them. In our group meetings involving six to eight people, we have sometimes discovered that each member had experienced one or more events that were improbable, and that we shared the same category of event.

Synchronicity-seeking can be fun, challenging, thought-provoking, inspiring, connecting, rejuvenating, and awakening. And best of all, we do not need research funding or fancy equipment (though digital cameras and recorders in contemporary smart phones can be useful).

In my own case, the synchronicity experiences in my life and my understanding of them have grown significantly as I have more deeply developed the following abilities and attributes:

(1) Watching,
(2) Surfing,
(3) Attracting,
(4) Participating, and
(5) Celebrating

In addition, the combination of all five explanations may have what physicists and systems scientists refer to as non-linear consequences—the whole may be more than the sum of its parts.

#1: Synchronicity Watching, with Discernment

Synchronicity watching is very much like bird watching. If you do not look for birds (or synchronicities) you probably will not notice them.

The better you are at looking for birds (or synchronicities) the more likely you will be to spot them.

The better your binoculars (or synchronicity-watching skills) are, the more birds (or synchronicities) you will be able to see.

The more you know about birds (or synchronicities), the better you will be able to spot them, and even capture images of them.

And finally, the more sophisticated you are about bird watching (or synchronicity watching), the better you will be about distinguishing between different species and subspecies of birds (or synchronicities).

The last point is critical, because in the case of synchronicity watching it is essential to learn to distinguish between non-synchronistic occurrences versus genuine synchronistic occurrences.

Extreme disbelievers/skeptics typically assume that *all* so-called synchronistic observations must be merely coincidences or the result of what is scientifically termed "perceptual priming" (i.e., the VW bug effect).

However, this assumption is mistaken. With sophistication comes discernment, as experienced bird watchers (and synchronicity watchers) know well.

#2: Synchronicity Surfing, with Caution

Second, similar to an avid and accomplished ocean surfer, I have become an avid and accomplished synchronicity surfer.

It can be said that we all live in a sea of synchronicities. However, for many of us the synchronicity seas are so calm that we do not notice or detect the ripples of synchronicities that surround us.

For some of us the synchronicity seas are choppier and we will notice waves of synchronicities from time to time.

Others of us actually live by the ocean and cannot only observe the synchronicity waves but we can readily swim in them.

A minority of us choose to take up the sport of surfing, and actively seek out the largest synchronicity waves to ride, while an even smaller group of us become "professional surfers."

Ocean surfers realize that the waves can be rough and even dangerous at times. And sometimes there can be Tsunami-size waves that leave destruction in their wake.

As you witnessed in this book, I have sometimes felt like I was experiencing "synchronicity overload" and "could not breathe" because of the number and magnitude of the synchronicity waves I was experiencing at the time.

It is important to recognize that ocean surfers do not *make* the waves; they know how to find them and then learn how to ride them. However, as explained below, synchronicity surfers can contribute to the appearance of waves of synchronicities.

#3: Synchronicity Attracting, with Openness

Third, just as magnets attract iron filings, it can be said that avid synchronicity seekers attract synchronicity filings.

And just as contemporary chaos and complexity theory describes mathematical attractors that somehow pull in patterns of organized information around them, it can be said that accomplished synchronicity attractors have the effect of pulling in patterns of synchronicities around them.

One way this happens is that when people hear that you are open to synchronicities, and they discover that it is safe for them to share synchronicities with you, they will not only more likely confess their personal synchronistic experiences to you, but they will even seek you out as well.

My experience has been that some of the increased synchronicity attracting is psychological and social in nature (the above example), and some of it is energetic or spiritual in nature (including so-called “paranormal”), as described next.

#4: Synchronicity Participating, with Questioning

Fourth, in the same way that people can intentionally design and organize information—from composing music, making sculptures, and writing novels, to designing computers, building airplanes, and constructing whole communities—it appears that people can sometimes manifest, or at least co-manifest, synchronous information and events.

A more appropriate word to describe this orchestration process is participating.

Probably the most extraordinary aspect of my supersynchronicity journey has been the discovery that to the extent that I “ask the universe” for information, the more likely I seem to “happen upon (or chance upon)" non-random events in my life. I put "happen (or chance) upon" in quotes for an important reason.

My conscious intentions seem to *foster* increased *occurrences*—not just increased *observations.* My use of the word *foster* is quite purposeful; my experience is that when I *try* to make things happen, or *actively* search for them, they typically do *not* occur.

But when I ask for things to happen for the best and highest good—*and I have no attachment to whether or not they occur*—they surprisingly more often occur. It is a kind of effortless seeking that requires an extraordinary effort to achieve!

The incredible complexity—and sometimes humor—associated with the intricate web of synchronicities I have encountered has led me to the conclusion that although I (and all of us) appear to be playing a creative role in the overall process, we are doing the creating with a small "c." There appears to be a Super-Creator with a capital "C" orchestrating the Big Picture. The terms "Super Mind" and the "One Mind" reflect this evolution of the synchronicity process.

The process appears to be more "two-way co-creative" than "one-way creative."

One aspect of so-called quantum weirdness is the observer effect, the thesis that the very act of measuring a quantum process affects it.

As scientists like Dr. Dean Radin, author of *Entangled Minds* investigate, and journalists like Lynne McTaggart, author of *The Intention Experiment* explicate, human attention and intention can alter physical, chemical, and biological processes to various degrees.

I have come to the conclusion that formulating some sort of a Quantum Synchronicity Theory (QST) will be required to comprehend the true nature of synchronicity.

Since QST incorporates consciousness at all levels, from the micro to the macro, it is in principle big enough to integrate the notion of a quantum holographic consciousness—in other words, the One Mind—as part of its foundation.

#5: Synchronicity Celebrating, with Gratitude

Finally, it appears that the more we enjoy the process of discovering synchronicities and celebrate their occurrence in our lives, the more frequently synchronicities occur.

With each passing year, I have become ever more comfortable in experiencing and honoring synchronicities. I express my heartfelt gratitude not only to the people who participate in my/our supersynchronicities, but to the inferred invisible conscious forces in the universe which make all of this possible.

I have developed an increasing number of synchronicity buddies. As a group we relish the surprising and playful ways that complex synchronicities connect us, and we delight in their creative occurrence.

People are sometimes startled by how animated and inspired I become when I am afforded the opportunity to share the apparent "magic" of supersynchronicities. And people sometimes respond to my thankfulness for synchronicity as if it is palpable.

My experience in working with many dozens of individuals who are highly credible observers and reporters of supersynchronicities in their respective lives is that as a group they are highly loving, caring, playful, and grateful people.

What we need most are open minds and open hearts. As Carly Simon reminds us, "I can see you have a change in mind. But what we need is a change in heart".

Acknowledgements

Now my own suspicion is that the universe is not only queerer than we suppose, but queerer than we can suppose.
J.B.S. Haldane, *Possible Worlds*

I learned about the above quote concerning the mystery and queerness of life and the universe, penned by the distinguished biologist J.B.S. Haldane, from the late Dr. Paul Pearsall in his beautiful book *AWE: The Delights and Dangers of Our 11th Emotion.*

Physicists talk about quantum "weirdness," and Dr. Haldane speaks about biological "queerness."

However, as you have seen, synchronicity—especially supersynchronicity—can be thought of as reflecting a condition of superweirdness/queerness. It is a state of unusualness that justifies our experiencing what Dr. Pearsall calls our "11th emotion," the feeling of awe.

I highlight the number "11" here to humbly acknowledge the fact that my personal synchronicity journey happened to begin with the number 11 (as described in Chapter 2), and I have repeatedly experienced the complex emotion of awe in spades.

It is a privilege for me to dedicate this book partly to Dr. Pearsall, who was an inspiring professional colleague and dear friend. *AWE* was published after Paul's untimely death, and when I received his book I was honored to discover that Paul had included an unanticipated acknowledgement to me.

Dr. Pearsall wrote:

> I express my aloha to psychologist Dr. Gary Schwartz not only for being my friend but for finding such awe in the mysteries of the world that he just can't stop researching what few scientists dare to study.

You may recall reading about a startling Type I Synchronicity involving Dr. Pearsall and his wife Celeste in Chapter 1. This book, this "aloha," is for Paul and his family.

The dramatic increase in the frequency of synchronicities that occurred in my personal journey over the past few years have paralleled the seemingly magical appearance of Rhonda Eklund Schwartz in my life. You were introduced to her in Chapter 1. It was she who first said the term "supersynchronicity" out loud to me, and directly contributed to the unanticipated tidal wave of synchronicities involving the prefix "super."

Some of the extraordinary supersynchronicities revealed in this book directly or indirectly involved Rhonda. She has become an exemplar of a successful synchronicity self-scientist and shares some of her remarkable synchronicity journey in her books *Love Eternal, New Edition* and the forthcoming *Seeing Heaven*. This book is here significantly because Rhonda is here.

When I first began this personal journey thirty years ago, I was a young tenured professor at Yale University, and I often felt alone on the tumultuous ride of increasing synchronicities that I continually experienced after moving to the University of Arizona. However, over the past few years, an ever-widening group of fellow synchronicity riders have come into my life. Not only have they served as beacons of encouragement and energy, but they have also provided essential feedback to keep the larger journey on a clear and compelling path.

Importantly, they helped me realize that not only is supersynchronicity a real phenomenon, but that the creative process of becoming an effective synchronicity watcher and explorer can be developed and shared.

My fellow synchronicity colleagues represent a diverse and impressive array of professions, including physicians, lawyers, scientists, postdoctoral fellows, business executives, research assistants, teachers, artists, administrators, editors, writers, psychology graduate students, healers, religious leaders, psychics, celebrities, and children. These synchronicity colleagues include Dr. Larry Dossey, whose seminal book *One Mind* helped frame my understanding of supersynchronicity.

I wish to gratefully acknowledge (using first names only, and in no particular order):

Bill, Clarissa, Ilsa, Bob, Sam, Ernie, Mary, Mark, Sheryl, Lynne, Shirley, Britt, Suzanne, Iris, Richard, Karen, Anne, Whitley, Tammy, Diane, Kelsey, Camille, Sarah, Jerry, Carrie, Chip, Jim, Natalie, John, Juan, Andrea, Ryoko, Jolie, Kathy, Krishna, Marty, Catherine, Rupert, Christopher, David, Bruce, Larry, Dean, Debbie, Doreen, Julie, Emily, Phil, Lynn, Kim, Skott, Jonathan, Monica, Izzy, Narayan, Maria, Linda, Arryne, Elizabeth, Russell, Hazel, Robert, Phran, Anastasia, Konstantine, Claude, Cynthia, Tom, Ginette, Dale, Cindy, Leslie, Allan, Nathaniel, Paul, Holland, Galen, Alex, Anthony, Dan, Clayton, Michael, Charlie, Mario, Lesley, Susanne, Dieter, Netzin, Bernd, Wulf, Deirdre, Marlene, Pat, Tanya, Vanessa, Kristine, Alexandria, and Roxanne.

Since there were multiple Mary's, Bill's, Kathy's, Jim's, Phil's, John's, Richard's, Mark's, Sarah's, Michael's, and Leslie's, the total list turned out to include more than 110 individuals. It was not until I prepared this list that I became aware of how extended and accomplished my Type III Synchronicity extended family has become.

I wish to thank literary agent and author William Gladstone, the editor of my first book and my mentor and friend, for his inspiring Foreword. It was Bill's visionary novel *The Twelve* that became the tipping point for me to complete the first draft of this book (as well as its forthcoming sequel).

I also wish to thank Dr. Stephen Brewer, Medical Director of Canyon Ranch in Tucson, who is a colleague, friend, and now fellow synchronicity explorer, for sharing his evidential Type II Synchronicity in the Introduction of this book.

Although my self-science journey of personal discovery had not been an active part of my formal professional life until a few years ago, it did transpire during my association with Yale University, the University of Arizona, and Canyon Ranch Health Resorts and Spas. Many of the individuals mentioned above—including faculty, students, health care professionals, business executives, administrators, research assistants, clerical staff, healers, and psychics—were or are associated with one or more of these visionary institutions. Directly or indirectly, these institutions have contributed to the emergence and evolution of my involvement with synchronicities, and they have my deepest gratitude and affection.

Special thanks go to the extraordinary team at Param Media (Andrea Blackie, Dr. John H Spencer, Juan F Tellez, and Ryoko Spencer). I met them through Dr. Mario Beauregard, a friend and colleague, and I was immediately inspired by their vision, goals, and abilities. Every aspect of *Super Synchronicity*—from the cover to the last page—has benefitted from their wisdom and skills. We have also experienced marvelous and evidential synchronicities throughout the process of birthing this book, and Dr. Spencer wrote a powerful Commentary. In the spirit of Dr. Pearsall, I think of them as the AWE Team.

I would also like to thank Dr. Mark Pitstick, Dr. Cecile Mielenz, and Darlene Martin, MA, for their careful review and editorial suggestions of the penultimate draft. Thanks to their loving attention, the clarity and precision of this book has been enhanced. And I would like to thank Dianne Havenner and Janet Eschenbrenner, two special synchronicity experiencers who took my workshop at Canyon Ranch titled Synchronicity and Spiritual Wellness, for encouraging me to select *Super Synchronicity* as the ultimate title for this book. If any book has taken a village to raise it, this is it.

Special thanks go to Robert Staretz, MS, a long-time colleague of the astronaut Dr. Edgar Mitchell who together published their integrative theory of the quantum hologram and consciousness in the *Journal of Cosmology*. After reading the penultimate draft of

Super Synchronicity, Bob not only suggested that I add a section on why supersynchronicities are important to Chapter 1, he literally gifted me with a first draft.

Finally, I would not be walking the walk, nor talking the talk, if I failed to acknowledge the apparent contributions of what some call "the other side," and what others refer to as "the greater spiritual reality."

Although it may be hard for some of you to believe—and it is often difficult for me to fathom as well—it appears that a number of deceased individuals, including Susy Smith and Marcia Eklund, several distinguished scientists (including Albert Einstein, David Bohm, and Nikola Tesla), and some controversial celebrities (including Harry Houdini, Sir Arthur Conan Doyle, and Michael Jackson) have contributed to the extraordinary synchronicities revealed in this book (and/or its sequel).

Moreover, scientific integrity requires that I acknowledge the apparent involvement of alleged "higher spiritual beings" such as Sophia (discussed in detail Part IV of *The Sacred Promise)* for key pieces of dramatic and evidential synchronistic information.

Last but not least, I must reverently acknowledge the apparent involvement of the One Mind—i.e. the Source, the Great Spirit, the Great Mystery, the Universal Intelligence, the Super Mind, the Infinite, the Sacred, the Divine, or what many people simply call God—in the apparent manifestation of supersynchronicities in all walks of life, including the strange unfolding of this book.

The truth is, if we take the totality of the evidence reported in this book seriously and with integrity, we are led inexorably to the hypothesis that some sort of infinite (and anonymous) Super Mind is co-scripting with us the super complex and strange play we call life. The title *Super Synchronicity* and the subtitle *Where Science and Spirit Meet* both honor this inevitable hypothesis.

What an awe-inspiring journey. Thank you all.

Note from the Publisher

In *Super Synchronicity,* Gary has beautifully illuminated the reality of synchronicity in a uniquely personal way that is grounded in scientific analysis. He is genuinely motivated to help others better their lives through an increased awareness of synchronistic events, and we are very pleased to contribute to his dream of "everyone experiencing at least one supersynchronicity in their personal lives"!

Multiple synchronicities also occurred throughout the process of our preparing *Super Synchronicity* for publication, and we are sure that many more await our discovery. We are all capable of experiencing synchronicities in our lives, observing them evolve and interconnect over time, and fortunately a formal background in science is not required. What is required is an open mind and heart, and a desire to dive more deeply into the mysteries of our existence.

We would also like to thank University of Arizona engineering instructor Jennifer Horner for her input on the cover design, and especially Canyon Ranch CEO Jerry Cohen, who reminded us of the importance of including a synchronicity duck! We hope that this book will help you to experience and better understand your own synchronicities, and for those who would like to grasp the key message as quickly as possible, Gary has provided essential readings below.

Recommended Reading

This is a brief reading list of relevant exemplary books and journal articles about coincidence and synchronicity.

Synchronicity in Science and Practice

Jung, C. G. *Synchronicity: An Acausal Connecting Principle.* 1960. Princeton: Princeton UP, 2011. Print.

Peat, F. David. *Synchronicity: The Bridge Between Matter and Mind.* New York: Bantam, 1987. Print.

Combs, Allan, and Mark Holland. *Synchronicity: Through the Eyes of Science, Myth, and the Trickster.* 1996. New York: Marlowe-Avalon, 2001. Print.

Grof, Stanislav. *When the Impossible Happens: Adventures in Non-Ordinary Reality.* Boulder: Sounds True, 2006. Print.

Hand, David J. *The Improbability Principle: Why Coincidences, Miracles, and Rare Events Happen Every Day.* New York: Farrar, 2014. Print.

Mackey, Chris. *Synchronicity: Empower Your Life with the Gift of Coincidence.* London: Watkins, 2015. Print.

Beitman, Bernard D. *Connecting with Coincidence: Synchronicity in Practice.* Deerfield Beach, FL: Health Communications, 2016. Print.

Synchronicity in Fiction

Redfield, James. *The Celestine Prophecy: An Adventure.* 1993. New York: Grand Central-Hachette, 2006. Print.

Gladstone, William. *The Twelve.* New York: Perseus, 2009. Print.

Science and the Paranormal

Tart, Charles T. *The End of Materialism: How Evidence of the Paranormal is Bringing Science and Spirit Together.* Oakland, CA: Noetic Books-New Harbinger, 2009. Print.

Radin, Dean. *Entangled Minds: Extrasensory Experiences in a Quantum Reality.* New York: Paraview-Simon, 2006. Print.

Powell, Diane Hennacy. *The Psi Enigma: The Scientific Case for Psychic Phenomena.* New York: Walker, 2009. Print.

Science, Spirituality, and God: Skeptical and Possible

Stenger, Victor J. *Quantum Gods: Creation, Chaos, and the Search for Cosmic Consciousness.* Amherst: Prometheus, 2009. Print.

Hagerty, Barbara Bradley. *Fingerprints of God: The Search for the Science of Spirituality.* New York: Riverhead-Penguin, 2009. Print.

Schwartz, Gary E. *The G.O.D. Experiments: How Science is Discovering God in Everything, Including Us.* 2006. New York: Atria-Simon, 2007. Print.

Dossey, Larry. *One Mind: How Our Individual Mind is Part of a Greater Consciousness and Why it Matters.* Carlsbad, CA: Hay House, 2013. Print.

Sample Journal Articles

Beitman, Bernard D. "Coincidence Studies." *Psychiatric Annals* 41.12 (2011): 561–562, 567–571. Web. 2 Aug. 2016.

Attig, Sheryl, Gary E. Schwartz, Aurelio Jose Figueredo, W. Jake Jacobs, and Karen C. Bryson. "Coincidence, Intuition, and Spirituality." *Psychiatric Annals* 41.12 (2011): el-e3. Web. 2 Aug. 2016.

Greyson, Bruce. "Meaningful Coincidences and Near-death Experiences." *Psychiatric Annals* 41.12 (2011): el-e5. Web. 2 Aug. 2016.

Schwartz, Gary E. "God, Synchronicity, and Postmaterialist Psychology: Proof-of-concept Real-life Evidence." *Spirituality in Clinical Practice* 1.2 (2014): 153–162. Web. 2 Aug. 2016.

Schwartz Gary E. "God, Synchronicity, and Postmaterialist Psychology II: Replication and Extension of Real-life Evidence." *Spirituality in Clinical Practice* 2.1 (2015): 86–95. Web. 2 Aug. 2016.

Schwartz, Gary E. "God, Synchronicity, and Postmaterialist Psychology III: Additional Real-life Evidence and the Higher Power Healing Hypothesis." *Spirituality in Clinical Practice* 2.4 (2014): 289–302. Web. 2 Aug. 2016.

Works Cited

Books and Articles

Andrews, Ted. *Animal Speak: The Spiritual and Magical Powers of Creatures Great and Small.* Woodbury, MN: Llewellyn, 1993. Print.

Berg, Phillip S. *Kabbalah for the Layman.* 1981. New York: Kabbalah Centre Books, 2012. Print.

Blackie, Andrea, and John H. Spencer, eds. *The Beacon of Mind: Reason and Intuition in the Ancient and Modern World.* Vancouver, BC: Param Media, 2015. Print.

Blount Jr., Roy. *HAIL, HAIL, EUPHORIA! Presenting the Marx Brothers in "Duck Soup," the Greatest War Movie Ever Made.* New York: Harper, 2010. Print.

Brewer, Stephen C., and Peggy Holt Wagner. *The Everest Principle: How to Achieve the Summit of Your Life.* Carlsbad, CA: Hay House, 2010. Print.

Connelly, Michael. *The Narrows.* Boston: Little, 2014. Print.

Cocks, Michael. "The Space Between: A Study in Synchronicity." *The Journal of Religion and Psychical Research* 5.4 (1982): 221–225. Web. 3 Aug. 2016.

Cussler, Clive. *Trojan Odyssey.* New York: Berkley-Penguin, 2003. Print.

Dossey, Larry. *One Mind: How Our Individual Mind is Part of a Greater Consciousness and Why It Matters.* Carlsbad, CA: Hay House, 2013. Print.

Eco, Umberto. *The Name of the Rose.* 1983. Trans. Richard Dixon. Boston: Mariner-Houghton, 2014. Print.

Ellerby, Jonathan H. *Return to the Sacred: Ancient Pathways to Spiritual Awakening.* Carlsbad, CA: Hay House, 2009. Print.

Freke, Timothy, and Peter Gandy. *The Jesus Mysteries: Was the "Original Jesus" a Pagan God?* New York: Ten Speed-Penguin, 2001. Print.

Gladstone, William, Richard Greninger, and John Selby. *Tapping the Source: Using the Master Key System for Abundance and Happiness.* London: Watkins, 2012. Print.

Haldane, John B. S. *Possible Worlds.* 2002. New Brunswick, NJ: Transaction, 2009. Print.

Hand, David J. *The Improbability Principle: Why Coincidences, Miracles, and Rare Events Happen Every Day.* New York: Farrar, 2014. Print.

Jung, C. G. *Synchronicity: An Acausal Connecting Principle.* 1960. Princeton: Princeton UP, 2011. Print.

Laszlo, Ervin. *Science and the Akashic Field: An Integral Theory of Everything.* 2004. 2nd ed. Rochester, VT: Inner Traditions, 2007. Print.

McTaggart, Lynne. 2007. *The Intention Experiment: Using Your Thoughts to Change Your Life and the World.* New York: Free Press-Simon, 2008. Print.

Parker, Robert B. *The Godwulf Manuscript.* New York: Dell-Bantam, 1973. Print.

---. *Crimson Joy.* New York: Dell-Random, 1988. Print.

---. *High Profile.* New York: Putnam-Penguin, 2007. Print.

Paulos, John Allen. *Irreligion: A Mathematician Explains Why the Arguments for God Just Don't Add Up.* 2008. New York: Hill and Wang-Farrar, 2009. Print.

Pearsall, Paul. *AWE: The Delights and Dangers of Our Eleventh Emotion.* Deerfield Beach, FL: Health Communications, 2007. Print.

Poe, Edgar Allan. "The Raven." *Poe: Poems.* New York: Knopf-Random, 1995. Print.

Powell, Diane Hennacy. *The Psi Enigma: The Scientific Case for Psychic Phenomena.* New York: Walker, 2009. Print.

Preston, Douglas, and Lincoln Child. *Brimstone.* 2004. New York: Warner, 2005. Print.

---. *The Cabinet of Curiosities.* London: Head of Zeus, 2014. Print.

Radin, Dean. *Entangled Minds: Extrasensory Experiences in a Quantum Reality.* New York: Paraview-Simon, 2006. Print.

Redfield, James. *The Celestine Prophecy: An Adventure.* New York: Bantam, 1988. Print.

Rollins, James. *The Doomsday Key.* New York: Harper, 2009. Print.

Salk, Jonas. *The Anatomy of Reality: Merging of Intuition and Reason.* New York: Praeger, 1983. Print.

Sams, Jamie, and David Carson. *Medicine Cards: The Discovery of Power Through the Ways of Animals.* New York: St. Martin's, 1999. Print.

Schwartz, Gary E. R., and Linda G. S. Russek. *The Living Energy Universe: A Fundamental Discovery that Transforms Science & Medicine.* Charlottesville, VA: Hampton Roads, 1999. Print.

Schwartz, Gary E. *The Afterlife Experiments: Breakthrough Scientific Evidence of Life After Death.* New York: Atria-Simon, 2002. Print.

---. *The Truth about Medium: Extraordinary Experiments with the Real Allison DuBois and Other Remarkable Psychics.* Charlottesville, VA: Hampton Roads, 2005. Print.

---. *The G.O.D. Experiments: How Science is Discovering God in Everything, Including Us.* New York: Atria-Simon, 2007. Print.

---. *The Energy Healing Experiments: Science Reveals Our Natural Power to Heal.* New York: Atria-Simon, 2008. Print.

---. *The Sacred Promise: How Science is Discovering Spirit's Collaboration with Us in Our Daily Lives.* New York: Atria-Simon, 2011. Print.

Schwartz, Rhonda Eklund. *Love Eternal.* New Edition. Vancouver, BC: Param Media, 2016. Print.

Stenger, Victor J. *Quantum Gods: Creation, Chaos, and the Search for Cosmic Consciousness.* Amherst: Prometheus, 2009. Print.

Strobel, Lee. *The Case for a Creator: A Journalist Investigates Scientific Evidence that Points Toward God.* Grand Rapids, MI: Zondervan, 2004. Print.

Tart, Charles T. *The End of Materialism: How Evidence of the Paranormal is Bringing Science and Spirit Together.* Oakland, CA: Noetic Books-New Harbinger, 2009. Print.

Movies, Musicals, and Documentaries

Contact. Dir. Robert Zemeckis. Perf. Jodie Foster, Matthew McConaughey, and Tom Skerritt. Warner Bros., 1997. Film.

Dragonfly. Dir. Tom Shadyac. Perf. Kevin Costner, Susanna Thompson, and Joe Morton. Universal Pictures, 2002. Film.

Evan Almighty. Dir. Tom Shadyac. Perf. Steve Carell, Morgan Freeman, and Lauren Graham. Universal Pictures, 2007. Film.

Life Afterlife. Dir. Lisa F. Jackson. Host: Linda Ellerbee. Perf. Larry Dossey, John Edward, Risa Gold, Elisabeth Kubler-Ross, Paul Kurtz, Sherwin B Nuland, Dean Radin, Linda Russek, Gary Schwartz, Charles T Tart, and Danah Zohar. Lucky Duck Productions, 1999. HBO Documentary.

Honk. By Anthony Drewe and George Stiles. Dir. Brandt Blocker. Royal National Theatre, London. 11 Dec. 1999. Musical Performance.

Romancing the Stone. Dir. Robert Zemeckis. Perf. Michael Douglas, Kathleen Turner, and Danny DeVito. Twentieth Century Fox, 1984. Film.

The Wiz. Dir. Sidney Lumet. Perf. Diana Ross, Michael Jackson, and Nipsey Russell. Universal Pictures, 1978. Film.

The Wiz. By William F. Brown. Dir. Geoffrey Holder. Majestic Theatre, New York. 5 Jan. 1975. Musical Performance.